# REACH FOR THE CROWN

THE LAND-DWELLER

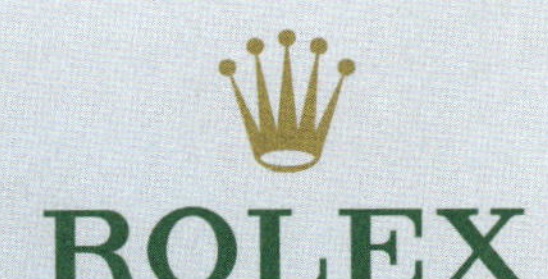

ROLEX

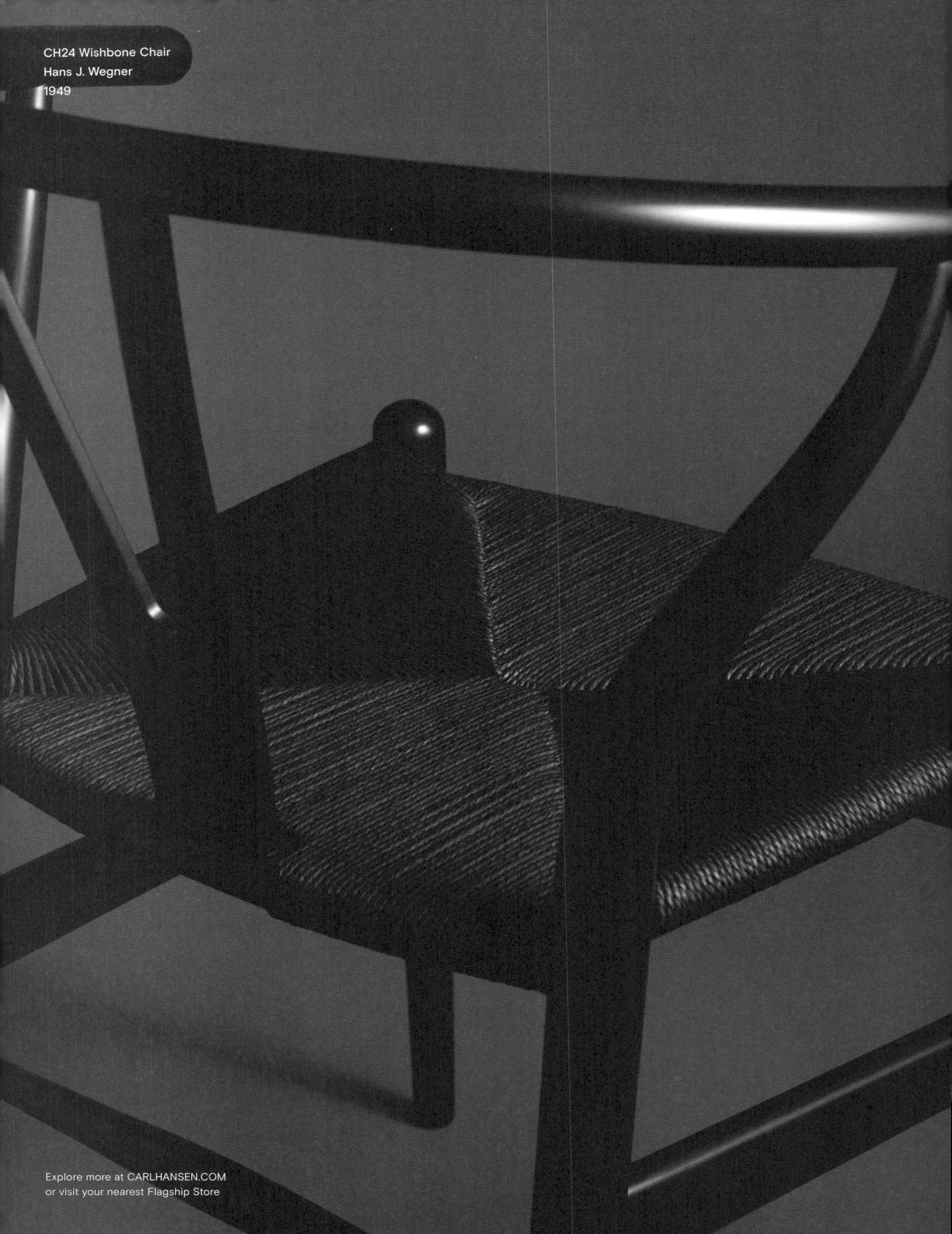
CH24 Wishbone Chair
Hans J. Wegner
1949

Explore more at CARLHANSEN.COM
or visit your nearest Flagship Store

# MAKING AN ICON

From start to finish, the Wishbone Chair undergoes 100 meticulous production steps – most of them completed by hand. The seat alone takes a master artisan an hour to complete using 150 meters of paper cord.

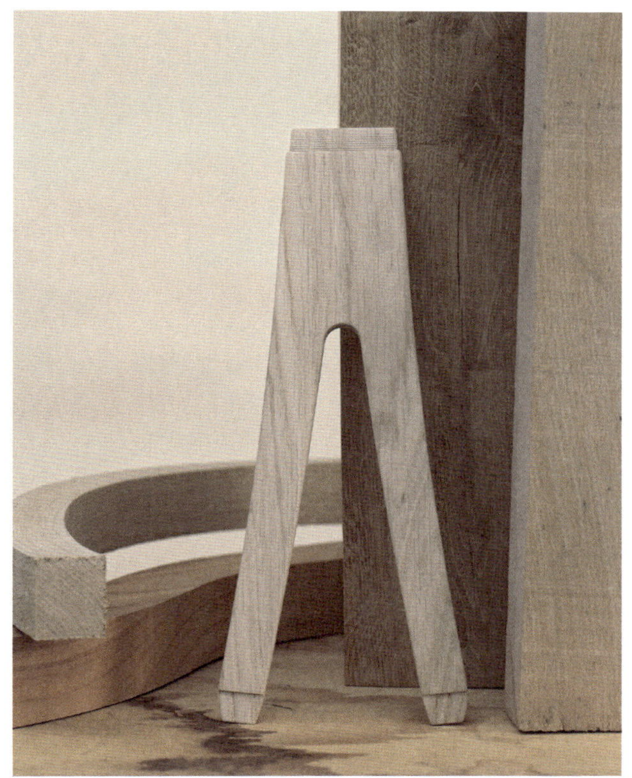

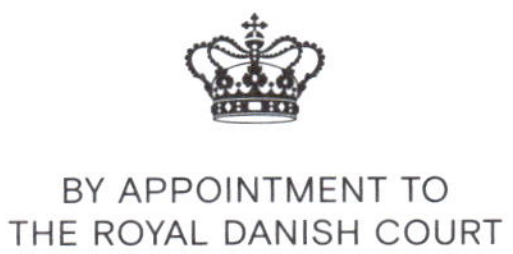

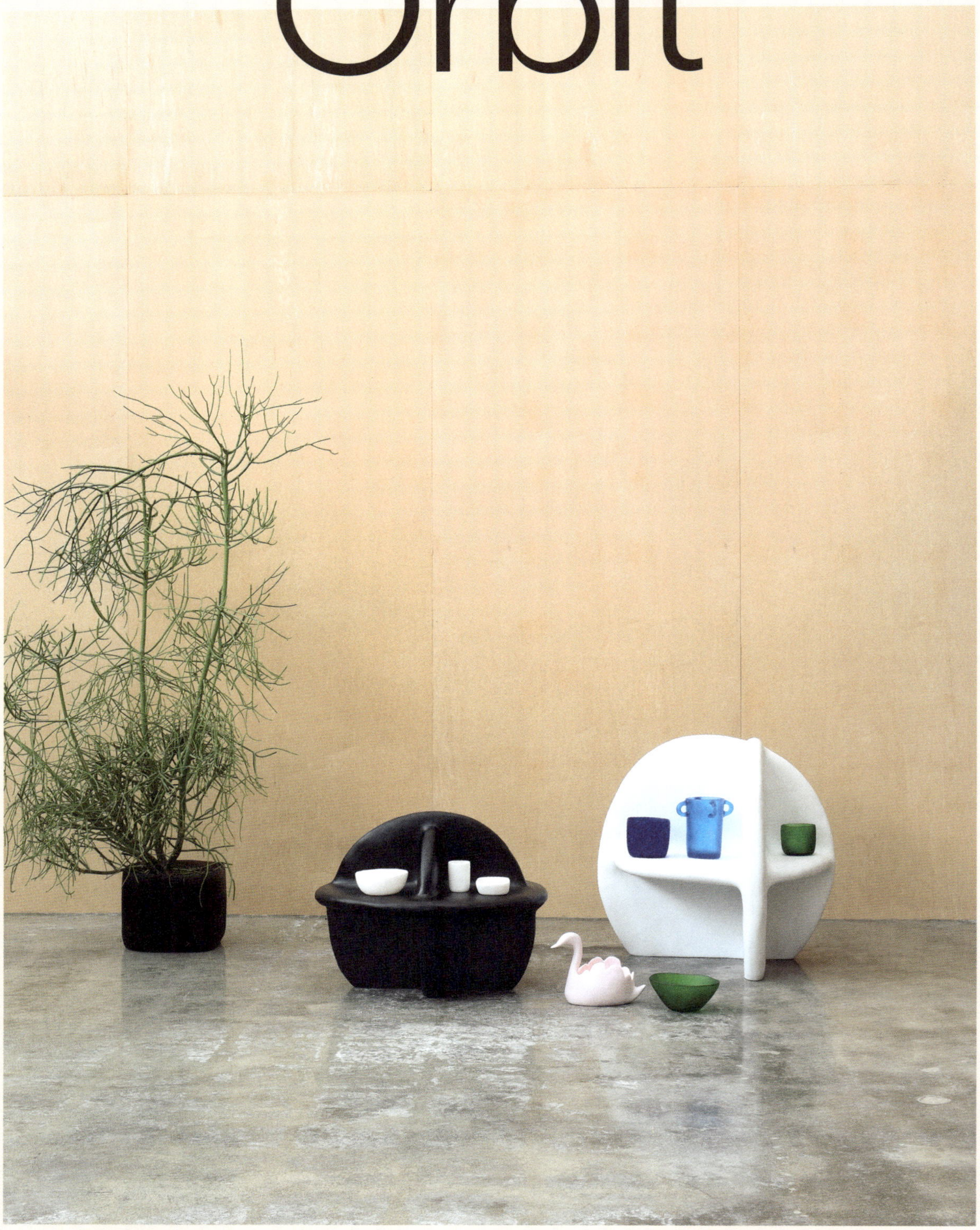

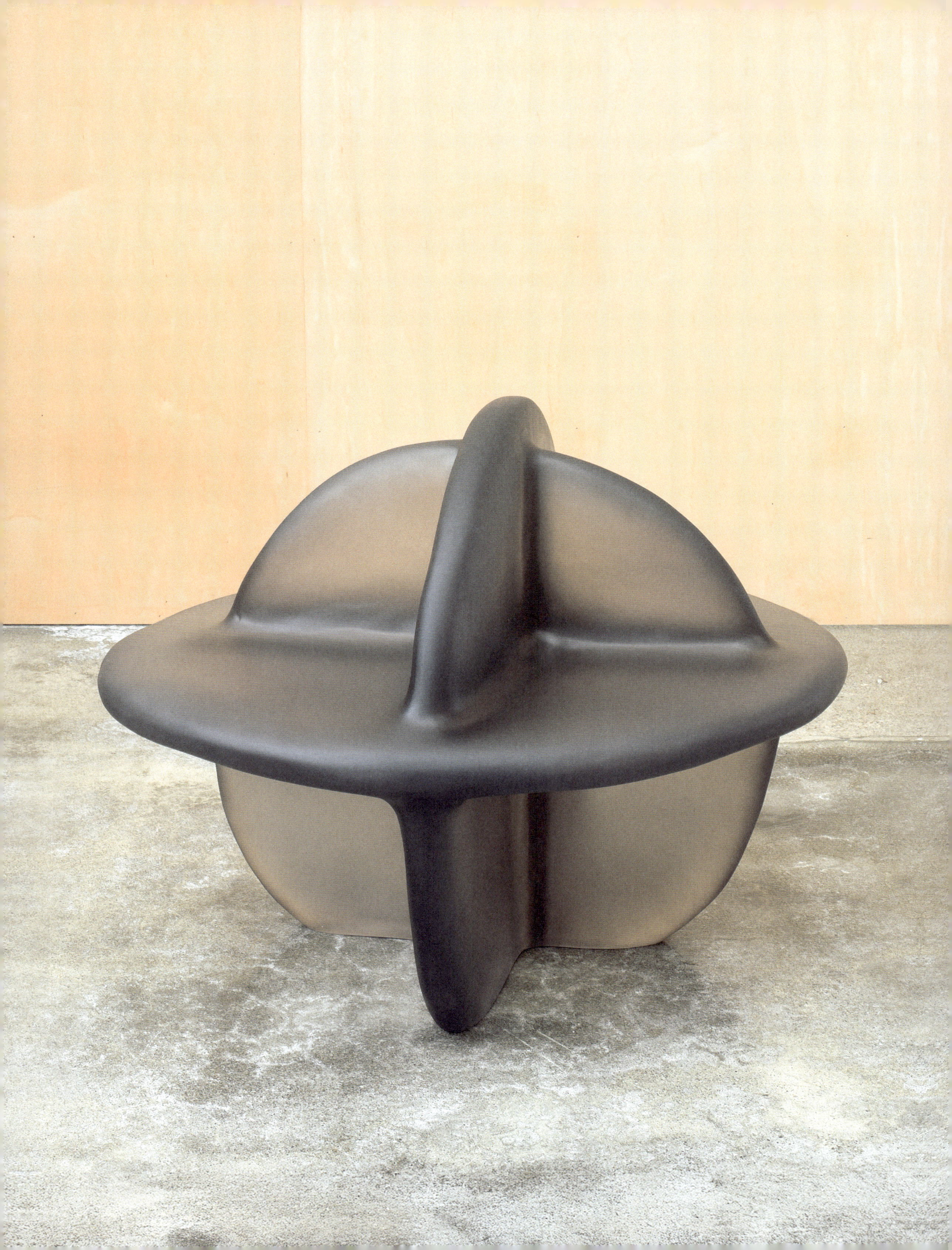

# KINFOLK


**TEAM**

—

EDITOR IN CHIEF — John Burns
DEPUTY EDITOR — George Upton
ART DIRECTOR — Isabel Lea
DESIGN DIRECTOR — Alex Hunting
COPY EDITOR — Rachel Holzman
PUBLISHING DIRECTOR — Edward Mannering
DIGITAL MANAGER — Cecilie Jegsen
ENGAGEMENT EDITOR — Rachel Ellison
STUDIO MANAGER — Victoria Benfeldt

—

CROSSWORD — Mark Halpin
PUBLICATION DESIGN — Alex Hunting Studio
COVER PHOTOGRAPH — Gregory Chong


**WORDS**

—

Precious Adesina
Julia Webster Ayuso
Petri Burtsoff
Ed Cumming
Benjamin Dane
Daphnée Denis
Donnie Dodson
Tom Faber
Salomé Gómez-Upegui
Kitty Grady
James Greig
Elle Hunt
Robert Ito
Francis Martin
Emily May
Shonquis Moreno
Ali Morris
Celine Nguyen
Poppy Okotcha
Sala Elise Patterson
Ellen Peirson-Hagger
Asher Ross
Rhian Sasseen
Ruby Tandoh
Jean Trinh
Hester Underhill
George Upton
Conie Vallese
James Vincent
Tom Whyman

**STYLING, SET DESIGN, HAIR & MAKEUP**

—

Summer Chen
Owen Lo Yuk Chi
Melissa Drouillard
Monaé Everett
Niklas Hansen
Una Ho
Cooney Lai
Aartthie Mahakuperan
Carolina Mizrahi
Jenny Shih
Shola Shodipo
Sarah Whiteside

**ARTWORK & PHOTOGRAPHY**

—

Gustav Almestål
Trent Davis Bailey
Ted Belton
Bliss Braoudakis
Gregory Chong
Hugh Davison
Adam DeTour
Oyè Diran
Nathan Wolf Grace
Florian Holzherr
Eugenio Intini
Cecilie Jegsen
Brian Kaiser
Chona Kasinger
Laird Kay
William Jess Laird
Alixe Lay
Austin Leis
Thea Løvstad
Yoshihiro Makino
Marina Martinez Marin
Julie Mayfeng
Paulius Petraitis
Peter Prato
Pixel Prof
Nathan Saillet
Robert Schlatter
Luisa Smith
Lisa Sorgini
Rich Stapleton
Staffan Sundström
Kutay Tanir
Aaron Tilley
Eric Van Nynatten
The Voorhes
Joe Whitmore

**PUBLISHER**

—

Chul-Joon Fark

# RICHARD MILLE

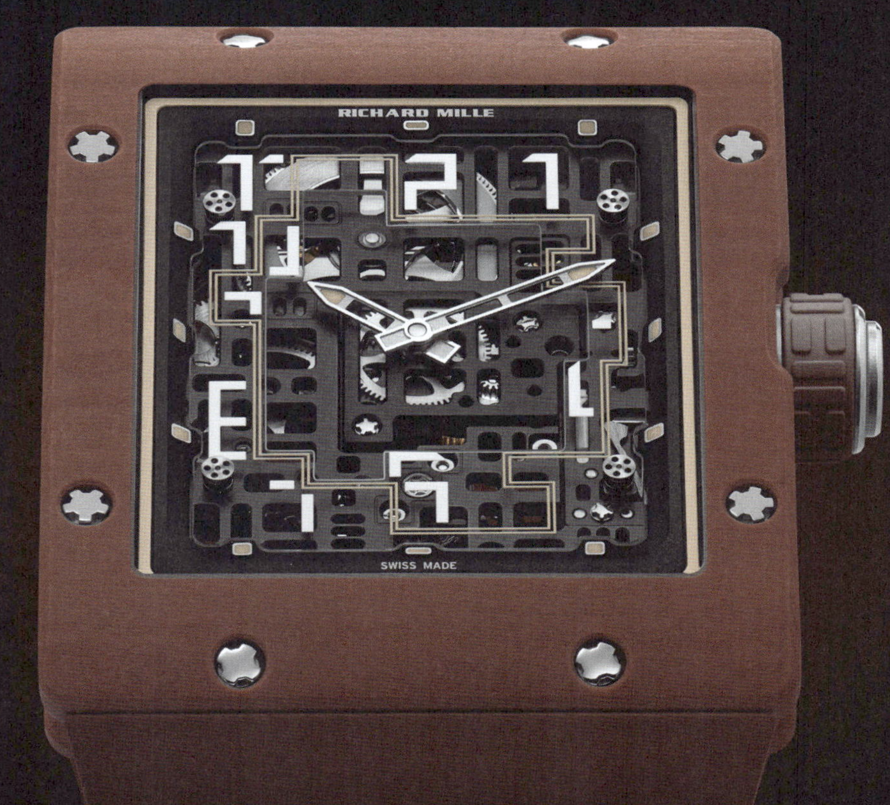


**RM 16-02 EXTRAFLAT**

In-house skeletonised automatic winding calibre
50-hour power reserve (± 10%)
Baseplate and bridges in grade 5 titanium
Platinum rotor
Case in Quartz TPT®

# A Racing Machine
# On The Wrist

# WELCOME
## History Special

We are living in a moment that feels unusually difficult to interpret. The international order that many of us grew up taking for granted appears to be unraveling, and what comes next remains unclear. It's at times like these that we turn to history for guidance—to search the past for patterns that might offer reassurance about the future. But if history teaches anything, it is that such clarity rarely arrives.

Yet history still matters, not because it predicts what comes next but because it shapes how the present is understood. The past functions as an active inheritance—a cultural and political undercurrent that informs the stories nations tell about themselves, the identities individuals construct and the structures of power that societies accept or challenge. In Issue Sixty, we examine history through this lens: as a field of interpretation continually being revised as new voices emerge and old assumptions are questioned. Across the issue, we hear from some of these voices—people reconsidering whose histories are relevant, whose have been marginalized and who ultimately has the authority to tell the story.

In London, we spend a morning with Nicholas Cullinan, director of the British Museum, who reflects on the challenge of stewarding the institution in an era increasingly defined by questions of restitution and accountability. In New York, Nikole Hannah-Jones—the Pulitzer Prize–winning journalist behind the 1619 Project—explains why revisiting foundational national narratives remains urgent today, while in Paris, writer Daphnée Denis examines the politics of remembering figures precisely because they were forgotten. Elsewhere, Zakia Sewell explores the folklore of the UK as communal archives passed between generations, while three descendants of world-changing figures reflect on the personal burden of inheriting their ancestor's legacy.

Elsewhere in the issue, we make a pilgrimage to Santiago de Compostela to meet David Chipperfield, the seminal architect known for his sensitive work with historic buildings. We also visit a series of homes, each with a history of its own: In Helsinki, the atelier apartment of artist Tove Jansson, preserved exactly as she left it; in Los Angeles, the glamorous midcentury properties restored by designers Ome Dezin, and Flamingo Estate, Richard Christiansen's botanical pleasureland.

One day, the period we are living through will be given a name and a place in the annals of history. For now, we can only be reminded that history is, in the end, simply the record of how people learn to live through their time. We hope this issue is one small contribution.

WORDS
JOHN BURNS

# HOUSE OF FINN JUHL

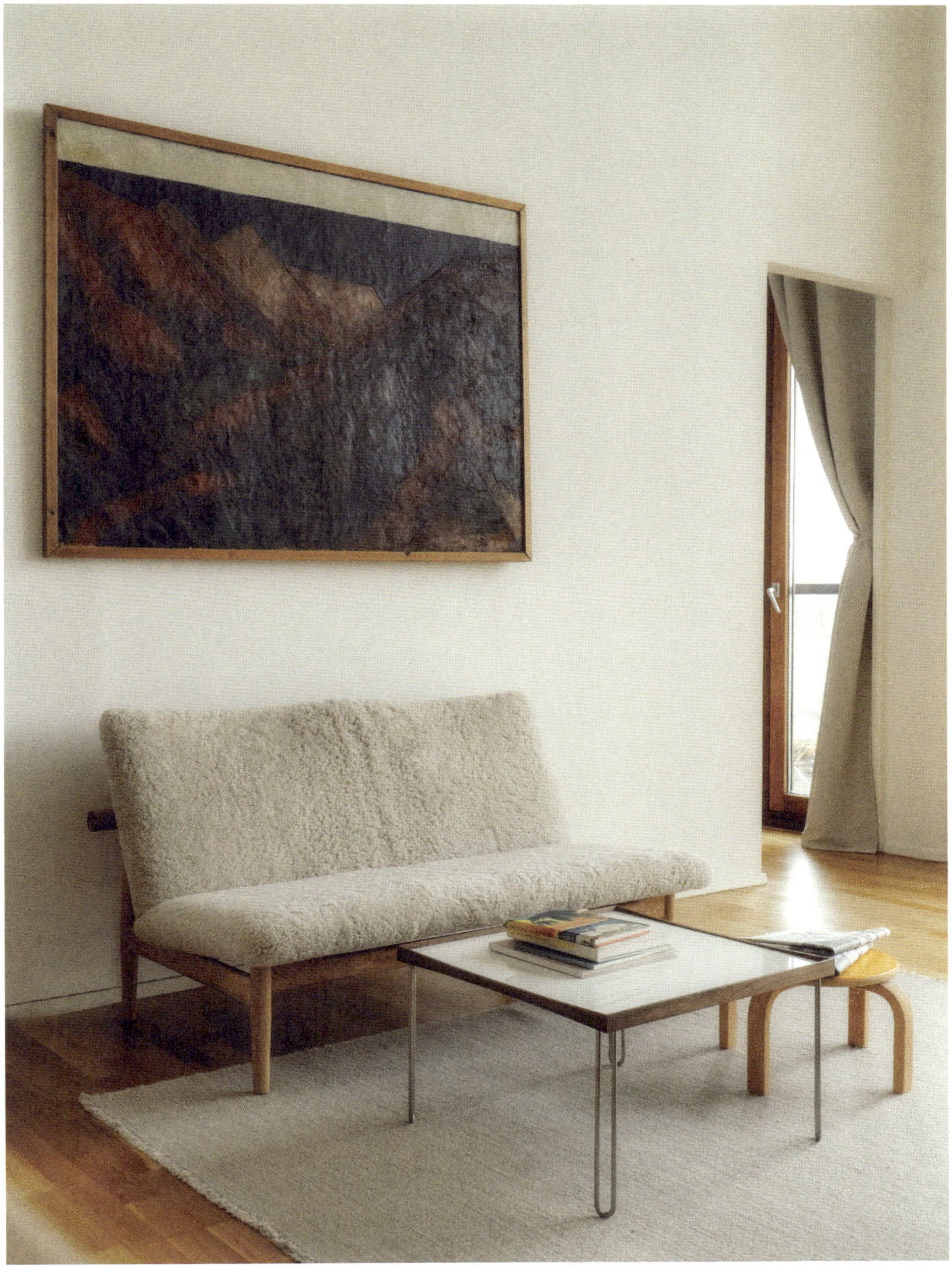

The Japan Sofa and the Tray Table by Finn Juhl.

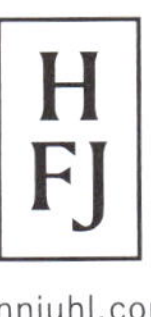

# STARTERS
## On love, time and nothingness.

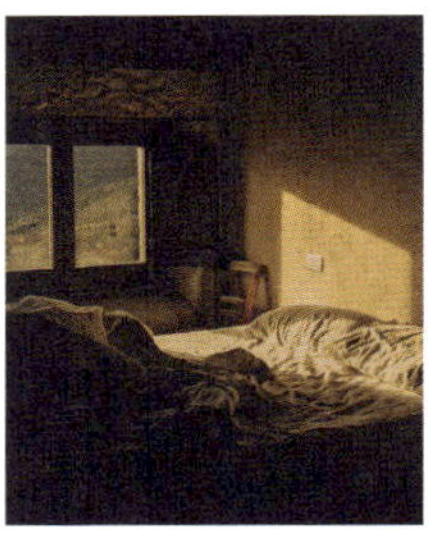





# FEATURES
## From Helsinki, Hong Kong and Los Angeles.

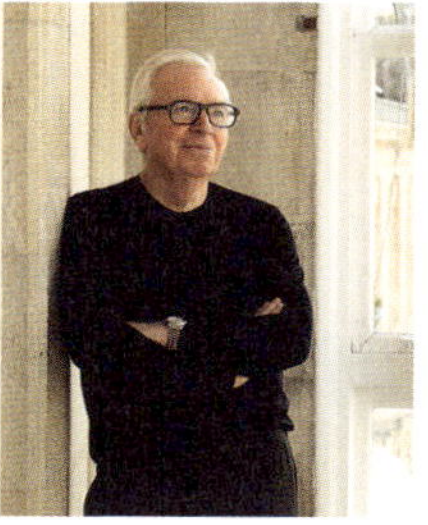



*"I'm doing it out of pure pleasure. It's totally indulgent on one level—but I enjoy it."*   ( David Chipperfield, P. 63 )

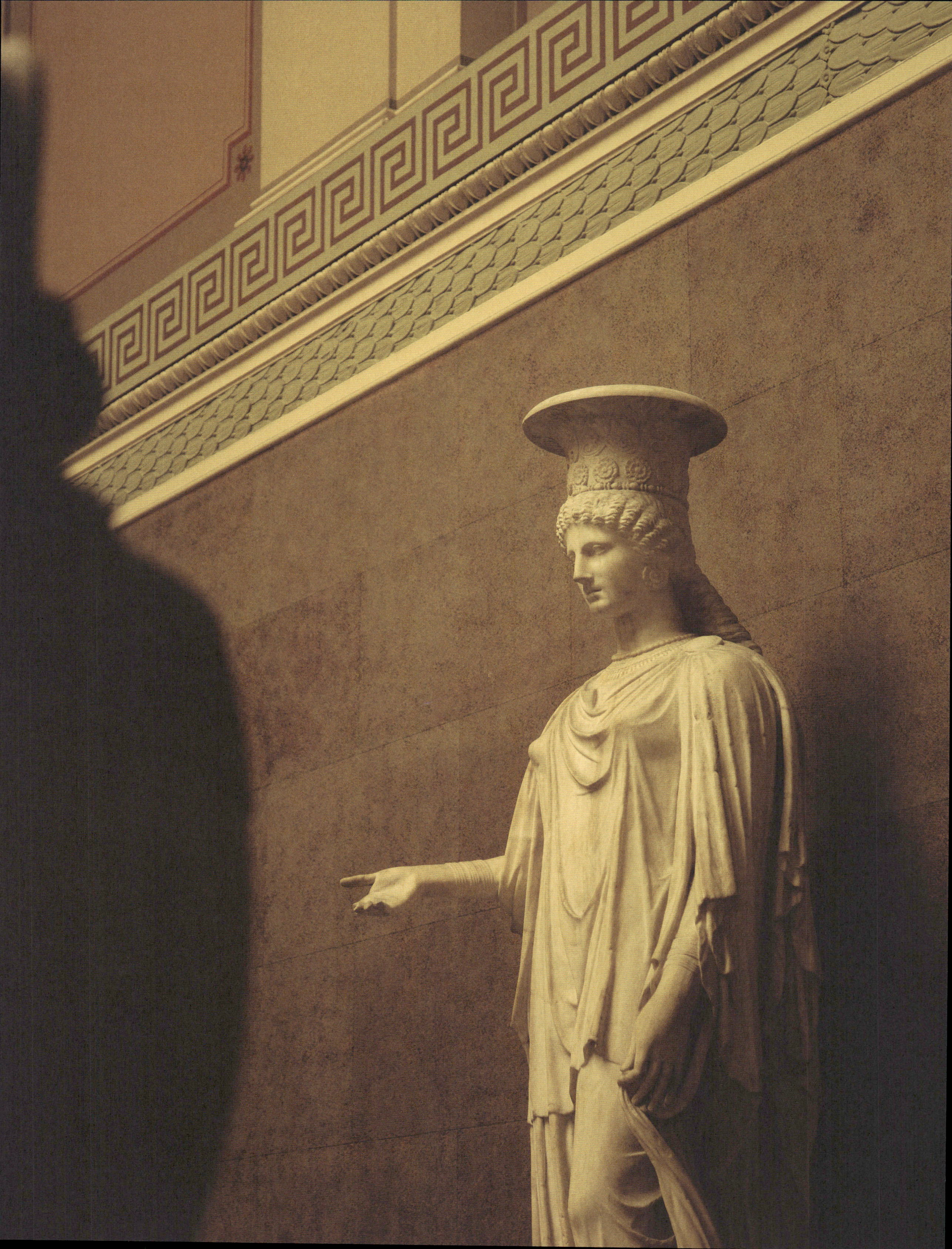

# HISTORY
## A path through the past.

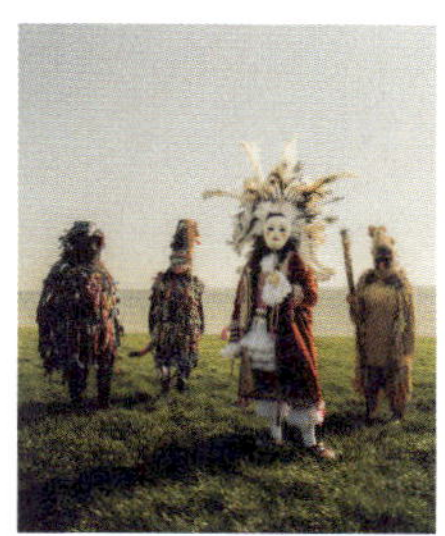





# DIRECTORY
## Culture and columns for summer.

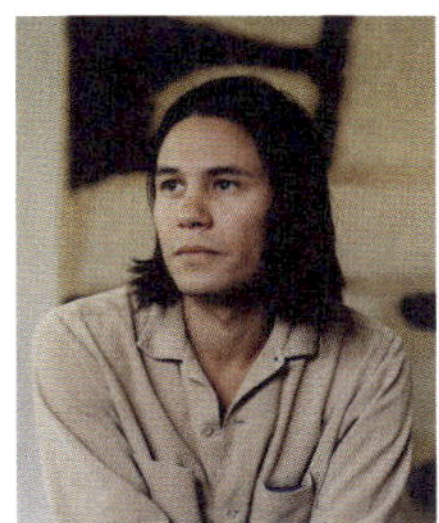

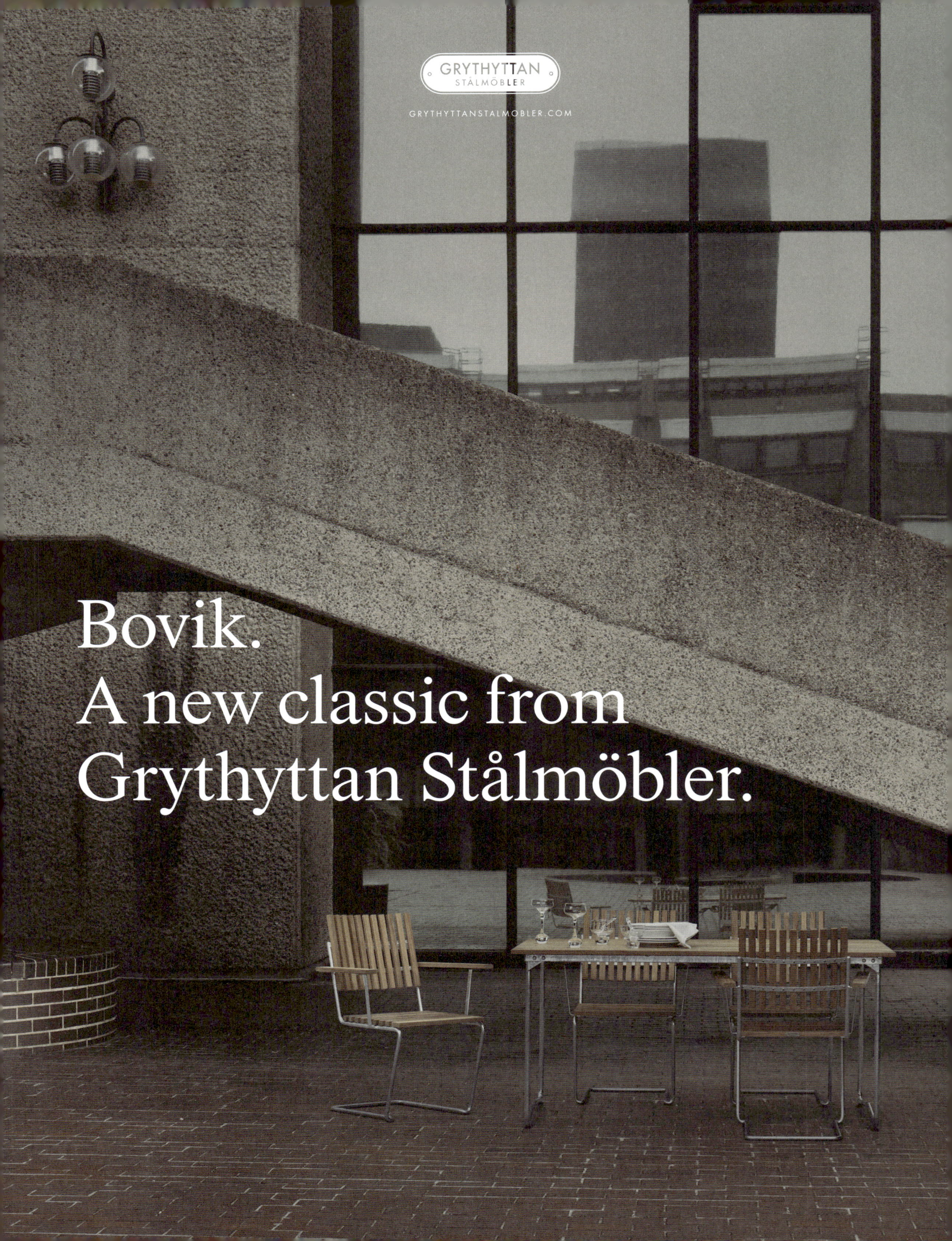

GRYTHYTTAN
STÅLMÖBLER
GRYTHYTTANSTALMOBLER.COM

Bovik.
A new classic from
Grythyttan Stålmöbler.

# Starters.

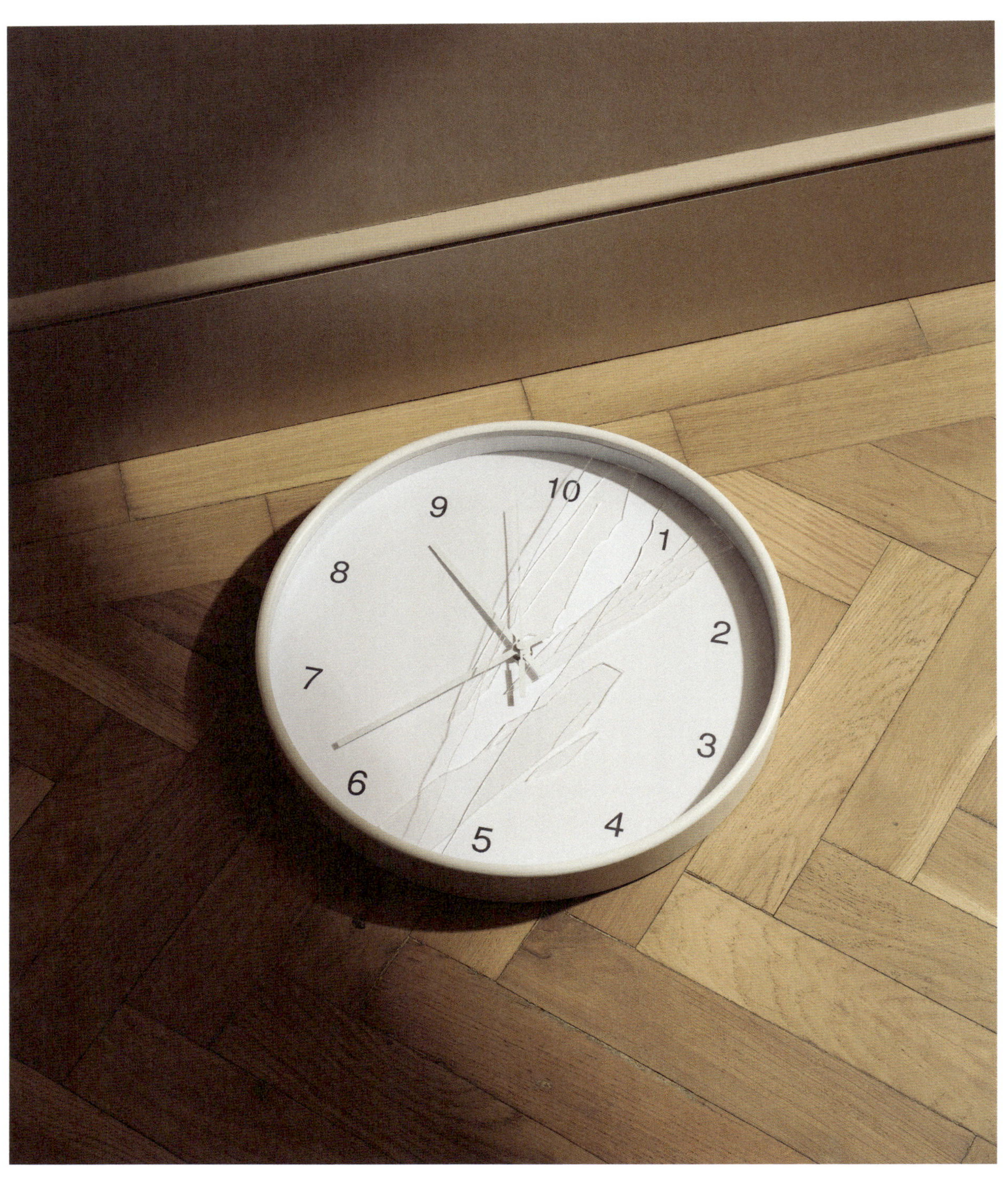

16

# SPECIAL MEASURES
## When days turned into weeks.

WORDS
ASHER ROSS
PHOTO
AARON TILLEY

In 1793, nine months after Louis XVI was executed, the revolutionary leaders of France's National Convention formally adopted the French Republican calendar. It was a period marked by violent revenge for social injustices and utopian visions of reform, and the new calendar was an attempt to liberate the flow of time itself from the shackles of the *ancien régime* and the church. The old Gregorian calendar, with its Catholic feast days, was replaced by a new system organized around agriculture, natural law and the decimal. The months were given new names—*Floréal*, the "month of flowers" (late April and early May) and *Fructidor*, the "month of fruit" (late August and early September), for instance—and were subdivided into three 10-day weeks. Laborers of the time complained that *décadi*, the tenth day of the week, marked for rest, came less often than the Sundays of the past.

With a new calendar came a new clock. Decimal time, introduced toward the end of 1793, similarly broke the day into 10 hours. Each of these hours contained 100 minutes, with each minute containing 100 seconds—meaning that a French revolutionary hour was about 2 hours and 24 minutes in standard time, while the revolutionary second was slightly shorter than it had been before—about 0.86 standard seconds.

Decimal time had already been in circulation as an idea among Enlightenment-era thinkers (Diderot included an entry on it in his *Encyclopédie*), and its establishment came amid a broad push to order weights, measures and currency according to the metric system. In theory, applying the idea to time would be a bureaucratic and statistical boon. It would be quite easy, for example, to calculate 60% of a day (6 hours), and times could be given in decimal form without calculation: 1.2345 decimal hours is the same as 123.45 decimal minutes, or 12,345 decimal seconds and so on.

Ideological pressure forced some to observe the system for a while, but it remained, for the most part, a matter of onerous conversion, rather than a liberator of habits. In 1795, after about 17 (standard) months, enforcement of decimal time was abolished. The revolutionary calendar lasted a bit longer, with Napoleon discarding it in 1806, just over a year after his coronation as emperor effectively ended the first French Republic.

While the metric system of weights and measures thrived and remains the global standard to this day, it can be tempting to see the failure of French decimal time as a cautionary lesson in revolutionary idealism.[1] Yet the spirit of the idea, in throwing off arbitrary constraints from the past and reshaping the world according to objective facts from nature, continued to capture the imagination. It's remarkable that many revolutions in world history—the Russian Revolution, the Chinese Revolution that ended the Qing dynasty, the Islamic Revolution in Iran—all attempted to reclaim the reality of time from what came before.

Like the French revolutionaries, we too live in an age marked by skepticism of hierarchies, words and assumptions inherited from a violent and oppressive past. Many now, as then, suspect that the world's order has served a privileged few, and are keen to dismantle the systems that have enabled it. We might wonder, along with the idealists at the National Convention, what energies and capabilities could be unleashed by throwing off the habits of the past.

Time, however, is a tricky thing, and our perception of it is not really governed by measures, whether they be in 24- or 10-hour increments. It's relative, both in the sense of physics and the observer's mood and experiences. Dread, boredom and anxiety can all make time seem to slow, sometimes agonizingly so. Joy, flow states and good company can make time pass pleasurably and quickly. Reclaiming the time that belongs to us is still a worthy and revolutionary act, but perhaps best conducted as a rebellion of one.

---

(1) The meter was originally defined by the French National Assembly in 1791 as one ten-millionth of the distance from the equator to the North Pole along a meridian passing, of course, through Paris. Since 1983, the meter has instead been defined as the distance light travels in a vacuum in 1/299,792,458 of a second.

In 1956, the Danish furniture designer Hans J. Wegner drew an apparently simple chair with a backrest curving to provide elbow support and a rounded seat that appears to float above the legs. Creating a prototype of the "Elbow Chair" proved to be so difficult, however, that it never went into production.

"It's incredibly complicated," says Knud Erik Hansen, the CEO of furniture company Carl Hansen & Søn. The structure that supports the seat alone is built from nine layers of veneer, pressed in a single operation with a special mold; the back is a large, steam-bent piece of wood that must then be precisely milled. In the 1950s, when the chair would have been built entirely by hand, the process would have taken weeks. Every manufacturer Wegner approached declined.

Half a century later, Hansen encountered the prototype in Wegner's studio and was determined to find a way to finally put it into production. At the factory, his craftsmen balked at the idea but Hansen looked to cutting-edge CNC capabilities, investing in a machine that could mill multiple backrests at once. What had once been "a terrible job" was now suddenly possible.

To suit taller bodies and modern table heights, the reissued Elbow Chair was raised by almost an inch, a change that Wegner's design studio had to give permission for. "We can't do anything at all to the design unless it's approved," Hansen says. It's a requirement that ensures manufacturers respect the original intentions of the designer and, for Carl Hansen, this is often central to choosing what the company reissues—a selection process that is part curatorial and part commercial.

"It's a combination of the story behind the products, the design—and, of course, whether we believe people will actually buy it," Hansen explains.

WORDS
BENJAMIN DANE
PHOTO
CARL HANSEN & SØN

# OBJECT MATTERS
## A good, old-fashioned revival.

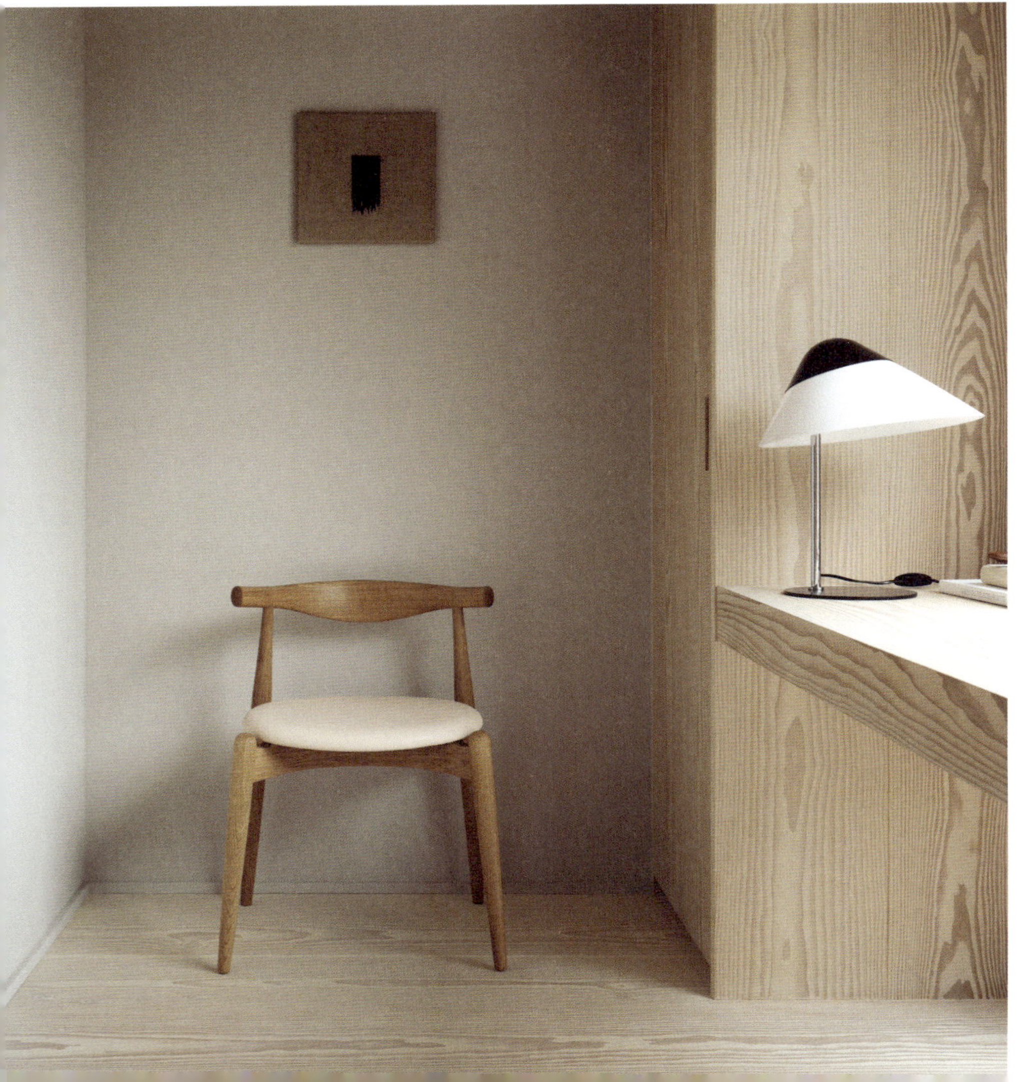

*The Bank of London and South America building:* This is an iconic Brutalist building in downtown Buenos Aires by the Italian Argentinian architect Clorindo Testa. It's just incredible, and I love that it's right across from a very traditional 19th-century building. One of the things I enjoy about Buenos Aires is the architecture—in just one block you can find so many different styles that together are somehow harmonious.

*A Woman Under the Influence, John Cassavetes:* Gena Rowlands' performance is so brilliant in this movie.

*Galerie Sardine:* I saw their recent show with Justin Bradshaw and Maria Robledo. Their space in New York is gorgeous and I loved how it brought together the artists' different worlds.

*Northern Argentina:* I go to the mountains, open landscapes and clear skies of the Salta and Jujuy provinces in the north of Argentina for the light, space and silence. It is calm and powerful at the same time, and the colors—pale rose, ocher, yellow, purple—change throughout the day. You can stay in a nice estancia, drink wine in bodegas and eat very good empanadas.

*Getz/Gilberto, João Gilberto and Stan Getz:* I simply love this album. It reminds me of some really nice moments in my life.

*A simple tortilla de papas:* Potatoes, onions, eggs and tons of olive oil.

*"El Remordimiento," Jorge Luis Borges:* My mom would recite this poem whenever I was sad. She knew it by heart and I would always sit and listen until she had finished.

*Mambo:* This restaurant opened last year and I went several times with friends when I was back in Buenos Aires in January. The space is open, the design clean and the food absolutely delicious.

*Autumn Sonata:* This is my friend Lilli's brand. She has an incredible line of towels and homeware, and I am always excited to see what she does next.

*The Journal of Philosophy:* I like to read random articles from *The Journal of Philosophy* that you can find online for free. The most recent one was "What Is Real Pleasure?" by Wilson D. Wallis, an American anthropologist, which was published in 1919. Reading philosophy is my way of learning to ask better questions and challenge habits of thought.

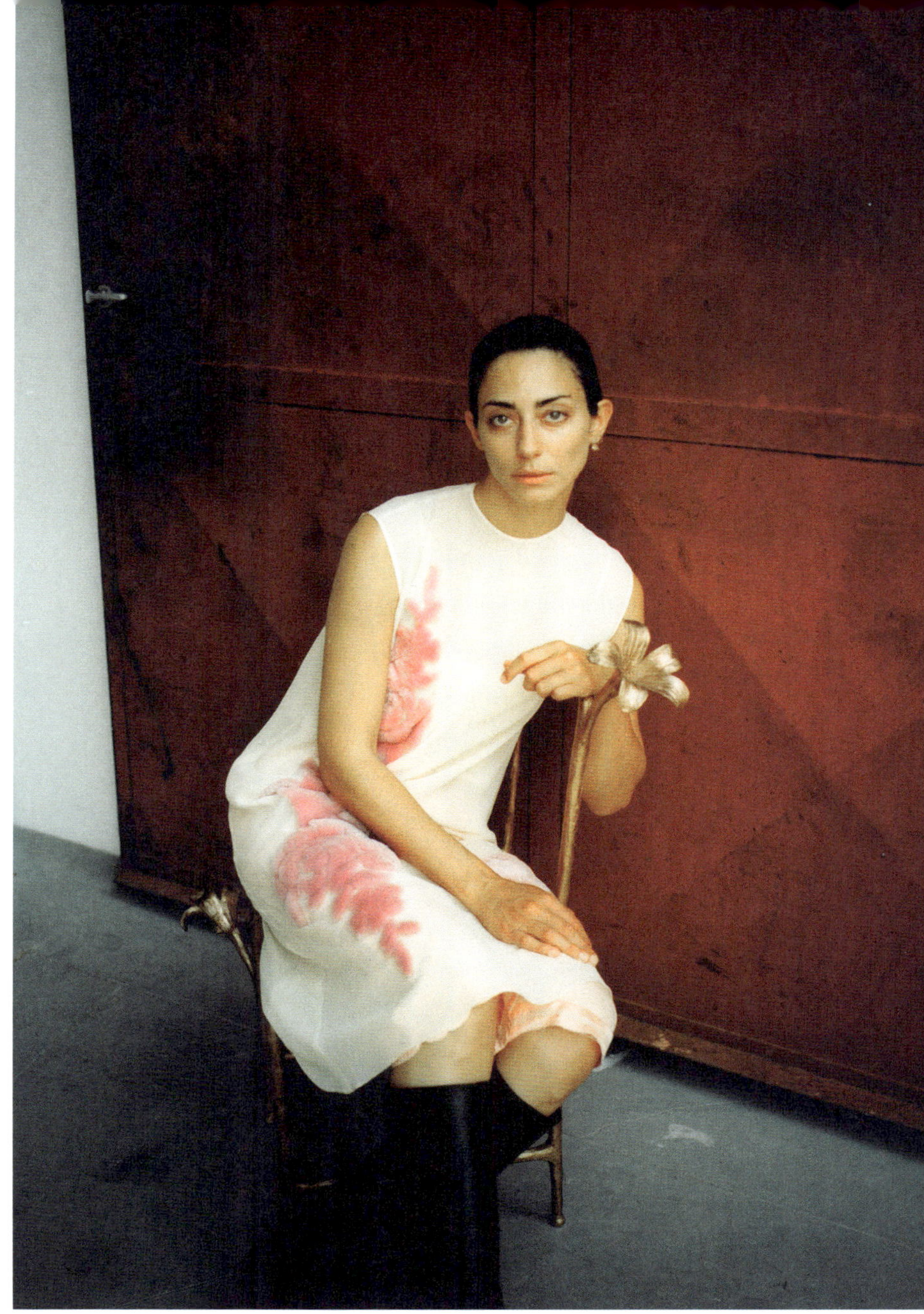

WORDS
CONIE VALLESE
PHOTO
EUGENIO INTINI

# STARTER FOR TEN
## Artist Conie Vallese's favorite things.

# THE GOTTMANS

WORDS
ROBERT ITO
PHOTOS
CHONA KASINGER

## The couple who can save your marriage.

John Gottman and Julie Schwartz met in 1986 when John, a psychologist, was a professor at the University of Washington. John had spent the previous 15 years researching what makes some marriages work and what leads others to divorce. It was an interest that Julie, a clinical psychologist, shared and five years into their own marriage, she began to wonder whether, rather than simply observing relationships implode, they could actually intervene and help.

For the past four decades, the Gottmans have been doing just that. As two of the world's most respected experts in marriage, the pair have helped countless partners to live and love better, based on what they've learned from the more than 55,000 relationships they've seen in workshops.

This wealth of experience has come to inform the Gottman Method, an approach to couples therapy that focuses on improving communication and strengthening emotional connections. Here they talk about why snuggling is good, blame is bad and how fighting, done right, can help.

ROBERT ITO: You've met a lot of unhappy couples. Is there anything they have in common?

JOHN: One of the things we noticed is that unhappy couples had developed a habit of only looking for their partner's mistakes and ignoring all of the good things they do. Couples therapy in the 1970s just assumed that couples who were unhappy weren't doing nice things for one another, and so in one of the interventions that was introduced at the time, people had to do nice things for one another even if they weren't in the mood. The problem was, it wasn't that they weren't doing nice things already, it was that their partner wasn't noticing those things. Noticing positive things and saying thank-you can really turn things around.

JULIE: Many, many couples have a partner who thinks they only need to say "I love you" once. Maybe at the altar or at the wedding dinner, and that's it. They stop. They don't keep saying "I love you." They don't keep reinforcing fondness and admiration in the relationship. But you really have to keep expressing that.

RI: So, say nice things. What else should couples be doing?

JOHN: There was a study with 70,000 people in 24 countries that showed that among people who cuddle, almost all of them said they had a great sex life, but only 4% of the noncuddlers said the same thing. Cuddling, which is really about nonsexual touch, releases oxytocin and decreases cortisol in the body, so it's a very health-giving thing and really affects people's sex life.

RI: In heterosexual relationships, when it comes to communication, who is usually the worst at it? I would tend to assume it's the guy.

JULIE: No, no. That's one of the mistakes people make a lot in couples therapy. When couples come in, they're terrified that the therapist is going to nail one of them as the bad guy, and that isn't the way it is. You have to look at the dynamic between the two. I imagine it as this golden sphere—you have to look at what

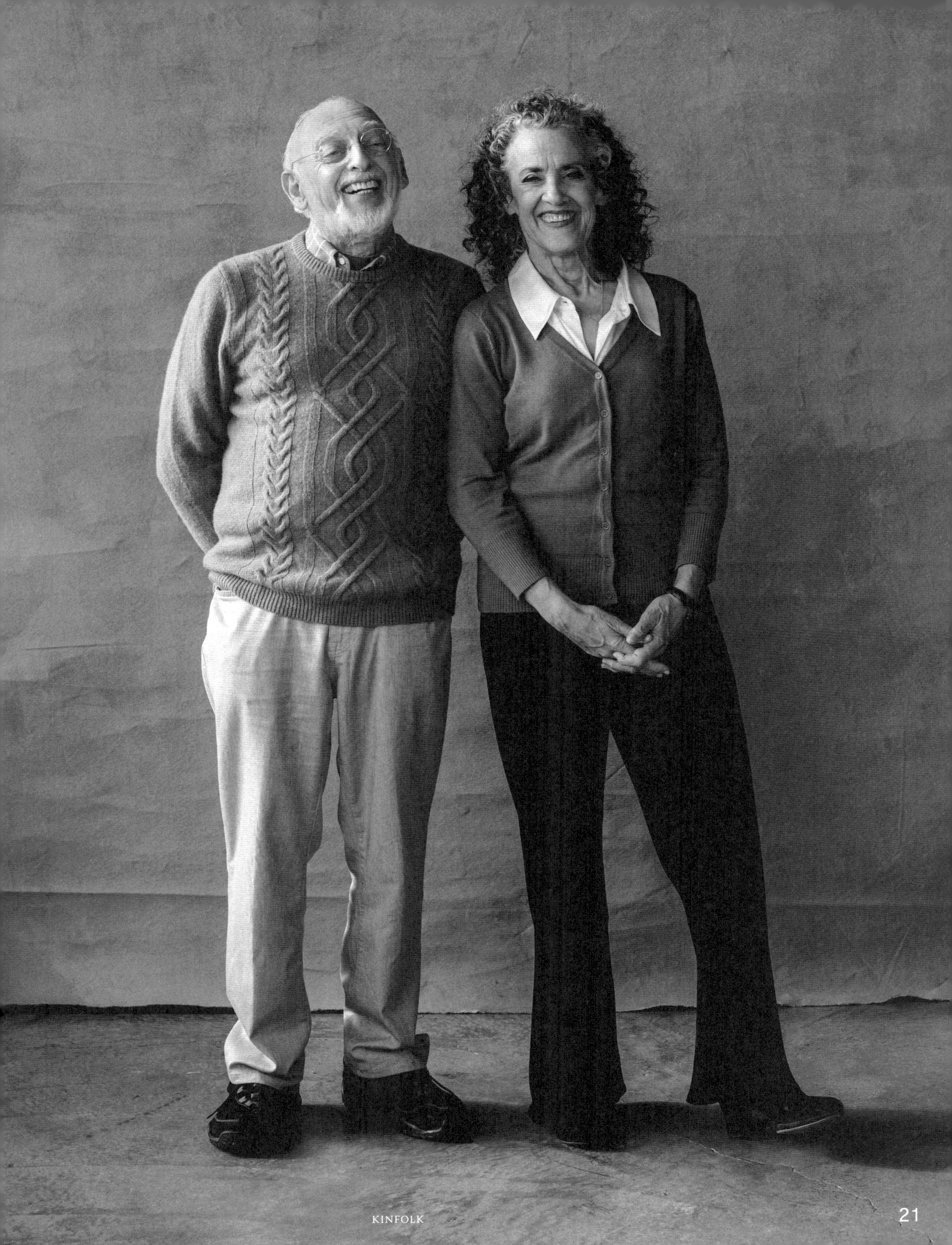

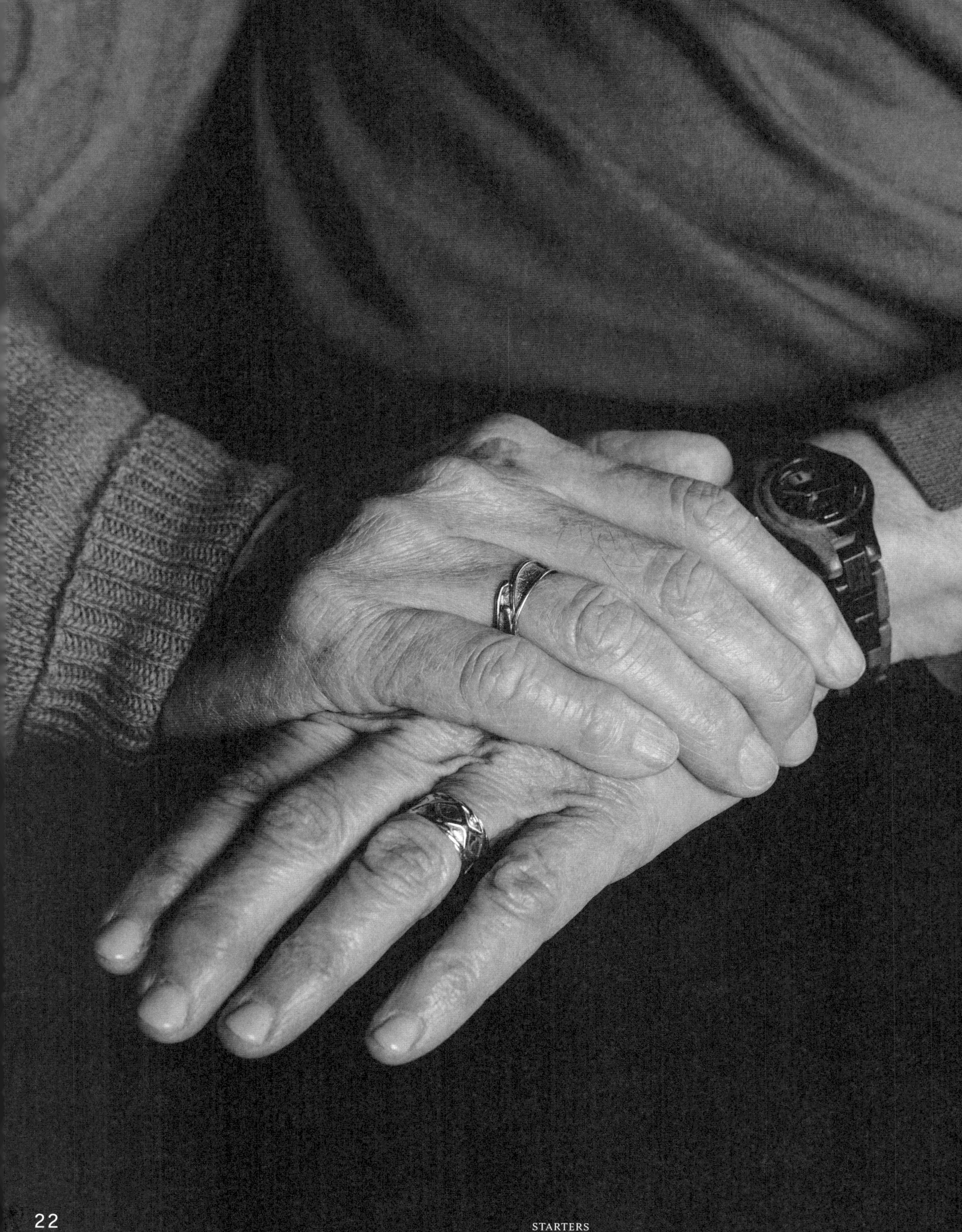



STARTERS

each partner is contributing to that world between them. Naturally, if somebody's critical, the other person is going to be defensive. That's a typical human dynamic, but one or the other is not at fault.

JOHN: A lot of therapies are oriented toward confronting the asshole, confronting the immature person in the relationship. I won't name the people who do that but they're pretty famous therapists. It just doesn't work. When you blame one person for all the problems, you're ignoring the dynamics of the relationship.

RI: What sort of relationship advice do people really struggle to implement in real time?

JOHN: I think it's downregulating defensiveness. This is what the masters are good at, the people who know intuitively how to have good relationships. When their partner is critical, rather than get defensive, they're much more likely to say, "Well, that's interesting. Tell me more about that. I want to know what you're feeling." I have an invention that really works for men; a notebook that you carry in your back pocket. When Julie wants to talk about our relationship, I take my notebook out very slowly, so I can delay my response. I keep breathing, and then I say, Okay, talk to me. I'm listening. And I start writing down what she's saying.

JULIE: He takes notes!

JOHN: I take notes, so I can then respond, nondefensively. It's my trick.

RI: How did the pandemic impact couples?

JULIE: During that first year, I was on the phone constantly talking about the ways couples could survive this, especially the quarantine period. A study found that couples who were already happy became happier during COVID because they had more time together. We were a great example of that. But the unhappy couples really fell apart—it was like the couple was in a pressure cooker and there was no escape valve. The pressure would build and build until there'd be an explosion. I thought of ways that couples could create some private space for themselves. It was actually so simple. You know how kids build forts out of couch pillows and sheets? I would have each partner build one of those. And when they went inside, they'd have pillows, they might have incense. They would go in that space, and nobody was to disturb them. Before COVID, many couples were used to more distance, at least during the part of the day when they went to work or took their kids to school. Well, all that was gone. So we had to create another means of doing that.

RI: Do you two fight? Is fighting a good thing for a relationship?

JULIE: It depends how it's done.

JOHN: Conflict is inevitable—and not only inevitable, but it really has a positive function. Conflict is the way that we love better over time, because when we encounter conflict, we realize that our partner is not thinking the way we're thinking. Conflict is a way to get closer to one another over time, and to stay close.

RI: I imagine a lot of people think you two don't fight.

JULIE: We try to take ourselves off the pedestal and show that we're all in the same soup. We're not perfect. We have just studied a lot of couples who are really good, and we've learned from them.

RI: Do you still meet people that make you go, Oh, that's a good thing to do—other people should try that?

JOHN: Absolutely. In fact, we're starting a series very soon in which we will interview a happily married couple every two weeks, and present their relationship on video, so people can see what a great relationship looks like.

RI: Any last words of advice?

JOHN: Learning to communicate well in a relationship is like learning to play a new instrument. To play the instrument well, you've got to really practice, and you have to correct your mistakes. Only then can you get better. If you don't put in the effort, it doesn't work.

—

> *"Learning to communicate well in a relationship is like learning to play a new instrument... you've got to really practice."*

( opposite )    John and Julie have been married for 38 years. They both had previous relationships that ended in divorce.
( previous )    The Gottmans in Portland, Oregon, where they have an office. The Gottman Institute is based in Seattle.

Samuel Lee has been working with stone for 15 years, carving new sculptures, restoring old ones and working to preserve the ancient craft. At London Stone Carving, working cooperatively with three other masons, he oversees the whole process, from quarrying the stone to installing the finished piece.

ELLE HUNT: What led you to stonemasonry?

SAMUEL LEE: It started with a fascination with stone itself. I grew up in Wiltshire, where there is really hard stone, called sarsen stone. One of my earliest memories is hitting it with one of my dad's chisels and getting a spark. I thought, "How do you do anything with this material?" I later learned that my grandmother's family had been stonemasons for 125 years, building churches.

EH: What's the modern-day pathway for the job?

SL: At 18, I went to stonemasonry college, which covered the architectural side of things, like basic moldings, blocks and building conservation. After two years, I moved to the City & Guilds of London Art School for a classical art education: the life drawing, modeling and observational skills you need to make three-dimensional things.

EH: What does a typical day look like for you at the workshop?

SL: With stone carving, you explore different themes with each job. One job could be on an ornament from 1340, requiring you to get into art and architectural history. Next is a statue of a dog, and you have to be an expert in the anatomy of a spaniel. Increasingly, people are bringing us things they've modeled on a computer, or 3D scanned, to copy into stone, which doesn't always work.

EH: How do you think the work has changed throughout history?

SL: Some clients want every step to be done with hammers and chisels, but we prefer a middle ground. Everything is finished and carved by hand, but we do use a machine to take the bulk off. Then we're literally doing the work as it's always been done.

EH: What's the outlook for the industry?

SL: I worry about being able to make a living, but we only need three or four big jobs a year to keep us going. It is so niche, you don't need more than 30 stone carvers in the country to maintain the industry.

Carving tends to be the first thing to be cut from budgets. It's a shame—throughout history, we've always had ornamentation, even with Brutalism. People enjoy these objects for hundreds of years.

# ODD JOBS
## Samuel Lee, stone carver.

WORDS
ELLE HUNT
PHOTO
NATHAN WOLF GRACE

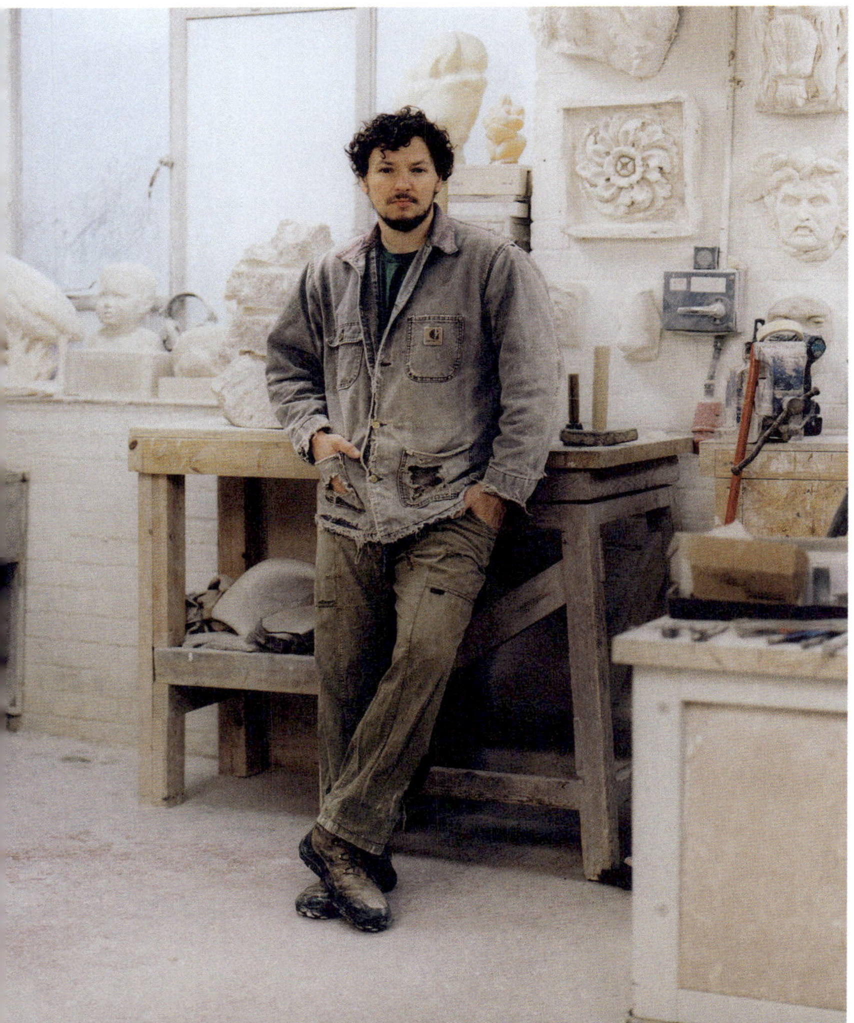

What happened on the day you were born? It can be oddly satisfying to find out—perhaps because it gives you a sense of how much the world has changed, or else because it offers clues about who you are, revealing how your life unfolds within a wider, collective history. At the very least, it's a fun way to pass an afternoon.

The archives of La Galcante, a small store in Paris packed with old newspapers and magazines, are dedicated to this unique purpose: selling the yellowed pages of old periodicals as keepsake birthday gifts. Founded in 1975 by collector Christian Bailly, the shop stocks some eight million newspapers dating back to the French Revolution, and takes its name from a playful contraction of *galerie* (gallery) and *brocante* (bric-a-brac shop). Inside, stacks of magazines cover two long tables, where you might find a copy of *Newsweek* from December 1992 next to 1972 issues of *Tintin*. On the back wall, daily newspapers are carefully classified into boxes by month and year; another shelf sorts them by themes such as "Sartre," "Walt Disney" and "Justice."

The store's current owner, Jacques Kuzma, first arrived as a student looking for a summer job and never left. One recent morning, while flicking through the papers in a box labeled September 1966, he picked up a call from someone in need of a prop for a film. "Ninety percent of my sales are birthday presents," he says. "But this year *Le Figaro* is celebrating its 200th anniversary, so I've sold quite a few to collectors and exhibition curators."

The National Library of France houses the country's vast press archives, which date back to 1631, but La Galcante makes that history far more accessible. "I've been surprised by how many young people come in," Kuzma says. "A lot of them are perhaps engaging with print for the first time. They stop, leaf through some magazines, ask questions. It's unexpected—and reassuring."

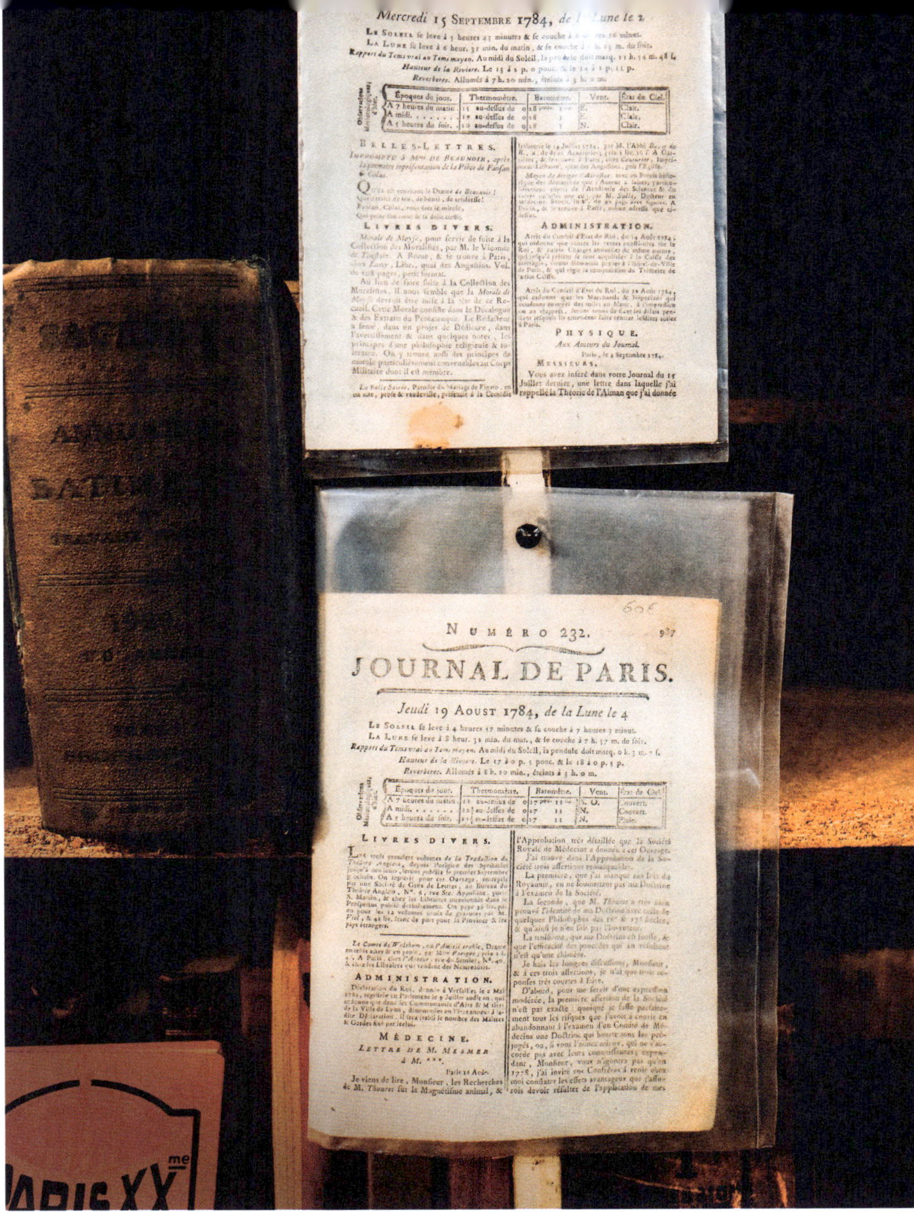

WORDS
JULIA WEBSTER AYUSO
PHOTO
JULIE MAYFENG

# CULT ROOMS
## La Galcante—a Parisian time warp.

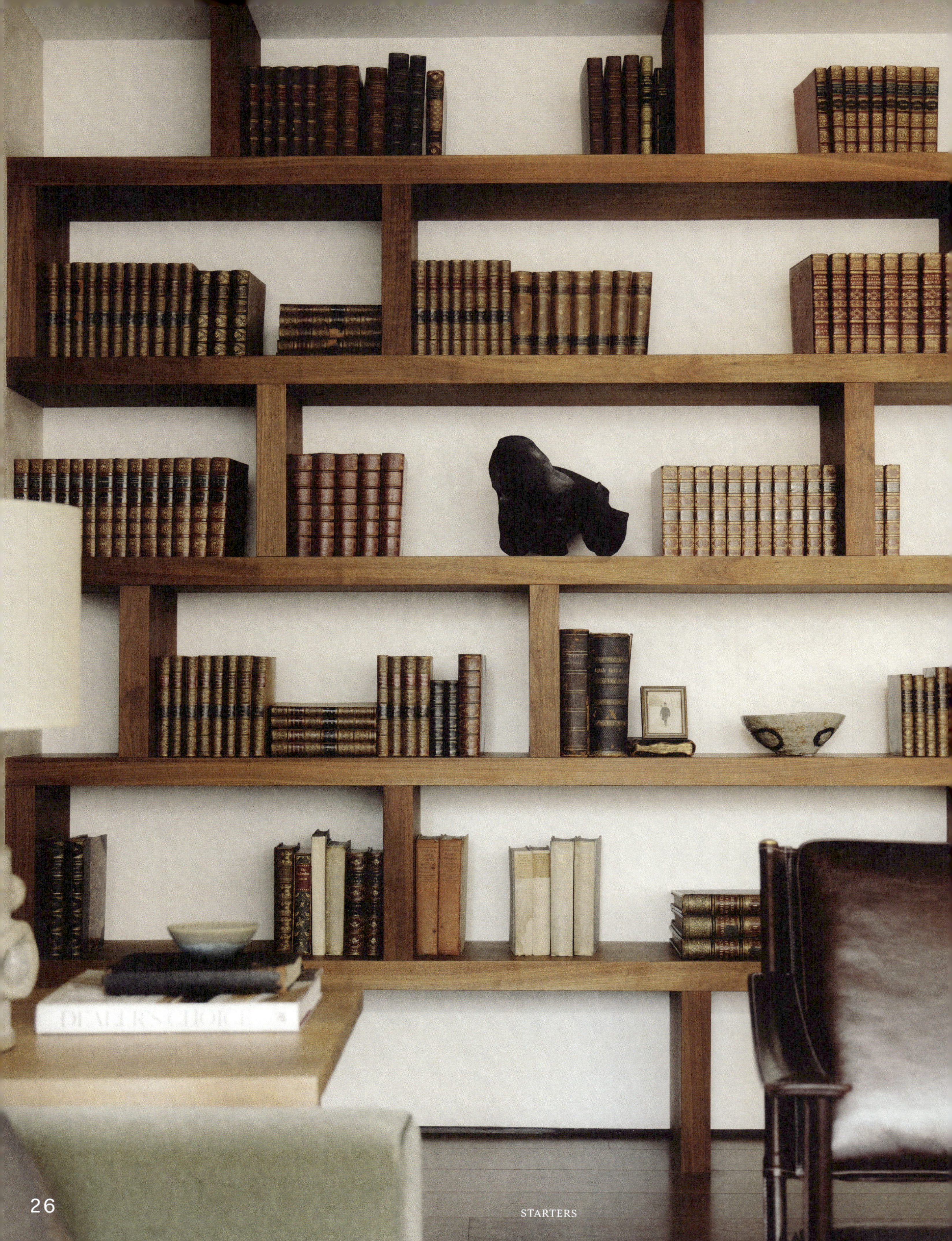

What constitutes a work of classic literature? T. S. Eliot, in a 1944 address to the Virgil Society in London, argued that a classic could be defined by its "maturity." "A classic can only occur," he maintained, "when a civilization is mature; when a language and a literature are mature; and it must be the work of a mature mind." Yet it is not exactly clear how Eliot, in his prickly way, defined maturity. "We cannot call the literature of the Elizabethan period, great as it was, wholly mature," he continues, neatly dismissing Shakespeare and Marlowe in one fell swoop.

Mark Twain, in a speech delivered at New York's Nineteenth Century Club 44 years earlier, took a more humorous approach to this question. A classic, he quipped, is "something that everybody wants to have read and nobody wants to read." It is easy to imagine the audience laughing self-deprecatingly, and it's a quote, originally attributed to a professor at Wesleyan University, that still gets repeated today. But while Twain's observation may be funny—and partially true—there's also something unsatisfying about it. After all, there are a whole host of reasons why certain books endure, even those that have, like Melville's *Moby-Dick* or the writings of Kafka, been dismissed, ignored or poorly reviewed during their authors' lifetimes.

While fashions in literature come and go, there is something attractive in the idea of a canon—if nothing else as a means of quality control when deciding what to read next. Perhaps this is why Morrissey, the musician and ex-frontman of the Smiths, insisted that his autobiography be published by Penguin's famous Classics imprint (Penguin justified its acquiescence by arguing that *Autobiography* was "a classic in the making"). At the same time, those who decide a canon's scope have wielded the term "classic" as though it were a weapon, allowing only a narrow swath of individuals from certain groups to be elevated to its place. Because of this, in recent decades there have been arguments in favor of what is called an "expanded canon," which makes space for writers who are women, or not white, or who work in non-European languages.

So, what *does* make a classic? Perhaps the best definition came from the Italian writer Italo Calvino in his 1981 essay on the subject: "A classic is a book that has never finished saying what it has to say." It's a book that is deeply engaged in a conversation that spans decades, countries, classes and creeds; a conversation that can otherwise be simply called "literature."[1] And to engage with this discourse, you don't need to be a certain type of person. You simply need to be curious enough to pick up a book.

As Virginia Woolf once wrote, "Literature is no one's private garden; literature is common ground." For a classic, that common ground is a useful one, creating touchstones and clues that allow the members of that worldwide and ageless secret society known as "readers" to find one another. There is no handshake required—only passion, good humor and an open mind.

---

( 1 )  Several of Calvino's own works have come to be considered classics, including *If on a Winter's Night a Traveler* and *Invisible Cities*, a novel in which the explorer Marco Polo describes a series of imaginary cities that all turn out to be Venice.

WORDS
RHIAN SASSEEN
PHOTO
WILLIAM JESS LAIRD



# WHAT MAKES A CLASSIC?
## A new answer to an age-old question.

# IMITATION CRAB
## A sideways scuttle to perfection.

Once there were only single-celled organisms, bobbing around in the primordial soup. A few billion years of evolution later we have golden eagles, baobab trees and Dua Lipa. It's a startlingly broad spectrum that suggests that such diversity will only continue to grow. But, in fact, it seems that many different species have arrived at the same place.

"Convergent evolution" is the name for the phenomenon by which organisms separately progress toward similar ends, like middle-class parents all ending up with the same "original" names for their children. It means we can legitimately ask the question: Of earth's cornucopia, which of those organisms comes closest to perfection?

Certain bats, birds and insects all worked out that wings might come in handy. At some point sharks (fish) and dolphins (mammals) acquired similar go-faster hydrodynamic forms. One study found that mammals have evolved to become anteaters (or at least ant-eating) not once but 12 times in history.

But as far as scientists can tell, no form is currently more desirable than that of the crab. At least five different crustaceans have evolved crab-like forms, a process called carcinization, going from being more lobster- or shrimp-like toward having a flat, rounded shell and a tail that is folded under the body. Some are in the sea, some are on land. They are so numerous that there is a term for them: "false crabs," impersonators at whom the true crabs presumably turn up their noses.

What is it about the crab form that makes it so well suited to the demands of modern existence? A few possibilities have been suggested: The small, concealed tail reduces the flesh available to would-be predators. The compact bodies are more efficient in terms of both structure and energy expenditure. And scuttling and hiding is easier with a flat shell than with a more rounded lobster-type one. Crabs can get along in all kinds of places.

Aside from better equipping a wide range of crustaceans to their respective environments, the apparent desirability of the crab form has also prompted a healthy supply of memes. A popular newsletter, *Today in Tabs*, includes a regular Today in Crabs section keeping readers abreast of crab-related news. And it is a running joke on the internet that Homo sapiens, too, are fated to assume a crab-like form, even if the biological consensus is that this is unlikely. Although humans remain subject to natural selection, we have developed the tools to interfere with it. As we outsource to machines not just physical tasks but intellectual ones, it seems more likely we will end up as the brain-dead, prostrate humans from *Wall-E* than as nimble, tough little crabs. Our loss.[1]

WORDS
ED CUMMING
PHOTO
THE VOORHES

(1) Many evolutionary biologists have speculated about how humans might evolve. Suggestions range from becoming taller, more lightly built and increasingly physically alike—with smaller brains—to splitting into entirely separate species or merging with machines.

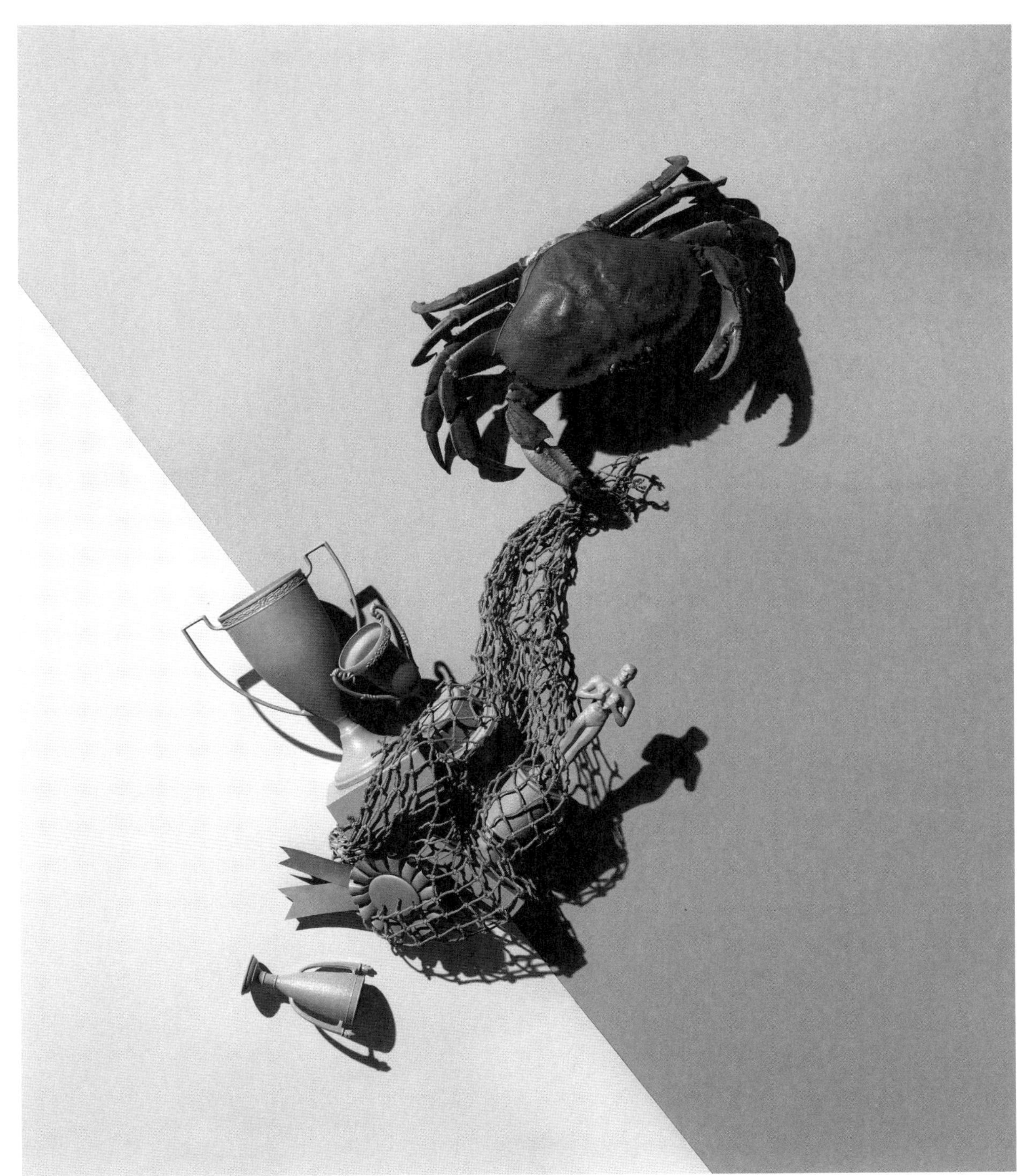

29

# WHAT ARE YOU WORKING ON?

WORDS
CELINE NGUYEN
PHOTO
TED BELTON

## David Michon's cult-favorite newsletter.

David Michon doesn't see FOR SCALE, the Substack newsletter he started in 2022, as a diktat of good taste, even though—as a former editor at *Monocle* and *Icon*—he would be well within his rights to issue one. Instead, he encourages his readers to develop their own critical faculties, offering them delightfully specific taxonomies of interior design—the "screenwriter aesthetic", "plinth culture" and "chair extremism"—as prompts. "Interior design is so important; we're affected by spaces, psychologically and emotionally," he explains. "But it should also feel fun. Things don't need to be stuffy and serious."

CELINE NGUYEN: What was the idea behind FOR SCALE?

DAVID MICHON: When my husband and I moved from London to Los Angeles, we brought nothing. We were furnishing our place with vintage stuff from resellers in LA and, as I was digging around, I felt an incredible energy that wasn't present in design magazines. It was important to me that FOR SCALE is connected to the real world. Substack was my first time writing editorially with my own tone of voice, not a magazine's. My posts are written very fast, which means they have to be topics I'm already passionate about.

CN: People tend to think that it's snobby and elitist to care a lot about taste. But FOR SCALE has a discerning voice that's still open to different points of view.

DM: There *are* some things that separate interesting, compelling interiors and less compelling ones, but I don't really like hierarchies of taste. The idea of an arbitrary tastemaker—I don't love that. Good critique is less about casting judgment and more about opening up questions. If something resonates with me, I ask why, instead of just saying, *This is cool now*. That's why I have these made-up aesthetics, like the "twink aesthetic." The intention is to show that you can make up your own—it's a way of observing something that you like, naming it, and making sense of it.

CN: What's exciting you about interior design at the moment?

DM: There are a trillion excellent people. Off the top of my head, there's Luke Foss, Aunt and 22RE in LA, Sarita Posada in New York, Marie-Anne Derville in Paris, Max Radford in London. LA is really great in design and interiors, because people make up their own rules here. There are designers who put together incredible interiors, but they feel loose, imperfect, where if you brought something home from a trip and put it on the table, it wouldn't disrupt everything. I'm allergic to spaces that feel tight and perfect, totally unlivable.

CN: What does the future of FOR SCALE look like?

DM: The print publication comes from my addiction to laborious projects that bring in almost no money. But it brings another dimension to the writing; it's so different seeing something in print. We're also doing a life drawing class at the Ace Hotel, with a nude model on cool vintage furniture, and an exhibition of photography with a friend of mine, Holly Hay, at the USM showroom.



"

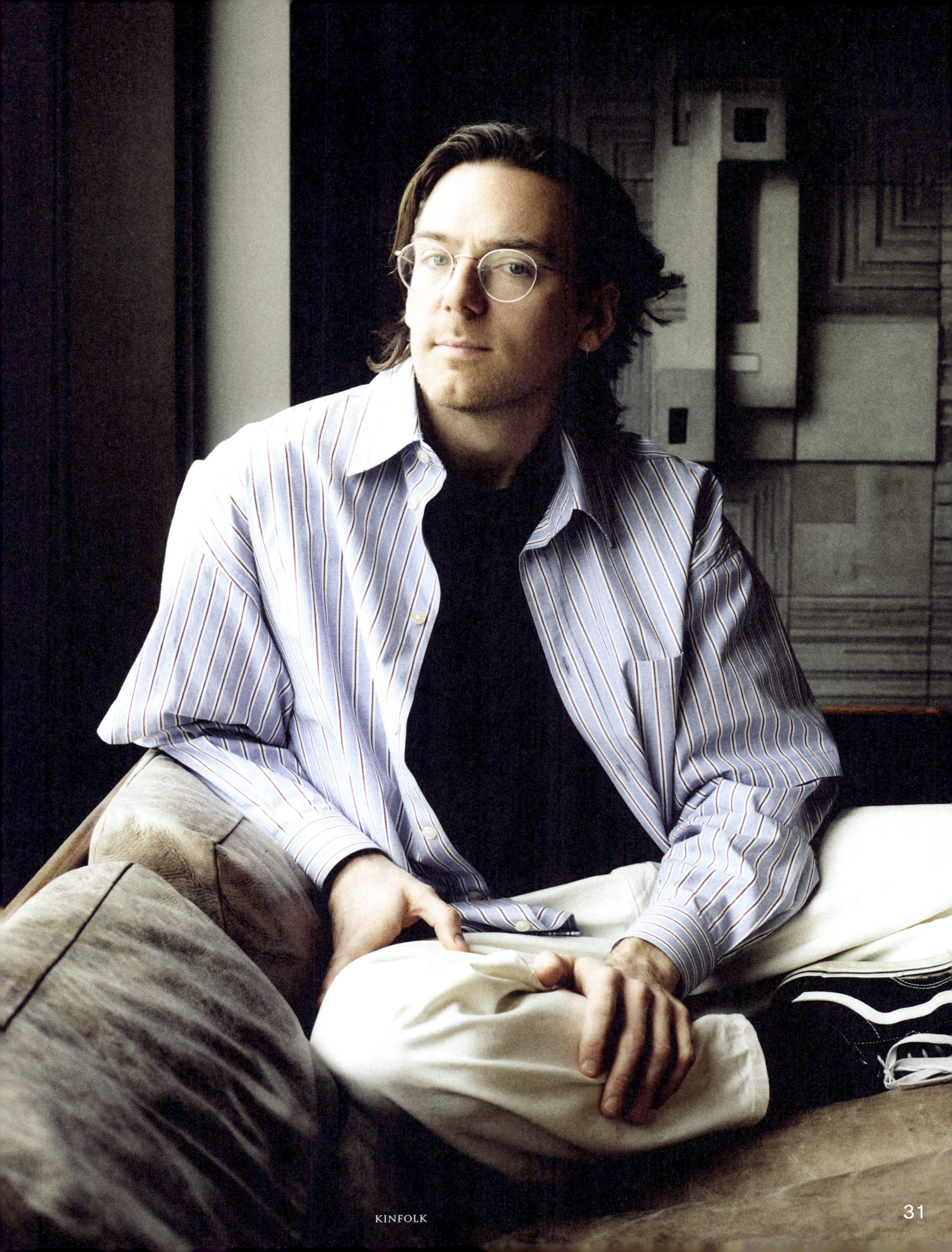

It's summer. A friend invites you to the park on a glorious day, but you decide instead to stay in and catch up on the series you're enjoying. Just as you're getting comfy on the sofa, however, the regret kicks in: You're squandering the good weather; on a day as nice as this, you really should be outside.

It's a feeling that has come to be known as "sunshine guilt," one that afflicts people in warmer and colder climates—a term that alludes to an almost universal imperative to make the most of the sun. And in many ways, we *should* regret not going out in good weather. Sunlight has been connected with health and vitality since antiquity and, more recently, science has backed this up; not only does it have natural mood-lifting qualities, boosting serotonin levels and increasing vitamin D production, but sunlight helps regulate our circadian rhythms and can even increase life expectancy. A 2024 study by the University of Edinburgh published in the public health journal *Health & Place* found a correlation between UV radiation and a lower risk of cardiovascular disease, even when the risk of skin cancer was taken into consideration.

And yet there is something liberating about staying in when you should be going out. It's an assertion of the fact that your days are yours to do with as you please and a rejection of a culture that celebrates optimization. Staying at home can be restorative in ways sunlight cannot. And besides, you can always justify the decision with your own small piece of scientific reasoning: The sun has risen for the past few billion years. It will rise again tomorrow.[1]

( 1 ) Or will it? It's a question philosophers have pondered for centuries. The belief that something will happen because it has happened before—such as the sun rising—is called induction, but we can never be completely certain that something won't go wrong with the sun overnight.

# NOBLE ROT
## The liberating power of sun shunning.

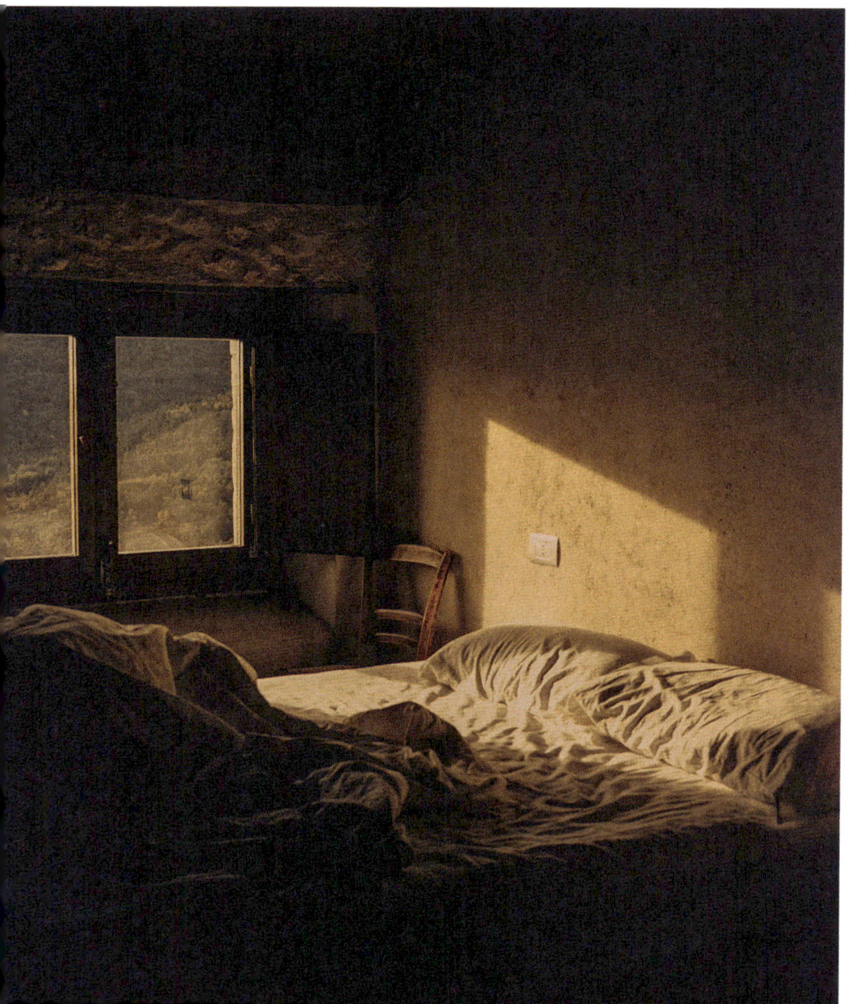

WORDS
PRECIOUS ADESINA
PHOTO
LISA SORGINI

WORDS
CELINE NGUYEN
PHOTO
NATHAN SAILLET

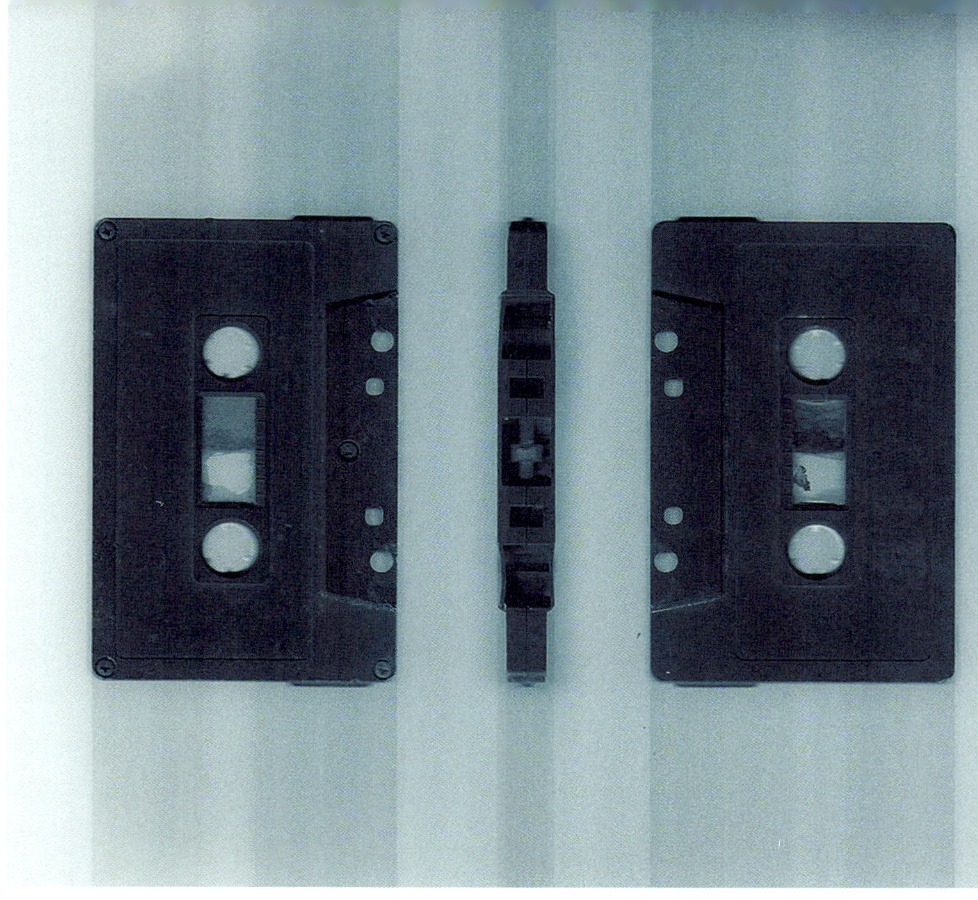

# TOTAL WIPEOUT
## On the digital dark age.

*The internet is forever* was once a cautionary cliché. The prevailing assumption was that everything uploaded online would be permanently and instantly accessible. We were told to not post impulsively, lest future lovers or employers unearth something embarrassing, and at the same time, we were encouraged to trust websites, software companies and digital devices with our most valuable memories, private messages and intimate data.

Now, several decades into Web 2.0, it turns out that the internet might have a shelf life after all—something AI founders would do well to remember. Take MySpace, one of the most widely used websites of the early 2000s. Home to countless online flirtations and burgeoning friendships, it also hosted fanpages that helped unknown musicians—Lily Allen, Arctic Monkeys and Adele, for example—become famous. But in 2019, the company confessed that everything uploaded before 2016—including 50 million songs—had been accidentally deleted. Another social media app, Vine, suffered a similar fate after it was purchased by Twitter and then discontinued. For several years, the company maintained an online archive but eventually, in 2019, it too disappeared off the internet. Those who didn't download their videos were bereft.

So what's the solution? When the popular web hosting service GeoCities was shut down in 2009, a volunteer archiving collective raced to download as many webpages as possible. In the last two years, similar volunteer projects have sought to preserve environmental and public health data that is no longer available on US governmental websites. But the valiant efforts of those preserving our digital past are often hampered by technology itself, with outdated file formats, degrading computer hardware and obsolete storage mediums like VHS tapes and floppy disks threatening to render much of the recent past unreadable.

For now, at least, it is possible to take matters into your own hands. As convenient as cloud storage and streaming services are, it is always advisable to back things up where possible—occasionally downloading your files, email and social media archives to a hard drive (or two) to ensure you will continue to be able to access them. And doing a little judicious curating—by printing out the best photos from your camera roll, for instance—can help make sense of the ever-increasing amount of content we produce. Long term, however, it's impossible to know if our .jpegs and .pdfs will be still readable in the decades and centuries to come. As a different cliché goes: Nothing lasts forever.

*Etymology:* A blend of "spud" (a digging implement) and "puddle," first recorded in 1630; a verb that means "to work feebly" and "to be extremely busy while achieving absolutely nothing."

*Definition:* The most mystifying thing about "spuddle" is its 17th-century origins. Working feebly may well be fundamental to the human experience, but it's hard to imagine how one could be incredibly busy while achieving nothing when ploughing a field, say, or going to war with the Dutch. That the word has enjoyed a renaissance in recent years—online forums are full of people identifying with the term—is less surprising. Spuddling is an inescapable fact of the modern workplace, particularly if you have the kind of job where you are required to stare at a screen for any stretch of time that far outstrips the human mind's capacity for true concentration.

Spuddling can be the result of unavoidable impositions on your time—whether that's being forced to answer a chain of Hydra-like emails that only invite further replies, or sitting through an hour-long Zoom meeting, chiming in occasionally with an insightful contribution ("Yep, sounds good!"). For the most part, spuddling should be best thought of as an honest, diligent and good faith form of procrastination, one that is less about tricking your employers into believing you're hard at work and more about tricking *yourself.* You might virtuously deny yourself the meager pleasures of scrolling through Vinted or reels of amusing animals, but still find that you're skirting around the task at hand—endlessly tinkering with a spreadsheet, say, or crafting a PowerPoint presentation with a Kubrickian attention to detail. There are, after all, many ways of technically "doing work" while achieving very little.

This behavior is both a product of the unreasonable demands of modern workplace culture and a failure to live up to its ideals of optimization and streamlined efficiency. It might be that, for you, four hours of spuddling is a necessary requirement for doing four hours of actual work. Even so, the sense of having achieved little for your efforts can leave you feeling at once exhausted and incompetent, frustrated and demoralized.

In his 2024 book, *Slow Productivity,* the self-help author and productivity guru Cal Newport proposes doing fewer things and at a slower pace in the hope of attaining a deeper level of focus. Perhaps one answer to spuddling is not to be more productive but to be lazier, to accept one's limitations and to embrace a centuries-old ethos of cheerful truancy.

WORDS
JAMES GREIG
PHOTO
KUTAY TANIR

# WORD: SPUDDLING
A term to take your time over.

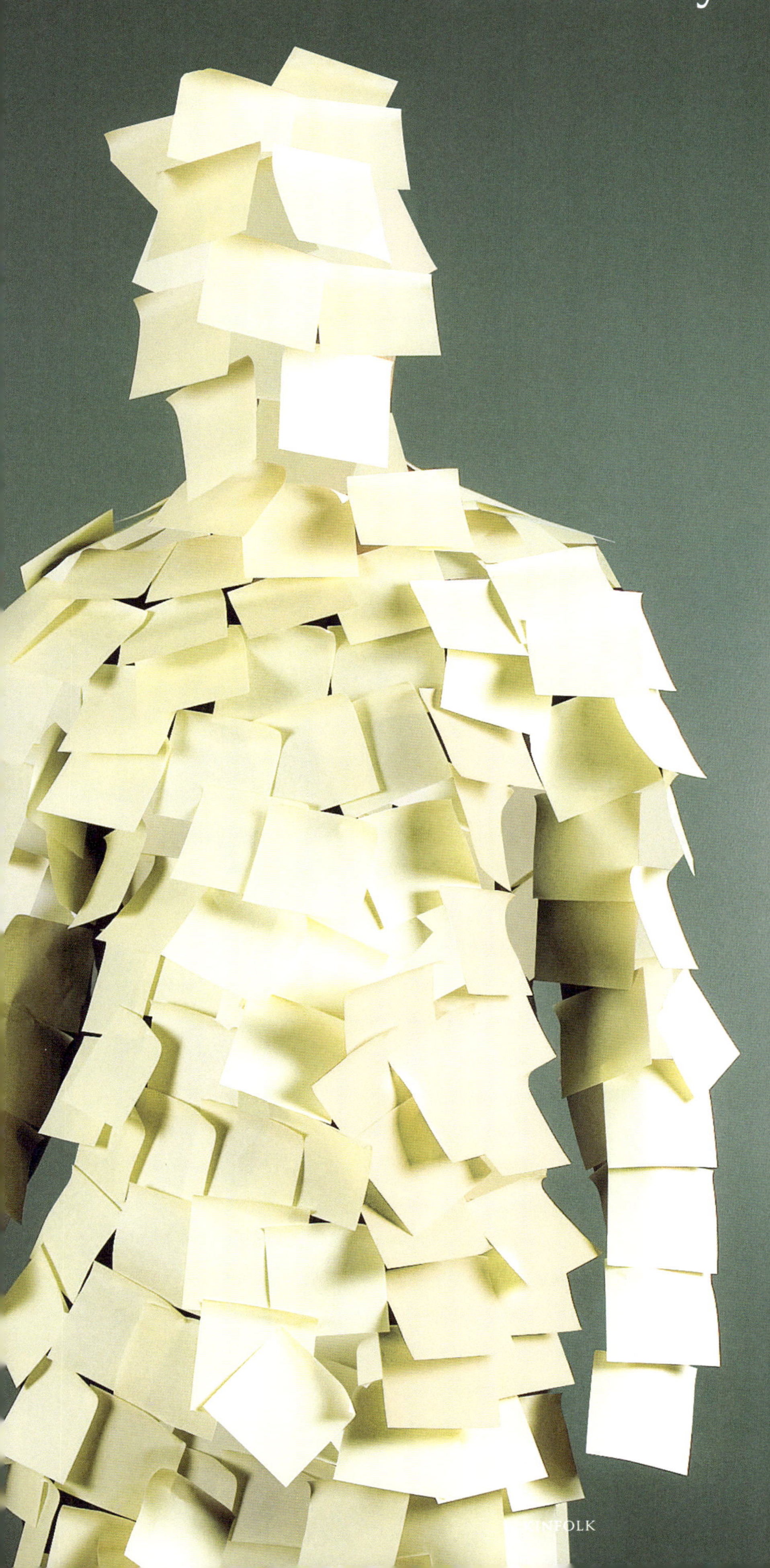

# A SHORT HISTORY OF NOTHING
How emptiness begets everything.

WORDS
TOM WHYMAN
PHOTO
AARON TILLEY

Jonathan Lear's 2006 book, *Radical Hope: Ethics in the Face of Cultural Devastation*, is haunted by the final testimony of Plenty Coups, the last great chief of the Native American Crow Nation. Plenty Coups had told the story of his life to the writer Frank B. Linderman in 1928, a few years before his death, but he refused to speak of what happened after the buffalo were cleared from the Plains and the Crow were forced to adopt a settled life on a reservation. He said: "When the buffalo went away the hearts of my people fell to the ground, and they could not lift them up again. After this nothing happened."

Lear is fascinated by this "nothing," partly because Plenty Coups' life on the reservation was filled with many achievements and events. Yet, as Lear understands it, for Plenty Coups "nothing happened" because, on the reservation, with his traditional way of life disappearing, nothing he did, or experienced, felt meaningful *to him*.

Here we have an understanding of "nothing" as abyssal: a void one might stare into; be trapped by. But "nothingness" can also be profoundly liberating, as it is into this void—this vacuum or lack—that possibility is born. When French existentialist Jean-Paul Sartre claimed that man was "the being through whom nothingness comes into the world," what he really meant was that we are able to negate whatever presently exists, to transform it; that we are *free*.

Sometimes, of course, it can feel like we will be trapped forever on the same endlessly downward roller coaster of boredom and decay. But it is precisely our thinking that *nothing matters* that might, provided the conditions are right, allow us to think about how to live *better*. For Lear, Plenty Coups was someone whose life gives us a hopeful example, since despite his sense that "nothing was happening"—that nothing really mattered for him—he never stopped living and trying in the hope that things that might *start* mattering again, both for himself and his people. It is only through nothing that anything becomes possible. We should look into the void with hope.

( 1 )  Other cultures have different ideas of nothing. In Zen Buddhism, *mu*, often translated as "no," "not" or "nothing," is used to negate the terms of a question and encourage a direct encounter with nothingness itself. In Sanskrit, *śūnya*, meaning "empty" or "void," describes a state of emptiness or absence and is theorized to have allowed the concept of the number "zero" to arise.

37

# COBBLED TOGETHER
## On the compulsion to collect.

I first picked up a rock during the COVID lockdown in 2020. On my daily walks through London, I would often come across abandoned roadworks; pavements were up-turned like archaeological digs, gloves and tools scattered about as though the workers had just gone for lunch. I don't know why, but one day, on a whim, I bent down and grabbed a granite cobblestone. It was about five inches in length, rough to the touch and worn by the passage of thousands of unknown feet. And so began my collection.

There are now rocks scattered throughout my home. They are mostly cobblestones and mostly granite, which is coarse and hard-wearing, with the occasional lump of the sandstone or slate often required by historical conservation or council specifications. I only take the discards and off-cuts, partly because I don't want to interfere with anyone's actual work, but mostly because they are more interesting. And every time I pick one up and take it home, I give it a label, noting the street I found it on and date of acquisition, as if cataloging them for a museum.

I could give you a half-dozen sentimental stories about why I do this; some waffle about reclaiming the city at a time when it felt closed off to me, or perhaps a comparison with *gongshi*, the rocks beloved by Chinese aesthetes that were thought to capture the essence of mountains in miniature, like stone bonsai.[1] My parents met through rocks, if that helps: My dad was a civil engineer and my mother working as a volunteer on an archaeological dig in York when the pair first exchanged looks over a pile of debris. But in truth, like most collectors, I simply obey a compulsion. I *like* rocks; how they look, and how they feel. And when they catch the sunlight in the morning and I stare at one over my cup of coffee I feel a sense of satisfaction and stability. Grounded, maybe, if you're feeling cute.

It helps, of course, that London was built with rock, and was only recently overlaid with more modern glass and steel. If you had pointed a camera at the city for the past few thousand years and played the footage back as a time-lapse, the rock would flow like water from a spring; bubbling up as forts and towers, frothing into churches and hostelries, demolished at times by fire and bombs but always renewing itself, directly from the earth. Not far from where I live there's an underground garage where you can see a section of old Roman wall from A.D. 110, unearthed during construction and now occupying bays 52 and 53, between the parked Toyotas and BMWs.

My favorite rock collection in London (besides my own) was also started in a private residence: in the home of John Soane, a Georgian-era architect who designed city landmarks like the Bank of England and filled his house with rocky treasures from antiquity. Soane's hoard is far grander than mine, of course. It includes Greek and Roman statues, pillars and pediments, funeral urns and bas-relief carvings, and even the sarcophagus of Egyptian pharaoh Seti I. (Oh what a rock that is! I'd sleep in it if I could.)

The house now functions as a museum, but the collection is displayed as Soane originally lived with it: a miscellany that crowds the rooms and walls, arranged solely for visual appeal. For Soane, the space was both library and laboratory, a place where he could consult fragments of the urban past and find inspiration for his work. I like to imagine him strolling among his rocks in the morning, clad in a bathrobe and sipping a cup of coffee; watching the sun fall gently on the rough stone, worn by time.

( 1 ) Humans have been collecting things for at least 105,000 years—archaeologists have found crystals in the Kalahari region of southern Africa where they do not occur naturally.

WORDS
JAMES VINCENT
PHOTO
ROBERT SCHLATTER

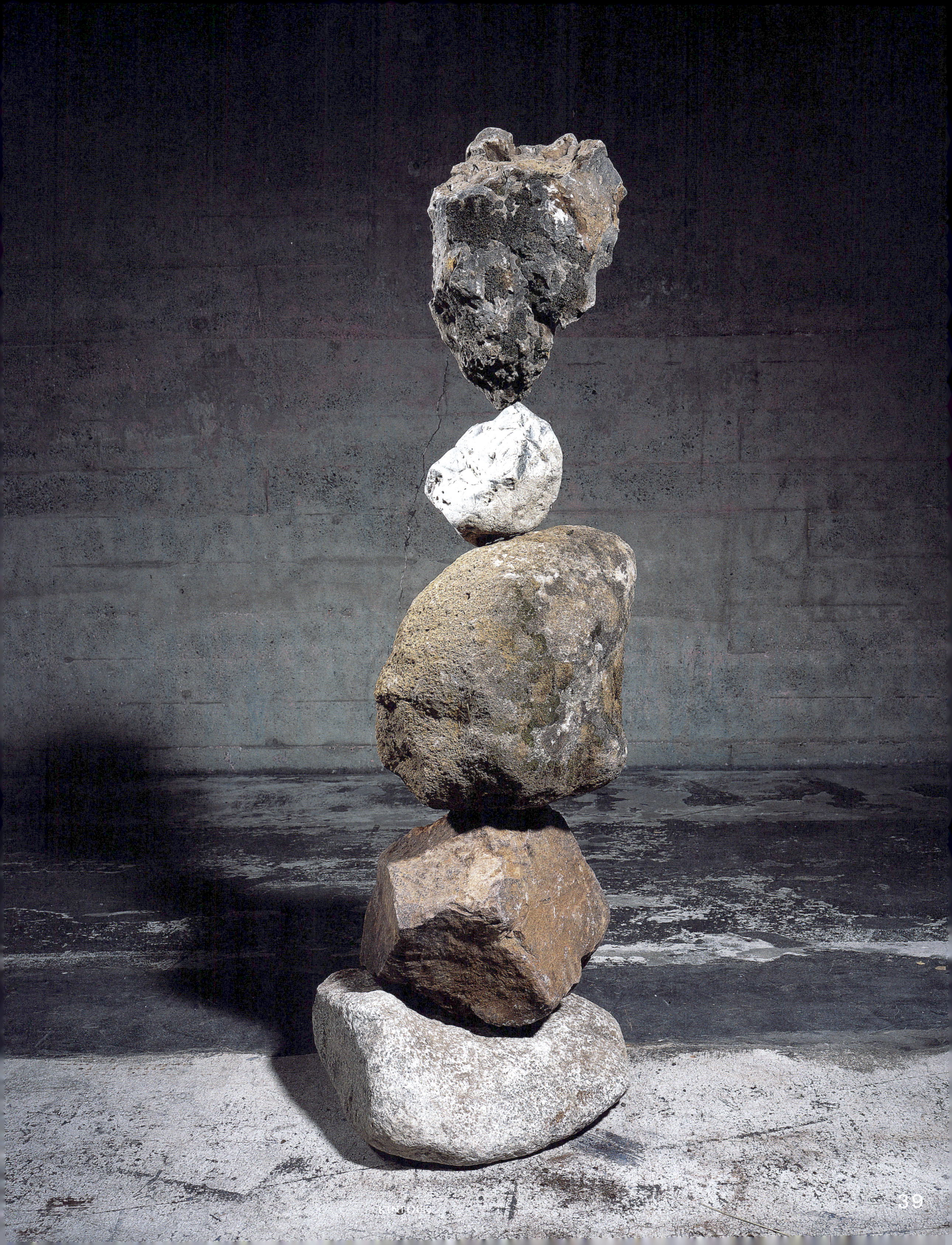

In practice, it's quite simple: You place a piece of paper over an engraving, headstone or seashell, rub it with graphite or charcoal or crayon, and watch as patterns and textures surface on the page. "Frottage," as the process is called (from the French verb *frotter*, to rub), has long been practiced by historians, artists and hobbyists. In 19th-century Britain, it became a popular way for people to create impressions of monumental brasses—the engravings laid into the floors and walls of churches and on tombs as funerary markers—as mementos of their trips.

While brass rubbing is used to make a copy of the subject, artistic frottage uses the same method to explore the unreal and the unintended. Stuck indoors on a rainy day in 1925, artist Max Ernst made a rubbing of a worn wooden floor, using its patterns to create fantastical forests and bird-like creatures. Salvador Dalí and other surrealists began to mine this source of serendipity, an expression of intuition and irrationality, and the technique remains part of the modern tool kit used today by Korean artist Do Ho Suh and Singaporean artist Simryn Gill, among others.

Rubbing unites aesthetics, history, identity and place. It can reveal something hidden in plain sight or allow us to see something familiar in a new light. It preserves the ephemeral and makes it our own—an act of conservation and creation; a copy with a distinct character. It's also a direct way to engage with your surroundings, whether you're traveling or stuck at home on a rainy day.

Today, digital technology offers another form of frottage: handheld scanners that capture depth, color and texture without touching (or damaging) their subject. The principle, however, is the same: to collect, contemplate and celebrate the incidental details that make up the rich fabric of our lives.

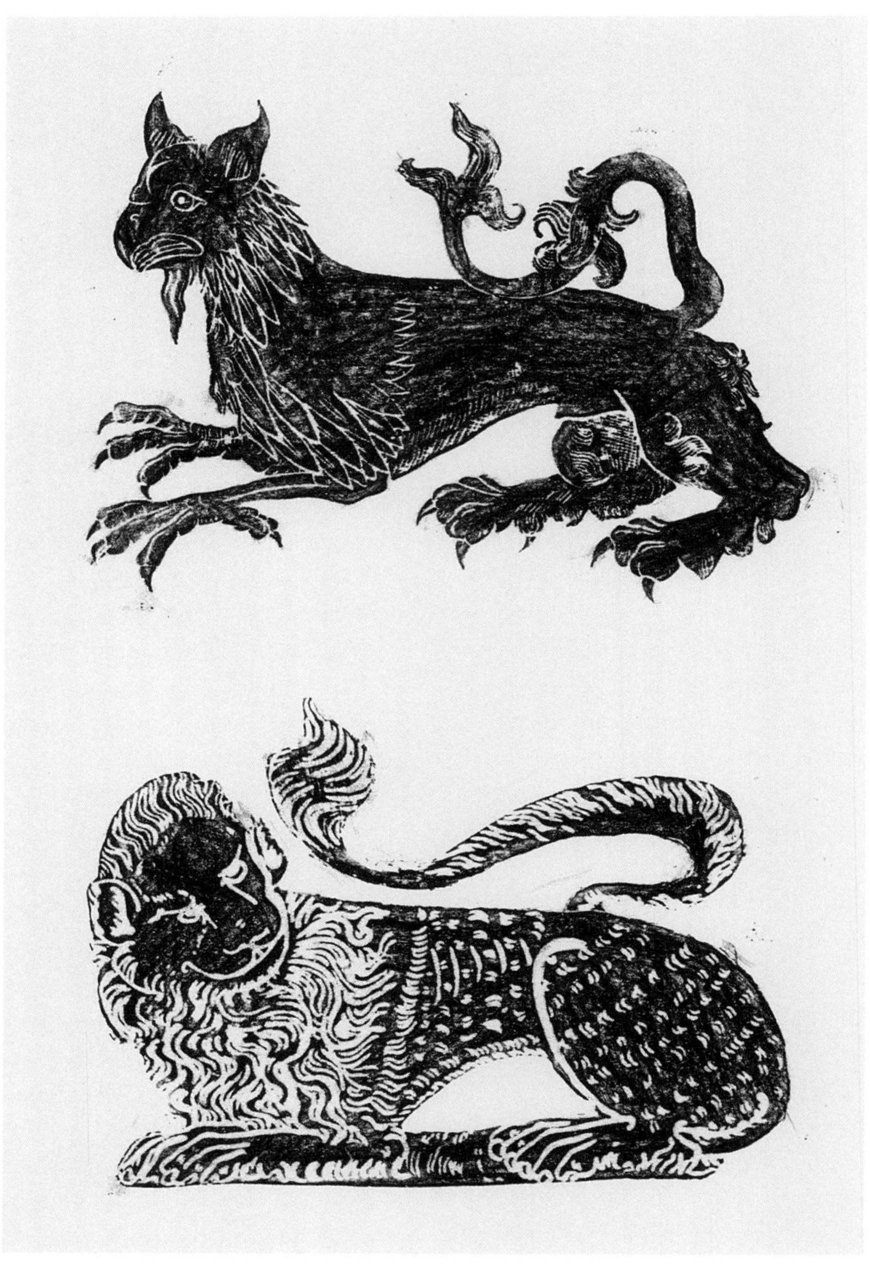

WORDS
SHONQUIS MORENO
ARTWORK
LUISA SMITH

# HOW TO: MAKE A BRASS RUBBING
## A guide to an antiquated pastime.

# Features.

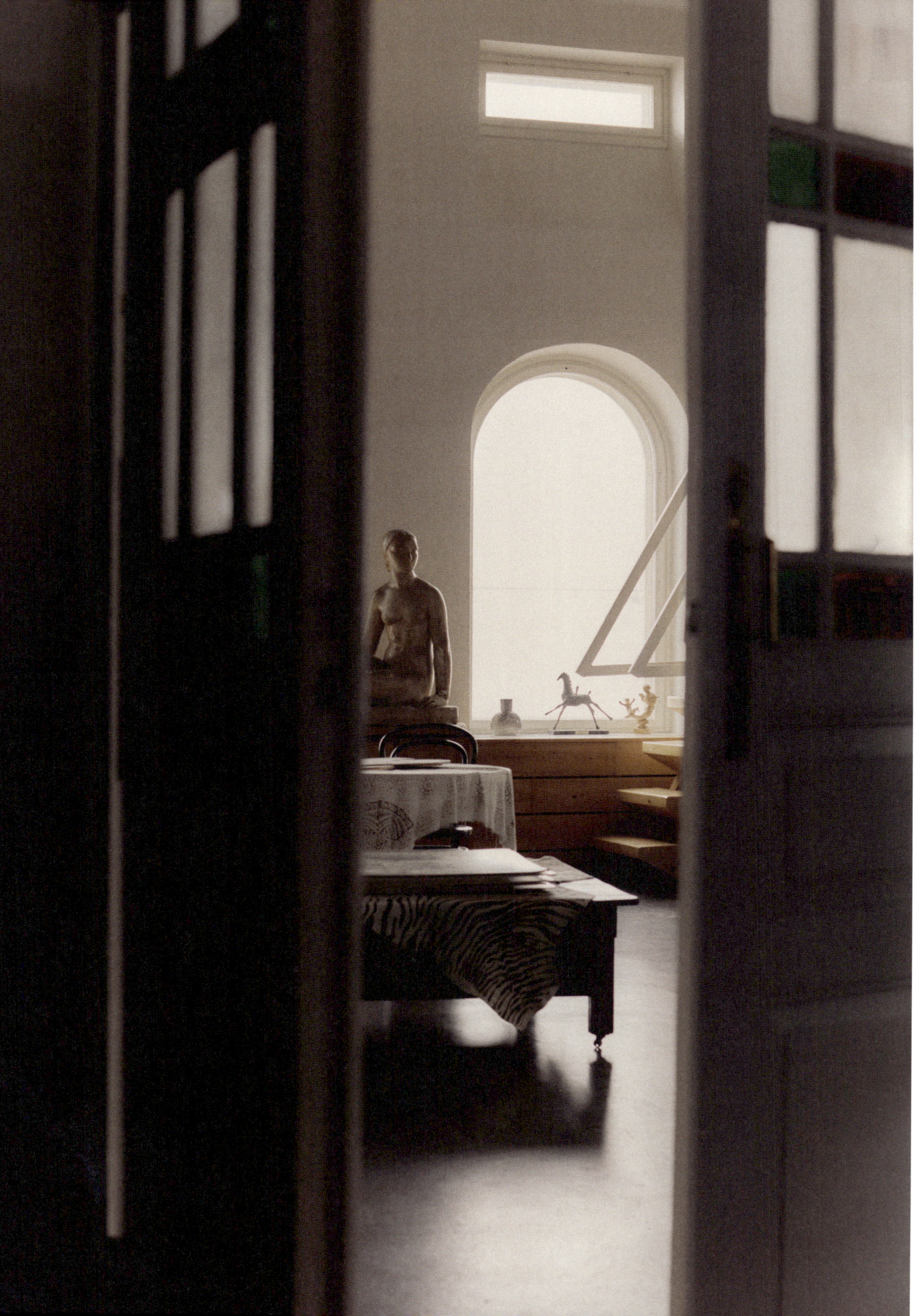

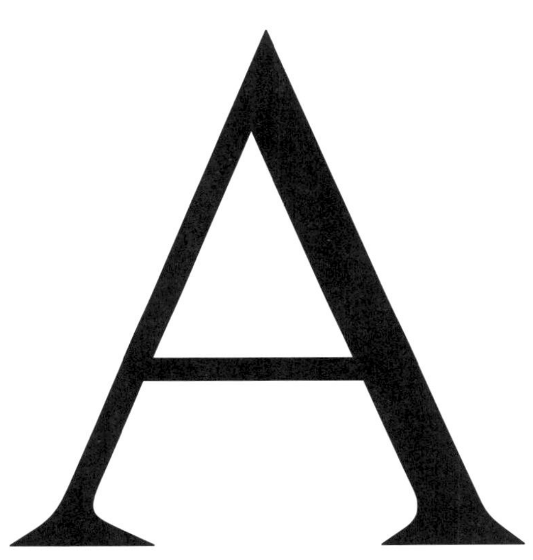


*Words*
Petri Burtsoff
*Photos*
Staffan Sundström


A ll too often, house museums lose their sense of home, with "do not touch" signs and modern alarm systems breaking the illusion of domestic life. This is not the case, however, at Tove Jansson's home and atelier in Helsinki. The attic space in the central Ullanlinna district—where Jansson wrote the Moomins, her bestselling series of children's books, and established herself as an artist— has been preserved almost exactly as it was when she died more than two decades ago.

The atelier is closed to the public, but for the rare visitor it tells the story of Jansson's artistic ambition. The soft Nordic light, which made it an ideal studio, still pours through the windows, the ceiling soars to nearly 16 feet and pine-paneled walls catch and reflect the pale winter sun. Books—in Swedish, German, English and Finnish, including everything from art to prose—line the walls in precarious stacks, and a long, timeworn workbench stands against the back wall. Three tall windows face south, overlooking rooftops, brick chimneys and distant church domes. From the mezzanine,

reached by a steep flight of stairs, you can catch a glimpse of the sea and the ferries slipping away in the icy waters toward Stockholm and Tallinn.

Jansson was 30 when she started living and working in the atelier and it quickly came to be an essential part of her practice. With the exception of summers—which she spent at her island retreat, Klovharun, in the Gulf of Finland—it was here that she came into her own as a painter and a writer, grew into one of the most notable artists of her generation and created the much-loved cartoon creatures that would bring her international acclaim.

> " Moving into the atelier
> began the most creative
> period of Tove's life."

"She had been wanting to find something like this for years," Jansson's niece, Sophia Jansson, recalls. "And once she moved in, she really didn't want to let go." It was late 1944 and the war between Finland and the Soviet Union was drawing to a close. The 1920s building had been bombed, leaving broken windows and a cold, bare interior. There was no proper kitchen, and the bathroom was rudimentary. In winter, the small side room where Jansson slept could drop to 42 degrees Fahrenheit; the atelier itself was often colder. Living here meant accepting discomfort in exchange for independence. "It was so cold that Tove used to paint with her outdoor clothes on," recalls James Zambra, her great-nephew.

And yet, despite the discomfort, Jansson stayed, slowly making the atelier her own over time—installing better heating and cooking facilities, and introducing practical additions such as shelves and tabletops. "Tove needed more space to fully embrace her creativity and artistic ambitions," says Jutta Tynkkynen, curator of the

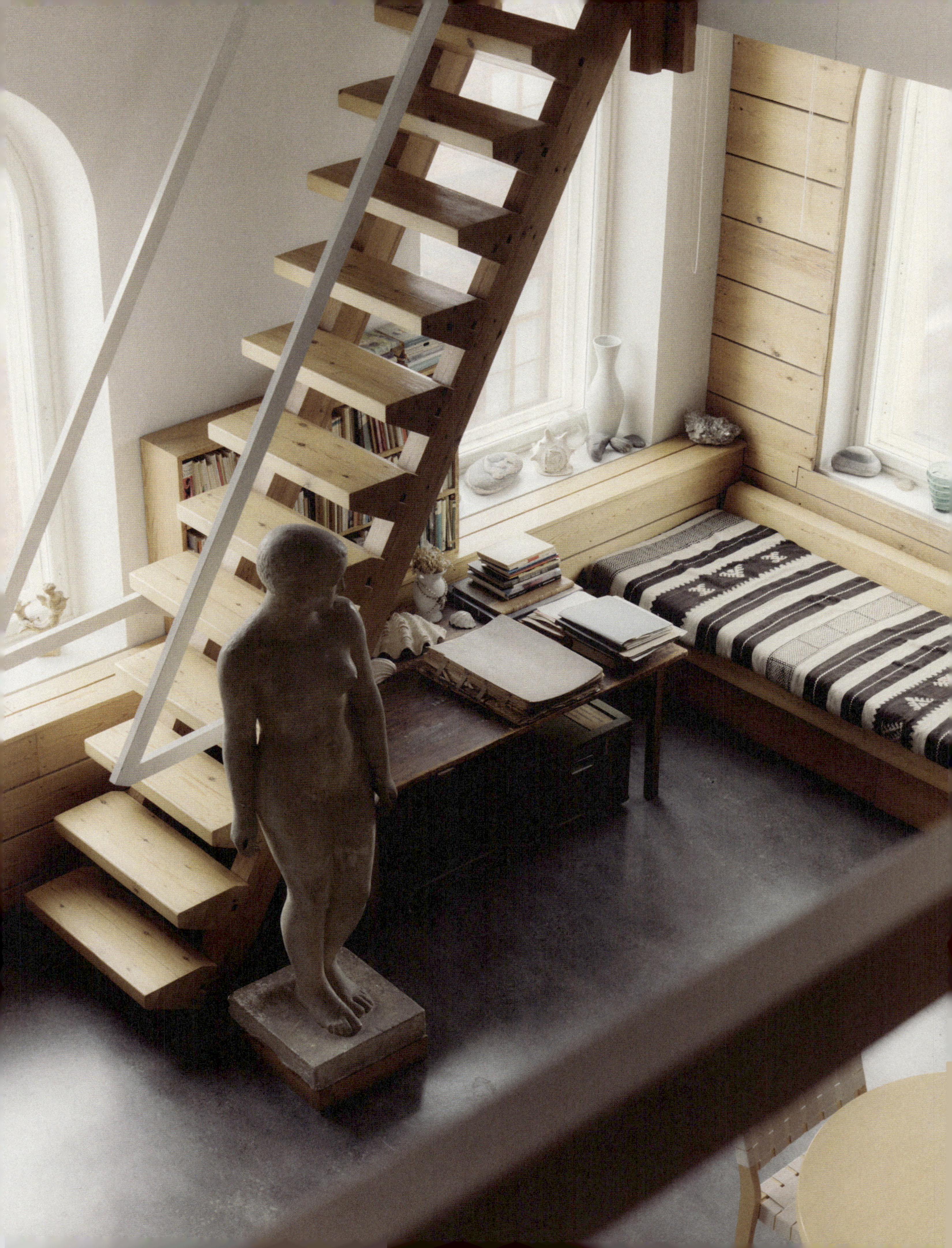

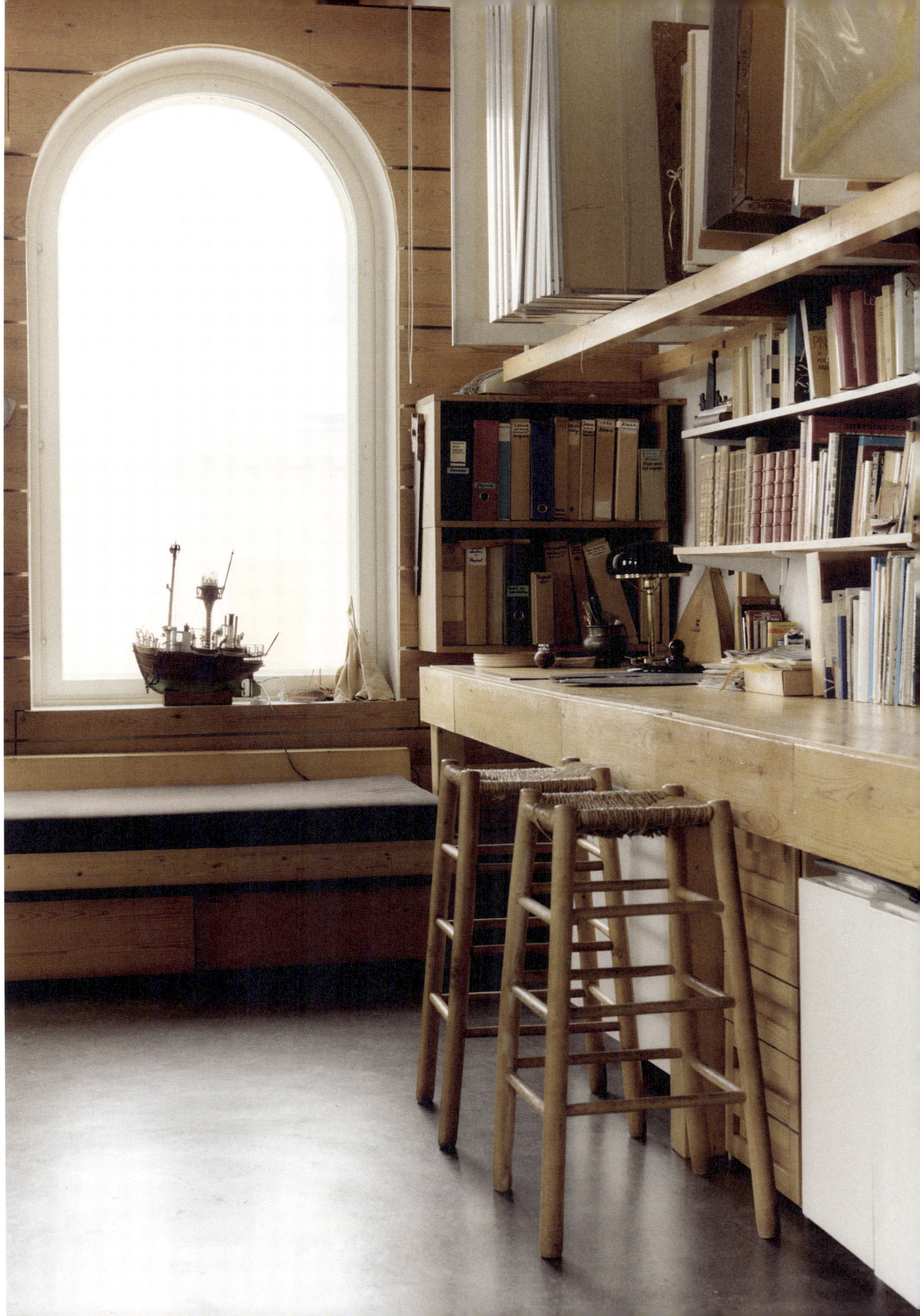

exhibition *Escape to Moominvalley* at Helsinki's Architecture and Design Museum. "The atelier gave her that. And having her own home gave her a sense of security about the future." That reassurance allowed her to take on larger and more ambitious projects, both in scale and in scope. "Moving into the atelier began the most creative period of Tove's life," says Tynkkynen.

Jansson's artistic journey had begun in the 1930s with formal training in Stockholm, Helsinki and Paris. She devoted herself to painting self-portraits, still lifes and intimate, often psychologically charged depictions of friends and family, while at the same time undertaking large-scale public murals that revealed her fascination with theatrical composition and narrative detail. The mood of her early work, often somber and subdued in palette, echoed the uncertainty and political tension that defined the era.

The Moomins appeared during the war years, initially as small, private sketches, before evolving into illustrated stories. What began as a personal, whimsical escape from the anxieties of the time slowly took on a life of its own, becoming a fully realized world: a series of whimsical, troll-like characters featured in books and comics that explore themes like family, adventure and philosophy. But even as the Moomin books brought Jansson international recognition, they remained closely bound to her visual art, both in style and in the themes they explored.

It's an approach that's reflected in the atelier: Easels, desks, shelves of books, stacks of drawings and unfinished canvases share the space, suggesting that Jansson did not silo her various forms of expression. "In her own mind, however, she was first and foremost a painter," says Tuula Karjalainen, her biographer.[1] "The Moomins were a source of income, but became somewhat of a burden for her eventually."

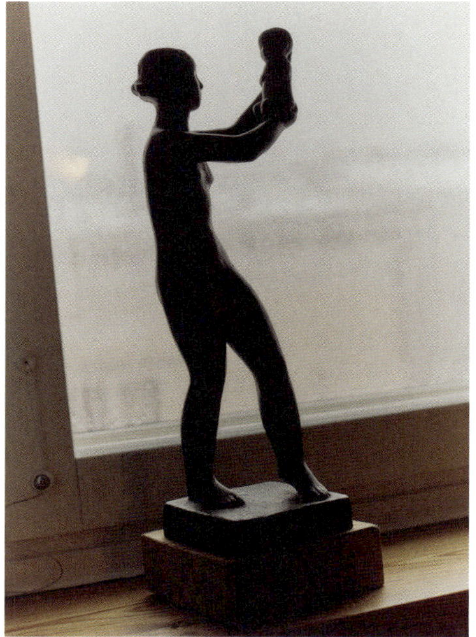

That may surprise those who know Jansson mainly as the creator of the beloved series. The first book was published in 1945, and all subsequent novels were written either here or at her island home on Klovharun. Yet, despite their commercial success, nothing in the atelier suggests prosperity. The home remains simple, almost austere, with no trophies or framed reviews.

Over time, as the years passed and the world shifted, Jansson's paintings grew lighter in both color and subject. Many of her works now reside in archives or museums, and her artistic sensibility can still be sensed in the orderly arrangement of brushes and palettes on the table, and in the canvases stacked neatly along the shelves. Jansson came from a family of artists, a lineage still visible in the atelier. Near the entrance, a cast-iron stove supports a small gas burner, its surface crowded with plaster studies—torsos and faces in gypsum—by her father, the sculptor Viktor Jansson.

## " It was so cold that Tove used to paint with her outdoor clothes on."

The most significant transformation of the atelier came with the renovation in 1962–1963. By then, Jansson could finally reshape the space entirely on her own terms. She enlisted architects Raili and Reima Pietilä—sister-in-law and brother of her partner, Tuulikki Pietilä—who were known for their organic modernism.[2] White pine panels replaced darker surfaces, and built-in shelves were added for storage. The addition of the mezzanine expanded usable space without compromising the room's openness.

After the renovation, Jansson slept beside the small mezzanine window, drawn by both warmth and the view of the sea, which she cherished, but later she moved her bed to the adjacent side room. Though the renovation introduced a more modern sensibility, it preserved the essential hierarchy: first, an atelier; then, a home. According to Sophia Jansson, when Raili Pietilä proposed installing a proper kitchen, she declined, opting instead for a bathtub—a small but telling prioritization.

Annukka Pietilä, the architects' daughter and Jansson's goddaughter, recalls how involved Jansson was in the project. She requested covered windowpanes so shadows would not shift across her canvases, and practical storage to lift paintings out of the way when needed. "Tove was very organized, and the atelier was always clean," Pietilä remembers. Though exacting, she

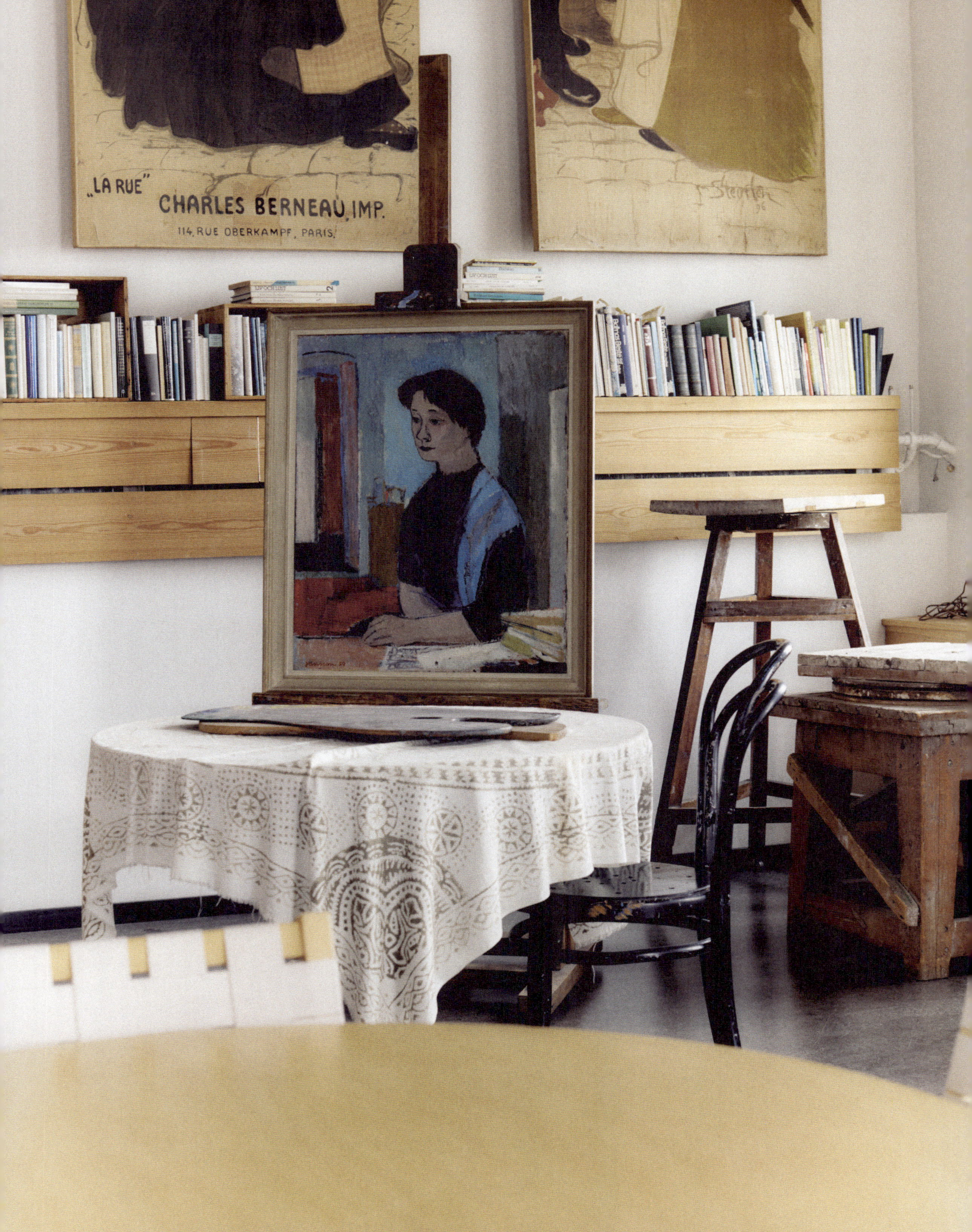
„LA RUE"
CHARLES BERNEAU, IMP.
114, RUE OBERKAMPF, PARIS.

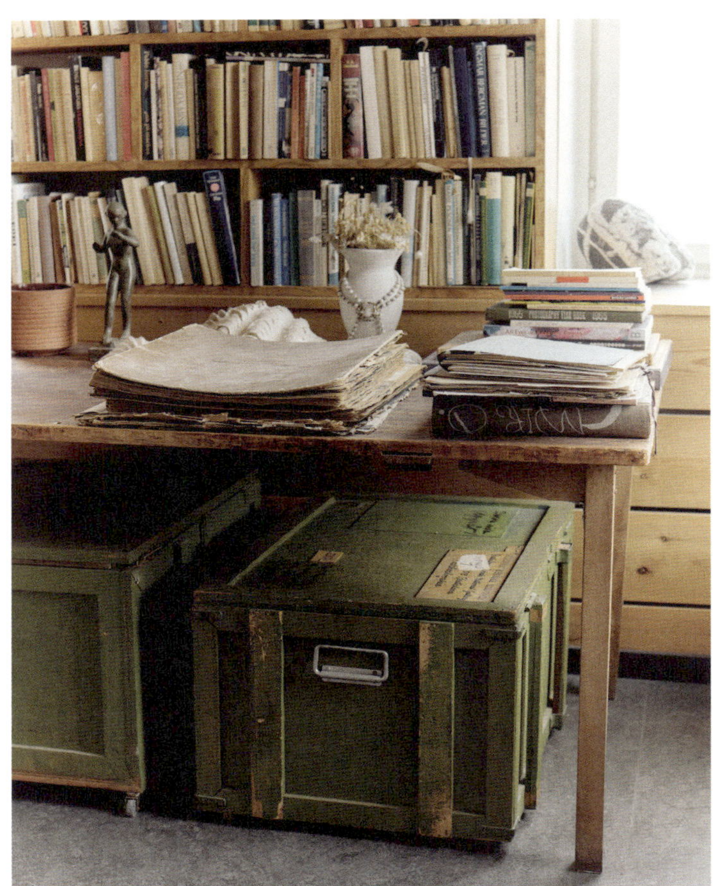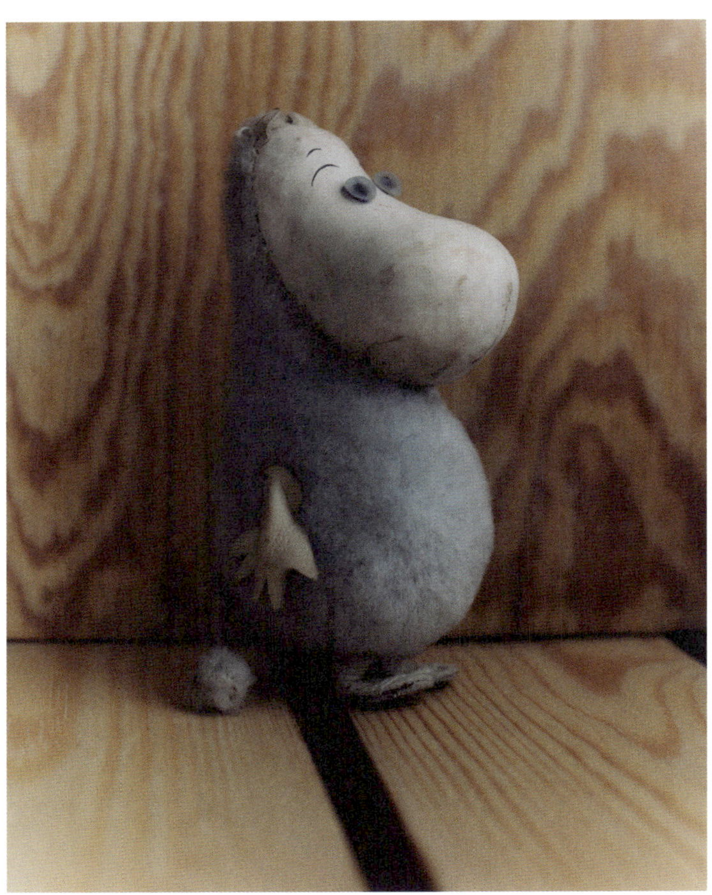

"In her own mind, however, she was first and foremost a painter."

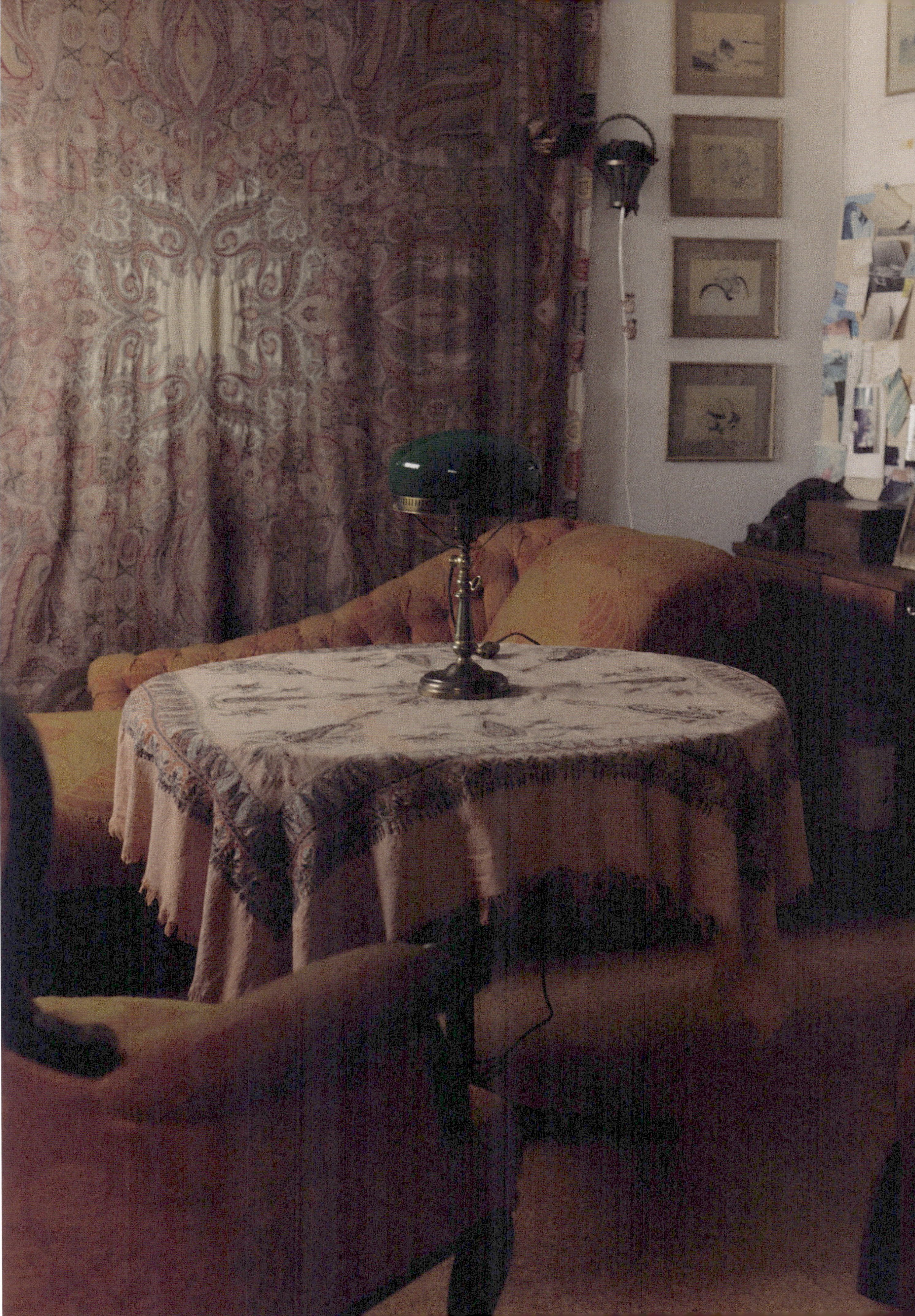

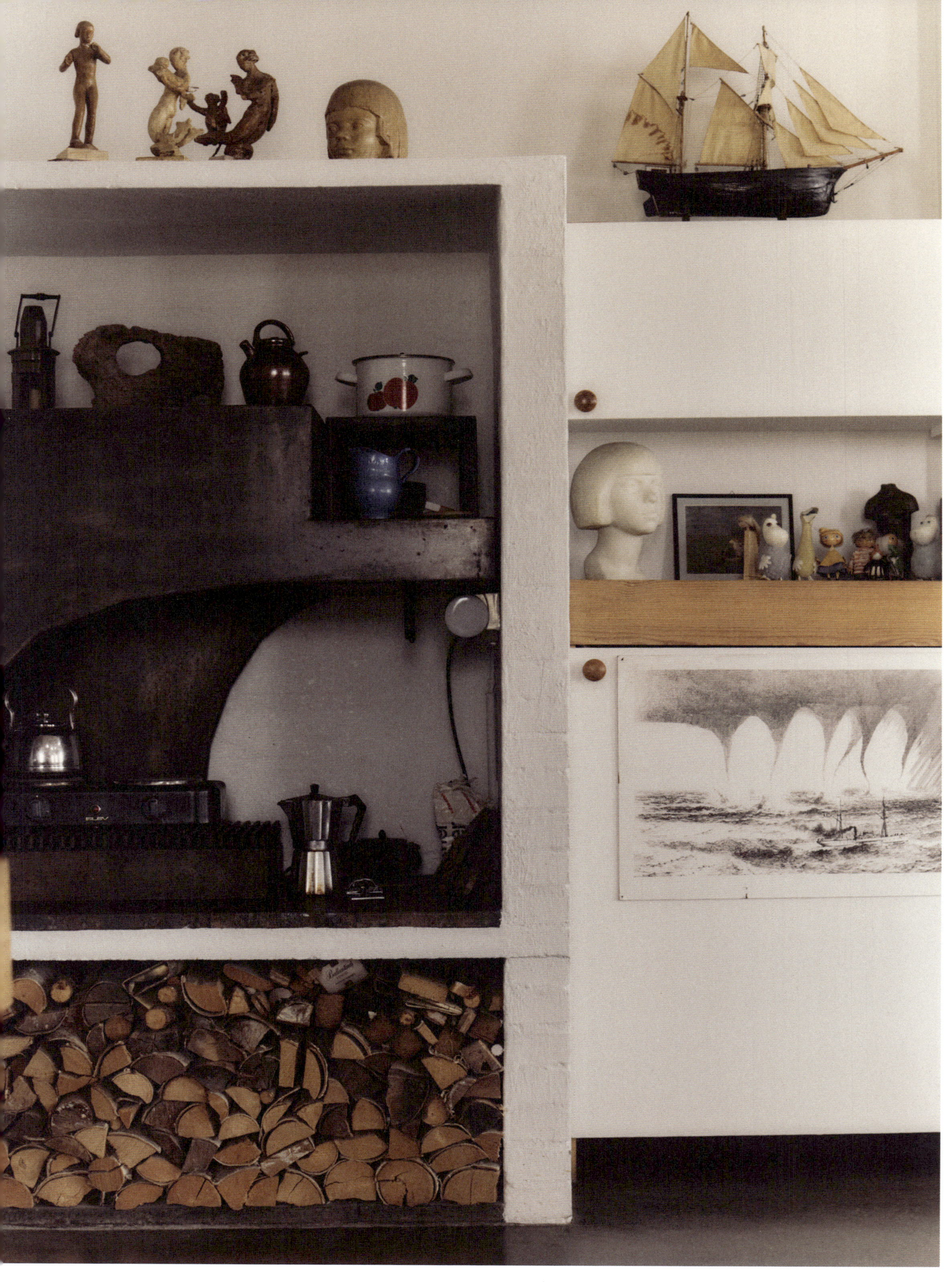

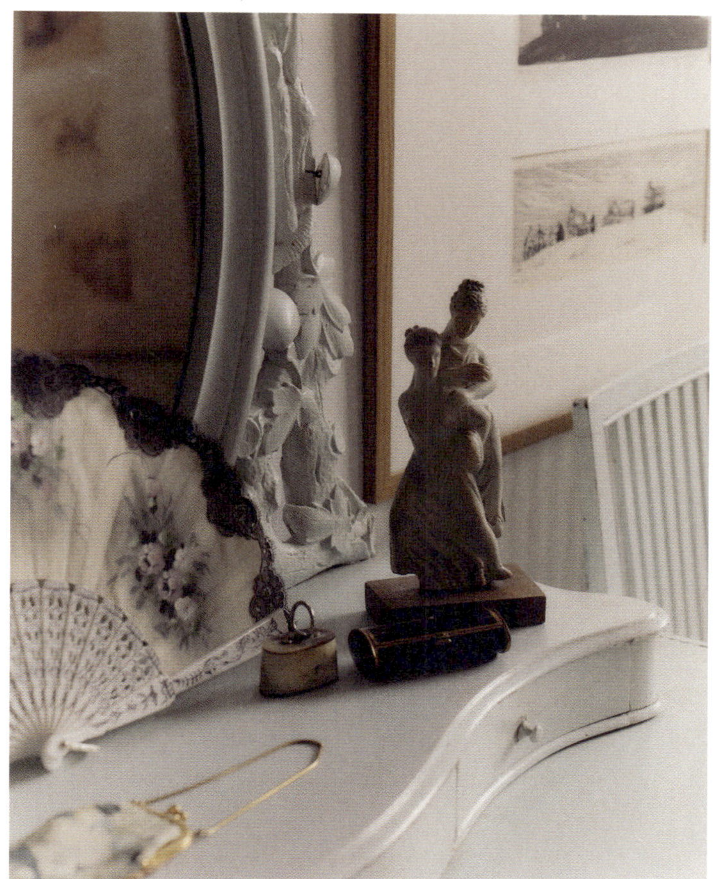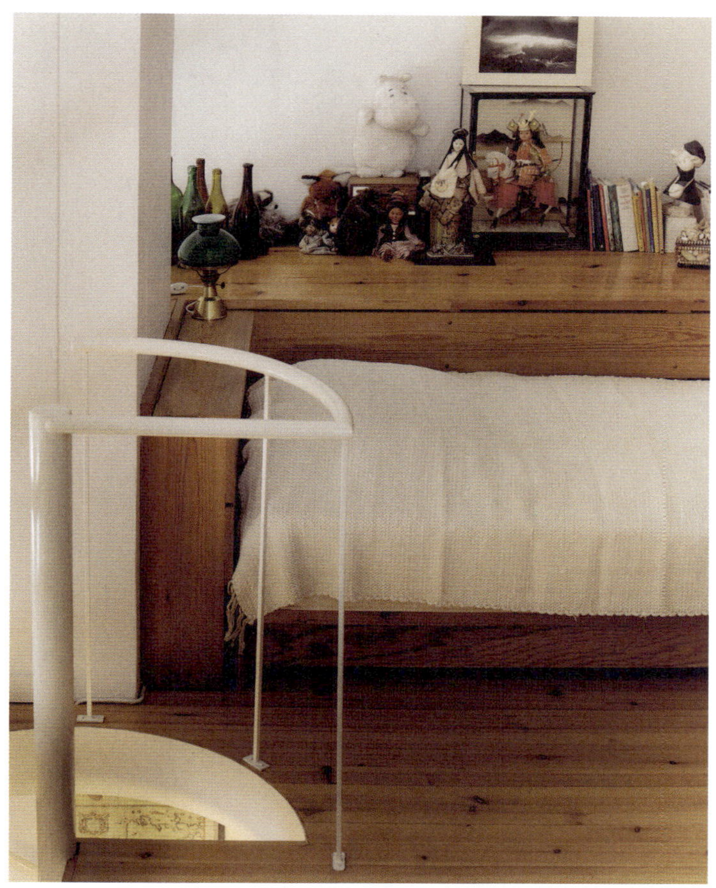

was also generous with the space. After the war, when music and dancing were scarce, friends and fellow artists gathered here. Jansson often hosted parties, and on New Year's Eve, the windows framed fireworks over the city, Pietilä recalls. Jazz and then later the Beatles played on the record player. In the summer, when she left for the island, other artists were invited to work here.

Jansson died in 2001, at the age of 86. Although she traveled widely, gained international recognition and experienced profound changes in her private life, the atelier was a constant for nearly six decades. After her death, it was entrusted to Moomin Characters Ltd., the company she founded with her brother Lars to manage her legacy. Early on, it was decided that the space would remain private. Necessary repairs were made—wiring replaced, windows sealed, smoke-darkened surfaces cleaned—but little else was altered. "We have fixed a few things," Sophia Jansson says, "but otherwise kept it in the original shape." Access remains rare and carefully considered, a choice that echoes Jansson's own reluctance toward spectacle.

To stand in the atelier today is to sense the breadth of Jansson's practice. Beyond the Moomins—now a $900 million global enterprise—she created hundreds of paintings, murals, political cartoons, novels and short stories. The atelier offers a full picture: not of a literary phenomenon alone, but of the artist she always wished to be.

( 1 )  Jansson has gained increased recognition as an artist in recent years, with major exhibitions such as *Tove Jansson—Paradise* at the Helsinki Art Museum in 2024 and *Houses of Tove Jansson* in Paris in 2023 reassessing her visual art alongside her wider creative output.

( 2 )  Organic modernism uses curves, natural materials and an integration with the surrounding environment to bring buildings into closer harmony with nature.

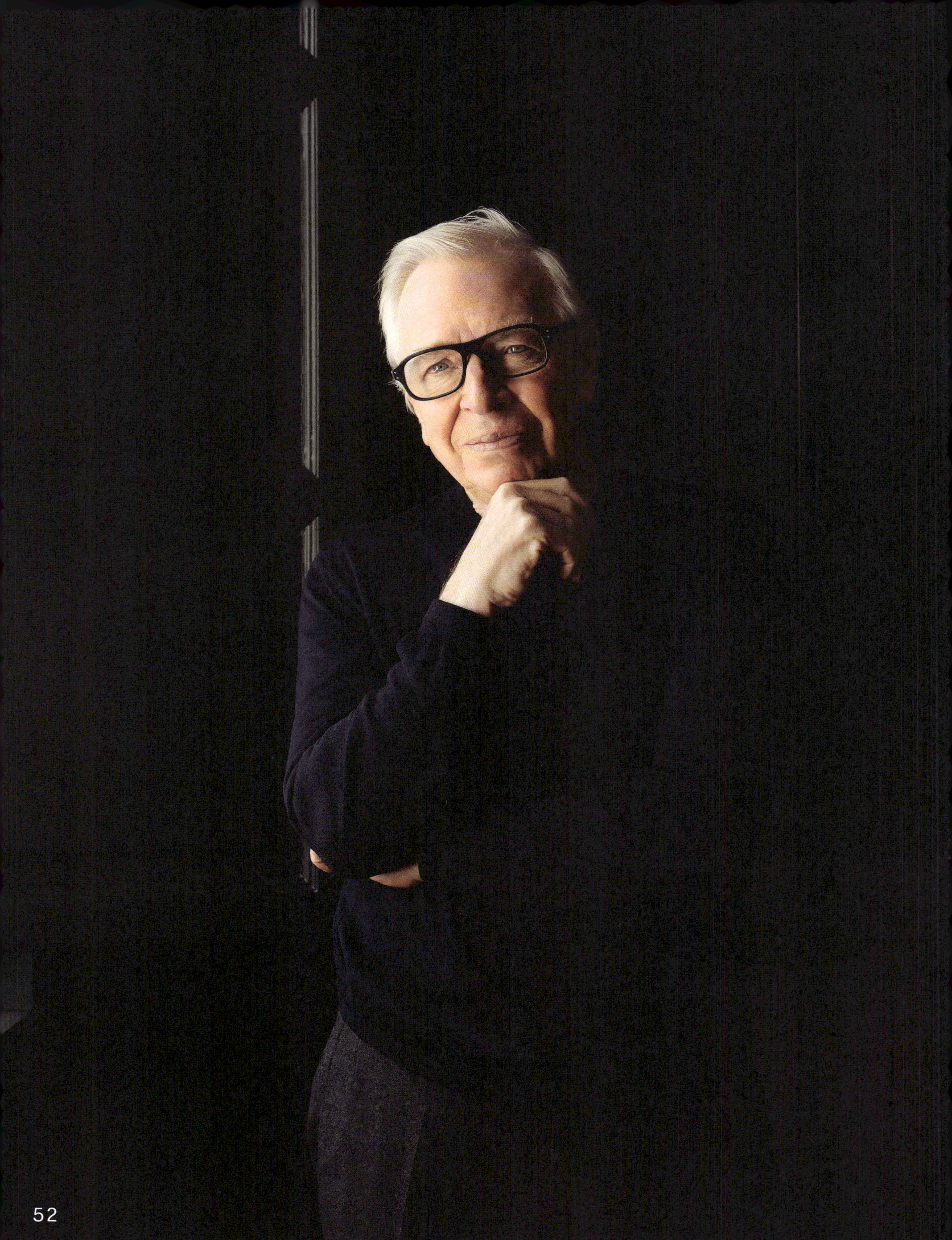

*Words*
Ali Morris
*Photos*
Cecilie Jegsen

The iconic architect working between past and present.

# DAVID

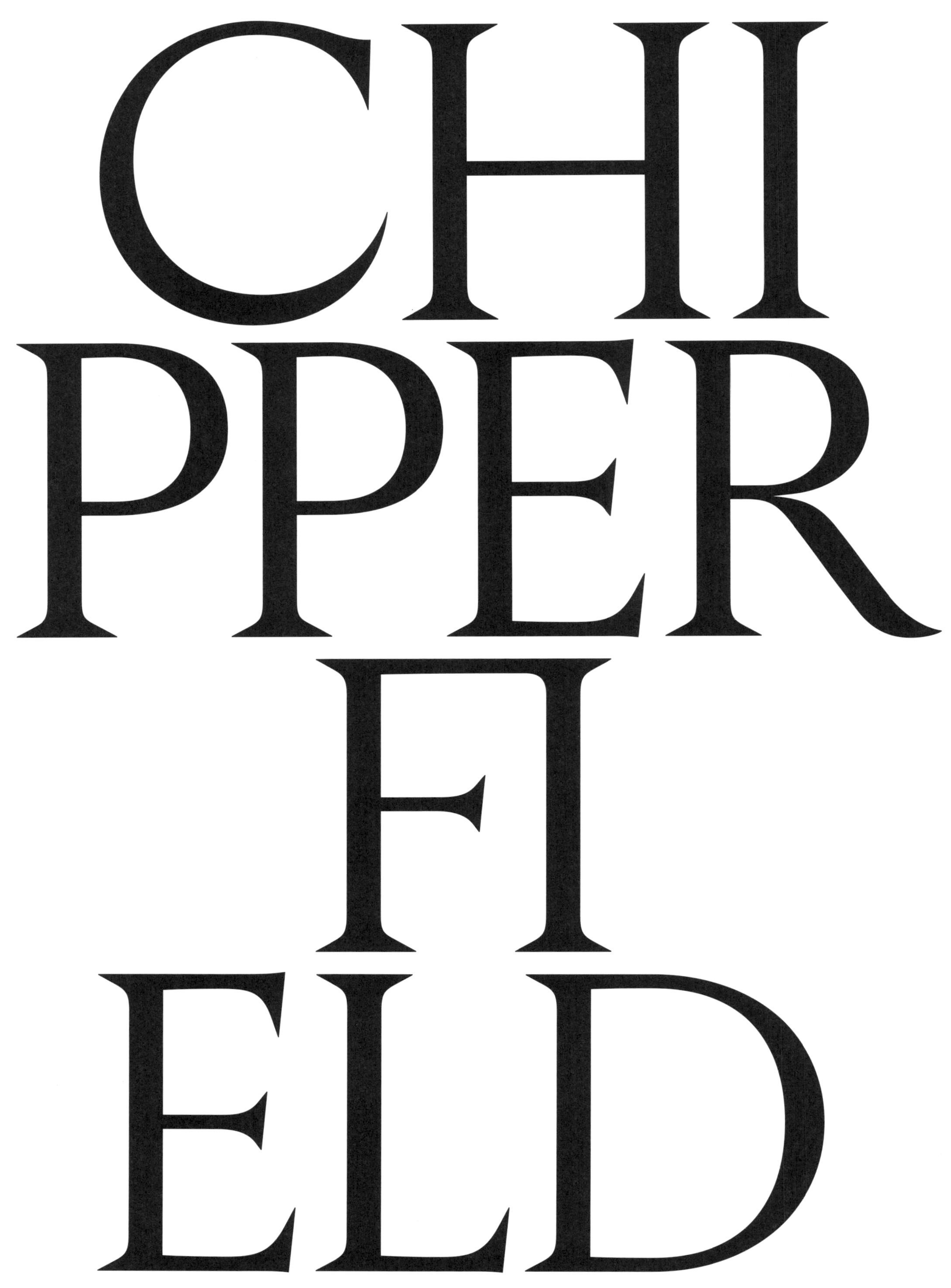

# CHIPPERFIELD

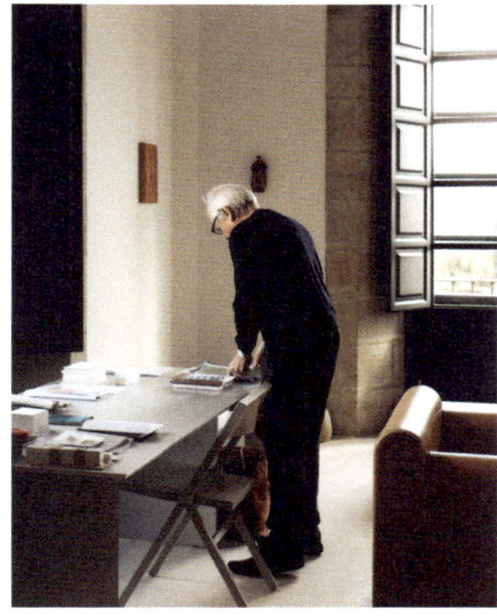

( above )
Chipperfield at home in his apartment, a private wing on the third floor of the Casa RIA building that also houses the foundation and architecture offices in Santiago de Compostela.

Tucked among the unassuming stone-fronted buildings of Santiago de Compostela in Galicia, northwest Spain—the traditional end point of the Camino de Santiago, where pilgrims arrive at the cathedral to visit the tomb of St. James—is an unlikely outpost of one of the most influential architects working today.[1] For much of his career, David Chipperfield has worked between London and Berlin where his internationally renowned practice has gained a reputation for considered, conscious architecture: offices, housing, civic buildings and, above all else, cultural projects that integrate their historical context and local culture. But in recent years, Galicia has become a working base for the architect. It's a place he knows well—he's been vacationing here for more than 30 years, after having designed a seafront retreat in nearby Corrubedo in the 1990s.

When it opened in 2022, the Santiago de Compostela office joined a network of studios in Milan, Shanghai, Berlin and London, where Chipperfield first founded his practice, David Chipperfield Architects, in 1985. Over the subsequent four decades, he became recognized for major commissions such as the restoration of Berlin's Neues Museum, Turner Contemporary in the UK, and the St. Louis Art Museum expansion in the US; he received a knighthood in 2010 and the Pritzker Prize in 2023. Chipperfield's work now spans Europe, Asia and North America, with projects in the works for Australia and Africa.

This corner of Spain—perched above Portugal and bordered on two sides by the Atlantic—has a distinctly un-Iberian climate, and it's an overcast February afternoon when I speak to Chipperfield at his practice's Santiago office.[2] It's located within Casa RIA, a former 19th-century sanatorium in the historic center of the city that is also home to Fundación RIA—a regional agency Chipperfield established in 2017 to support environmental and spatial planning initiatives across Galicia. Part workshop, research hub, exhibition space and public restaurant, the building operates less as a headquarters than as a civic platform, with projects running the gamut from car parking to forestry issues.

Seated at a conference table in one of the meeting rooms, framed by orderly white bookshelves, Chipperfield speaks openly, pausing at times to choose his words carefully—aware, perhaps, of the responsibilities that come with articulating ideas beyond the scale of a single building: "Ten years ago, I was invited by the then-president [of Galicia, Alberto Núñez Feijóo] to give some advice to the government about planning," he says, explaining how he came to be based in Santiago. "That turned into a decision to create a foundation which coincided with a shift in the architectural profession—a need to think about how we contribute to social and environmental issues, not just the commercial ones."

( 1 )   More than 500,000 pilgrims walk the Camino de Santiago each year, starting from various points across Europe. The pilgrimage—traditionally undertaken by Catholics, though today open to all—can take anywhere from five days to over a month, depending on the route and starting point.

( 2 )   There are more than 70 words for rain in Galician, including *orballo* (light drizzle), *poalla* (fine rain that soaks slowly), *babuña* (a slimy, persistent drizzle) and *treboada* (rain accompanied by thunder).

The city—the political capital of Galicia, a semiautonomous region—offers the foundation direct engagement with a government that holds significant administrative power. It's an area that has long grappled with rural depopulation, land use and economic transition, and these questions shape the foundation's work.[3] "A typical architectural practice waits for projects to happen, and then designs them," Chipperfield explains. "Whereas the foundation team works in the community—we stimulate projects. It's a different idea of the role of the architect."

The building itself is part of this experiment: a testing ground for ideas that privilege reuse over replacement, collective process over singular authorship. There is no grand entrance or overt branding to announce Casa RIA (named after the Galician *rias*, or inlets, that punctuate the coast). Instead, the foundation has embedded itself discreetly into the historic fabric of the town, opposite the municipal food market and overlooking a public park. The ground floor houses an exhibition space open to the public; upstairs, a conference room—"a big living room," as Chipperfield puts it—hosts regular talks and debates, and the top floors accommodate visiting students. A working garden supplies produce for the community-focused restaurant directed by chef Iago Pazos, reflecting the central role that food plays in the foundation's thinking about territory and sustainability.[4]

Despite this emphasis on collective process, Chipperfield himself has become synonymous with a particular architectural sensibility. His work has come to represent a counterpoint to the era of architectural spectacle and exuberance, offering instead restraint, material discipline and continuity. Though now best known for his work with historic structures and cultural institutions, Chipperfield's path to prominence was less direct than it might appear in retrospect.

Born in 1953 and raised on a farm in Devon in the southwest of the UK, Chipperfield was initially drawn to veterinary medicine, but lacked the necessary grades. He entered architecture via art school before studying at London's Architectural Association in the 1970s. Early roles with Richard Rogers and Norman Foster exposed him to the emerging language of high-tech architecture, but his own practice has evolved along a more restrained trajectory. The UK offered limited opportunities for the fledgling architect, and a series of shop designs and retail concepts for Issey Miyake took him to work in Japan. He set up his temporary Tokyo office in 1987 at the height of the bubble economy and completed three small buildings—the Gotoh Museum in Chiba, the Toyota Auto Kyoto, and the Matsumoto Corporation Headquarters in Okayama.

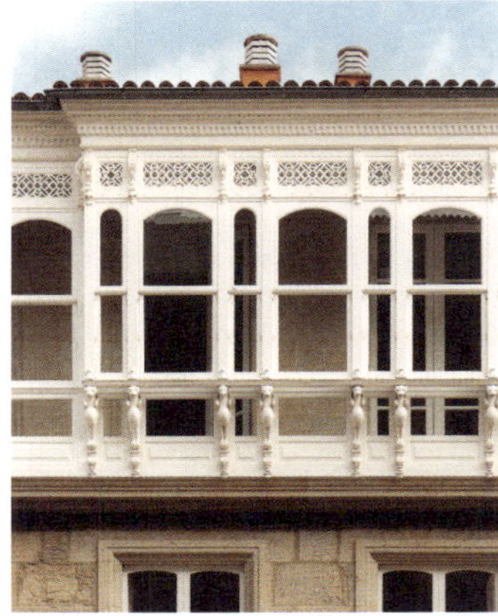

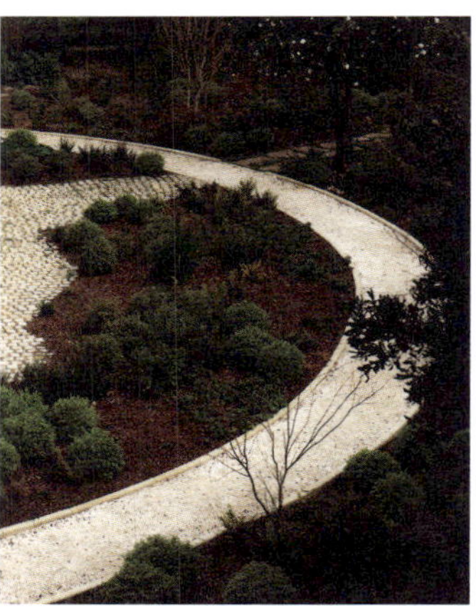

( above )
The vegetable garden and orchard of Casa RIA. Produce from the garden is regularly delivered to A Cantina, the building's canteen, where it complements ingredients from the local market and appears in daily meals.

( 3 )   Galicia, home to around two and a half million people, is one of Spain's poorest regions, though paradoxically it is also associated with a high quality of life. Galician women have a life expectancy of 87 years—among the highest in Europe.

( 4 )   Chef Iago Pazos has spent more than a decade shaping Santiago de Compostela's restaurant scene through projects closely tied to the city's historic market and local producers.

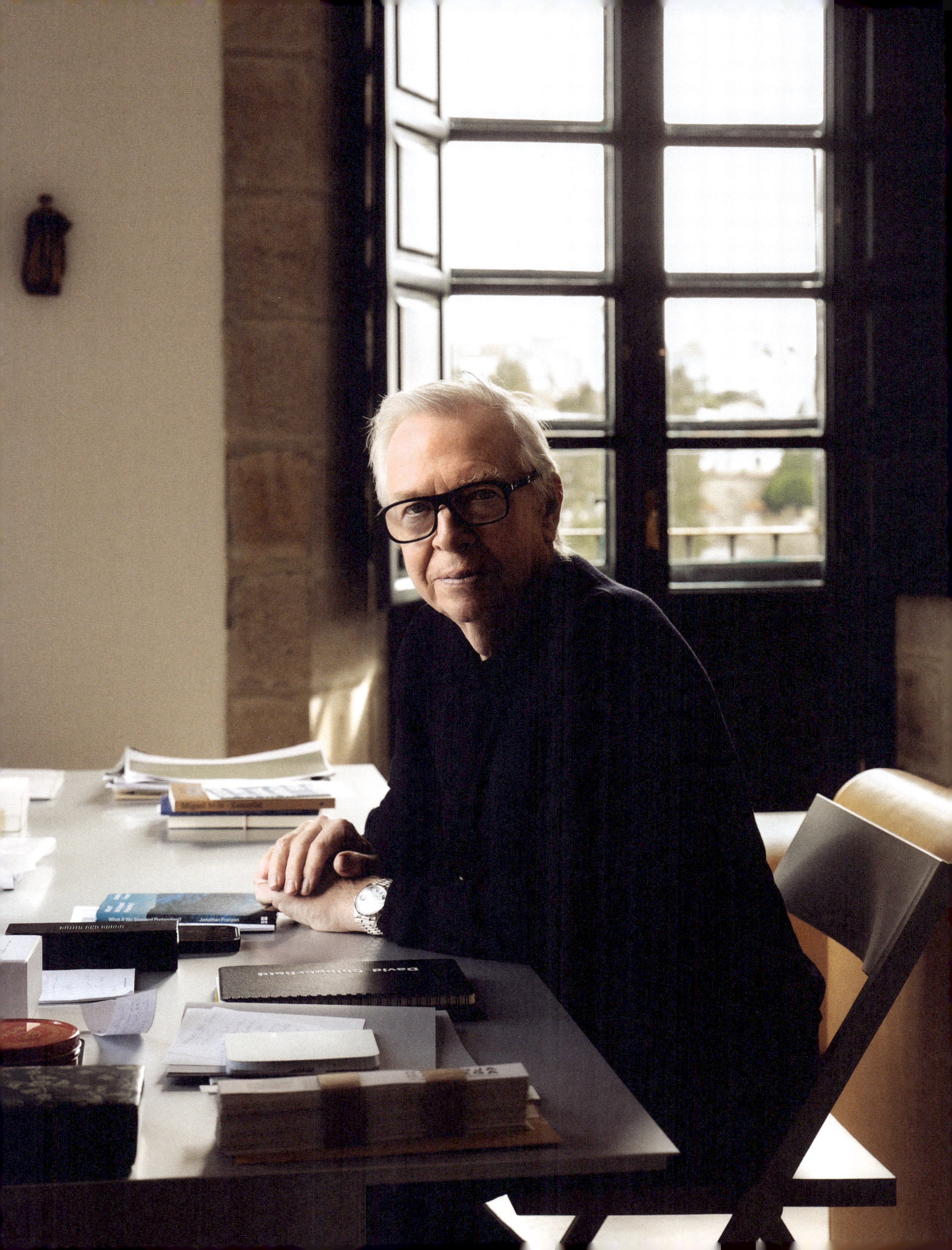

Having found his feet in Japan, Chipperfield later returned to Europe with a growing confidence. In contrast to the formal exuberance of his mentors, he had developed a language defined by sobriety, continuity and calm. And increasingly, his work—including a cemetery extension in Venice and museum and civic projects in Milan and Salerno—became concerned with how new architecture might sit alongside that which already exists.

Yet, as Chipperfield is quick to point out, the idea that architecture should consider itself part of a broader civic whole was hardly a new approach. Venice, he suggests, offers the clearest example: "If you go to St. Mark's Square in Venice, your perception is of quite a uniform space. But those buildings were created by different architects over 150 years. Why is there conformity? Because each architect felt that there was a responsibility between individual action and the collective representation of what one does."

> *"Anything which has been built by somebody else should have some value and significance. Before we knock it down, we should take it seriously."*

In 2022, he added his own chapter to St. Mark's Square through the restoration of the 16th-century Procuratie Vecchie, the arcaded building at the square's northern edge. After it had been closed to the public for centuries and used primarily as offices, Chipperfield's practice carefully reconfigured the structure to house the Human Safety Net foundation, opening its upper floors for the first time in 500 years.[5] The intervention is restrained but exacting: Historic fabric is repaired rather than replaced, and new insertions are precise yet deferential.

In Berlin, these sensitivities were tested at a different scale. The German capital is a place where reconstruction, memory and continuity are lived realities, and questions about how to build with history are part of the civic conversation and carry a greater emotional charge. Chipperfield's restoration of the war-damaged Neues Museum, undertaken with Julian Harrap Architects, would push his ideas to their limits—and ultimately come to define his engagement with history and memory.

Originally designed by Friedrich August Stüler and completed in 1855, the Neues Museum suffered extensive bombing during the Second World War and stood as a ruin for more than half a century, largely forgotten by East Germany. After the Berlin Wall fell and the country was reunited, its reconstruction took on national significance. Chipperfield won the international competition to restore and complete the museum in 1997 with a design that approached the project as an act of repair—edging out Frank Gehry's entry, which treated the ruin as an opportunity for reinvention.

(5)    The Human Safety Net is a nonprofit foundation established by Generali, one of the world's largest insurance companies. It runs two programs—supporting vulnerable families with children under six and helping refugees find employment or start businesses—and operates in 26 countries.

Rather than reconstructing what had been lost, Chipperfield proposed stabilizing the surviving structure and completing it using new brickwork, concrete and pale stone that would sit harmoniously alongside the original fabric. In the finished scheme, bullet-scarred columns have been preserved, fragments of frescoes dissolve into bare wall and new staircases thread through rooms where ceilings once collapsed.

Although the museum is celebrated as a benchmark in contemporary conservation today, the approach was controversial at the time. Many questioned why the building could not simply be rebuilt as it once was—a response Chipperfield acknowledges as "logical and emotionally understandable." "If you accept that everything which has survived is original, then you have to consider what it means to repair it," he explains. "If it was a painting or a sculpture, you wouldn't immediately cover everything as if it were new again. The priority must be the surviving material—and that material must remain readable."

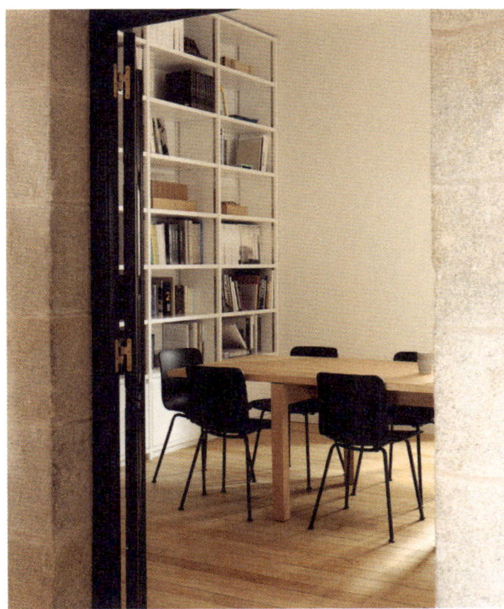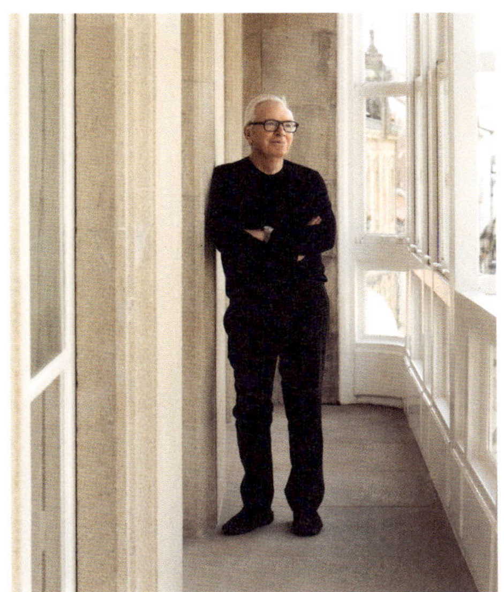

The project demanded a prolonged process of dialogue with curators, politicians and the public in order to gain consensus; the five years of planning saw protests against the project from heritage groups such as the "Save Museumsinsel" initiative, who argued that the visible integration of war-damaged remnants "defaced" or "downscaled" the original 19th-century structure.[6]

"This was the architect not being a sort of forceful genius—coming with a vision and telling everybody that's where it's got to be—but instead being a leader of discussion and debate," Chipperfield says, reflecting on how the decade-long project challenged traditional notions of architectural authorship. "The reward was that it meant a lot more to people than it might have done if we had just done exactly what they wanted in the first place, but it required persuasion and engagement."

(6)     In contrast to Chipperfield's approach to the Neues Museum, the neighboring Berlin Palace—also heavily damaged during the war—was reconstructed to resemble the original as closely as possible, to a design by the Italian architect Franco Stella that sees the Baroque facades conceal a modern concrete structure.

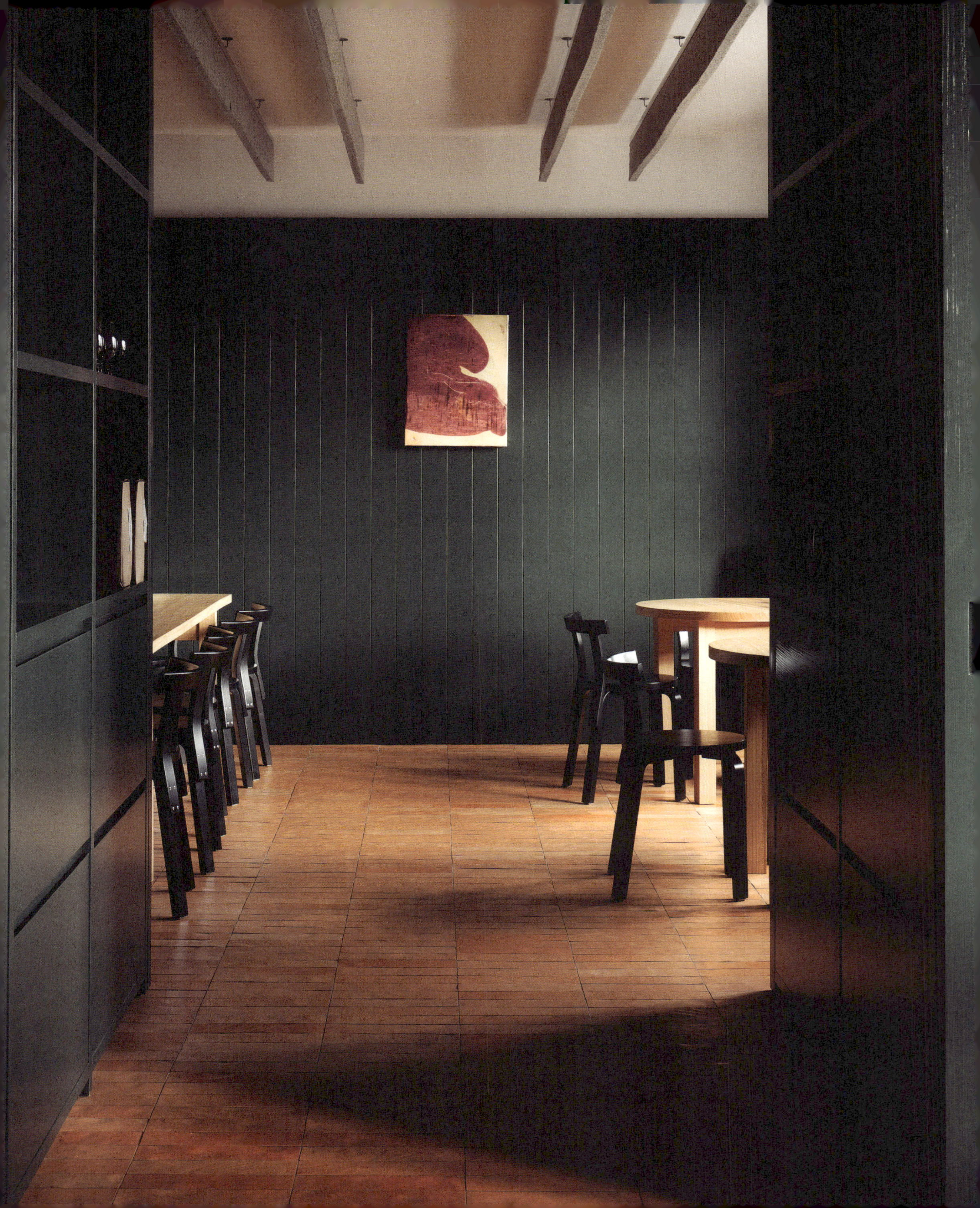

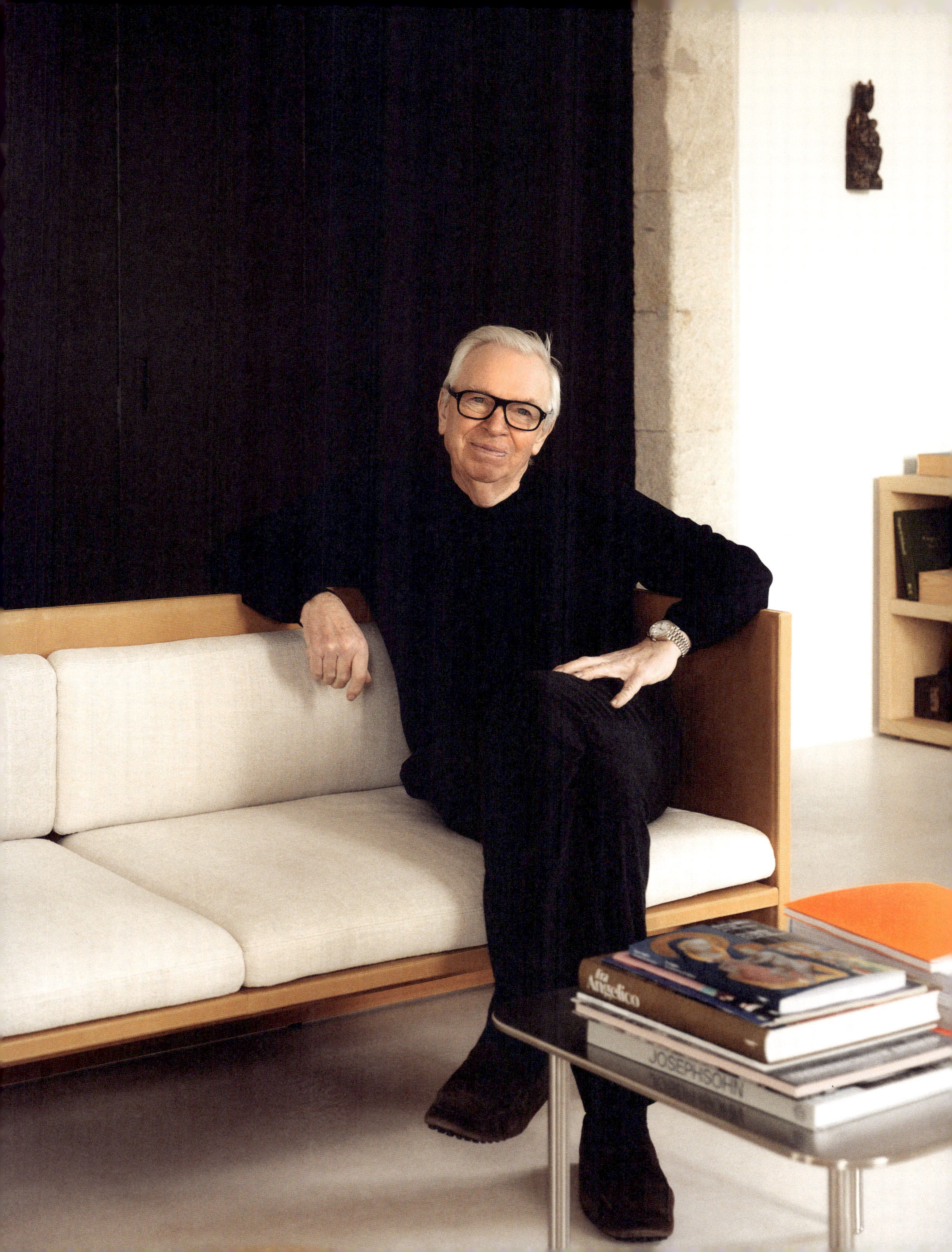

The experience proved career-defining for both Chipperfield and his studio, marking his emergence as a major international architect. He opened an office in Berlin in 1998 after securing the Neues Museum project, and the city has remained an important base for the practice ever since. The office today—housed in a former piano factory in Mitte—is also home to the practice's product design team, David Chipperfield Design.[7] His subsequent commission for the James-Simon-Galerie on the city's Musuem Island further embedded him within Berlin's cultural landscape.

Chipperfield argues that architecture must be understood not only as the production of buildings, but as part of a wider cultural and material continuum. Across projects in historic contexts, his practice regards the existing urban fabric as something to be stabilized, interpreted and continued. As with the Neues Museum, any new interventions operate in dialogue with what already exists. At the Royal Academy in London, for example, an enclosed concrete bridge was used to form a new public route between two listed buildings—Burlington House and Burlington Gardens. And in Shanghai, the Rockbund Art Museum transformed the 1930s Royal Asiatic Society Building, China's first public museum, through careful repair. "Anything which has been built by somebody else should have some value and significance," he says. "Before we knock it down, we should take it seriously."

Such thinking has particular resonance in an era shaped by climate urgency. A growing awareness of materials as finite resources—and the embodied carbon released through demolition—has reinforced the importance of Chipperfield's approach. "There's only one thing we absolutely know: that repurposing an existing building is better than building new," he explains. "If you can reuse a building, you're already in front of the game."

Like food, he argues, architecture also reflects where things come from and how they are understood over time. It can be treated as a commodity, a form of real estate, or as part of a shared cultural knowledge about how we live and use resources. The tension between these two positions has shaped much of the built environment in recent decades, often privileging market value and individual expression over collective continuity.

Architecture, he argues, is inseparable from memory and meaning—an idea he articulated when he accepted his Pritzker Prize—the most prestigious award in architecture—in 2023:[8] "As an architect, I'm in a way the guardian of meaning, memory and heritage. Cities are historical records, and architecture after a certain moment is a historical record. Cities are dynamic, so they don't just sit there, they evolve. And in that evolution, we take buildings away and we replace them with others. We choose ourselves, and the concept of only protecting the best is not enough. It's also a matter of

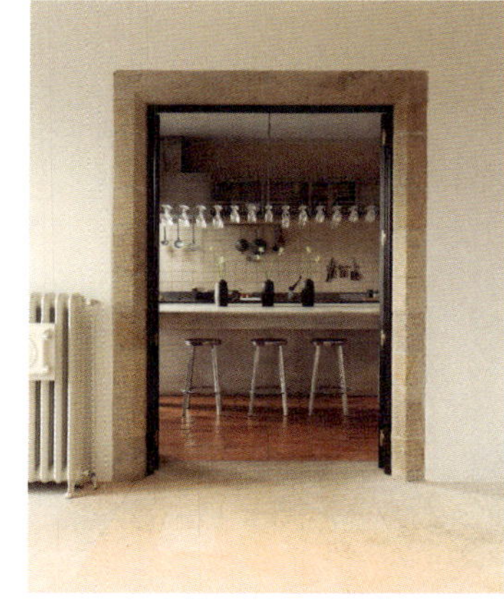

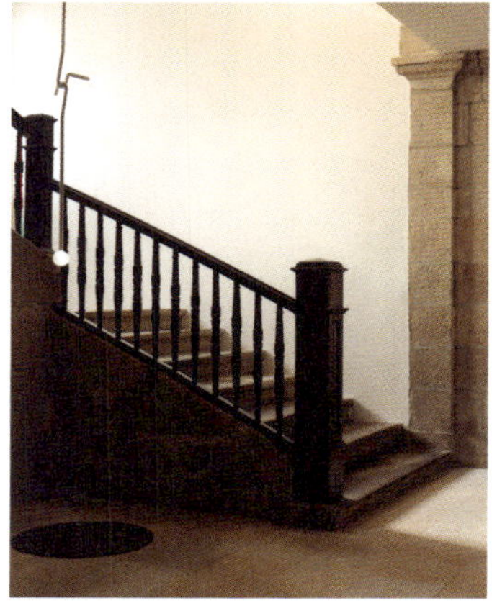

( above )
A Cantina, the building's public restaurant, is led by chef Iago Pazos. Located beside Santiago's market square, it serves as a gathering place that connects the foundation with the surrounding community.

( 7 )    Notable products designed by David Chipperfield Design include Tonale, a series of kitchenware products inspired by the paintings of Giorgio Morandi, and a reinterpretation of the classic moka pot for Alessi, launched in 2019.

protecting character and qualities that reflect the richness of the evolution of a city."

Postwar architects of the 1950s and '60s—the generation who taught Chipperfield—were deeply involved in shaping cities and public institutions, contributing to housing programs, universities and cultural infrastructure as part of national rebuilding efforts. By the late 20th century, however, the profession had largely retreated into designing within predefined commercial, political and planning constraints. "We learned that decisions that are made in planning can be much more important than the decisions that we make by the time the problem arrives on our desk," Chipperfield explains.

*"There's only one thing we absolutely know:
that repurposing an existing building is better than building new. If you can reuse
a building, you're already in front of the game."*

Fundación RIA seeks to extend the methodology developed at the Neues Museum into the civic and territorial frameworks that shape development itself. In Galicia, the foundation reengages with planning decisions and the conditions in which architecture takes place, creating platforms for collective reflection and operating as a forum for analysis, mediation and long-term thinking around the often invisible decisions that shape the region's landscapes, towns and infrastructures. "The work we're doing here is a continuation," he says. "We're trying to do things on behalf of others—and sometimes they don't want you to. But this is a house of discussion and dialogue."

Recent projects include planning the integration of circular forestry, agriculture and livestock systems into multifunctional landscapes in the Barbanza Mountains; transforming a traffic-dominated road in the nearby coastal town of Palmeira into civic space through a masterplan developed with port users and residents; and piloting sugar kelp cultivation in the Ría de Arousa to explore its potential for carbon capture, nutrient removal and economic diversification.

Chipperfield sees this shift in his role as an architect as a natural consequence of the later stage of his career. "I'm in an extremely privileged position in my life and my profession now," he acknowledges. "I've received the Pritzker Prize—I don't really need to build more individual projects to establish a name for myself. I'm comfortable, so perhaps I can think more broadly than I might have at 35. I can experiment a little, and now there are 18 young architects [working within the Fundación RIA] who are part of this experiment too."

Is he thinking about his legacy, or is it simply the next logical step in his career? "I'm doing it out of pure pleasure," he smiles. "It's totally indulgent on one level—but I enjoy it."

( 8 )     In its announcement, the prize described Chipperfield as "radical in his restraint." "The work of David Chipperfield unifies European classicism, the complex nature of Britain and even the delicateness of Japan. It is the fruition of cultural diversity."

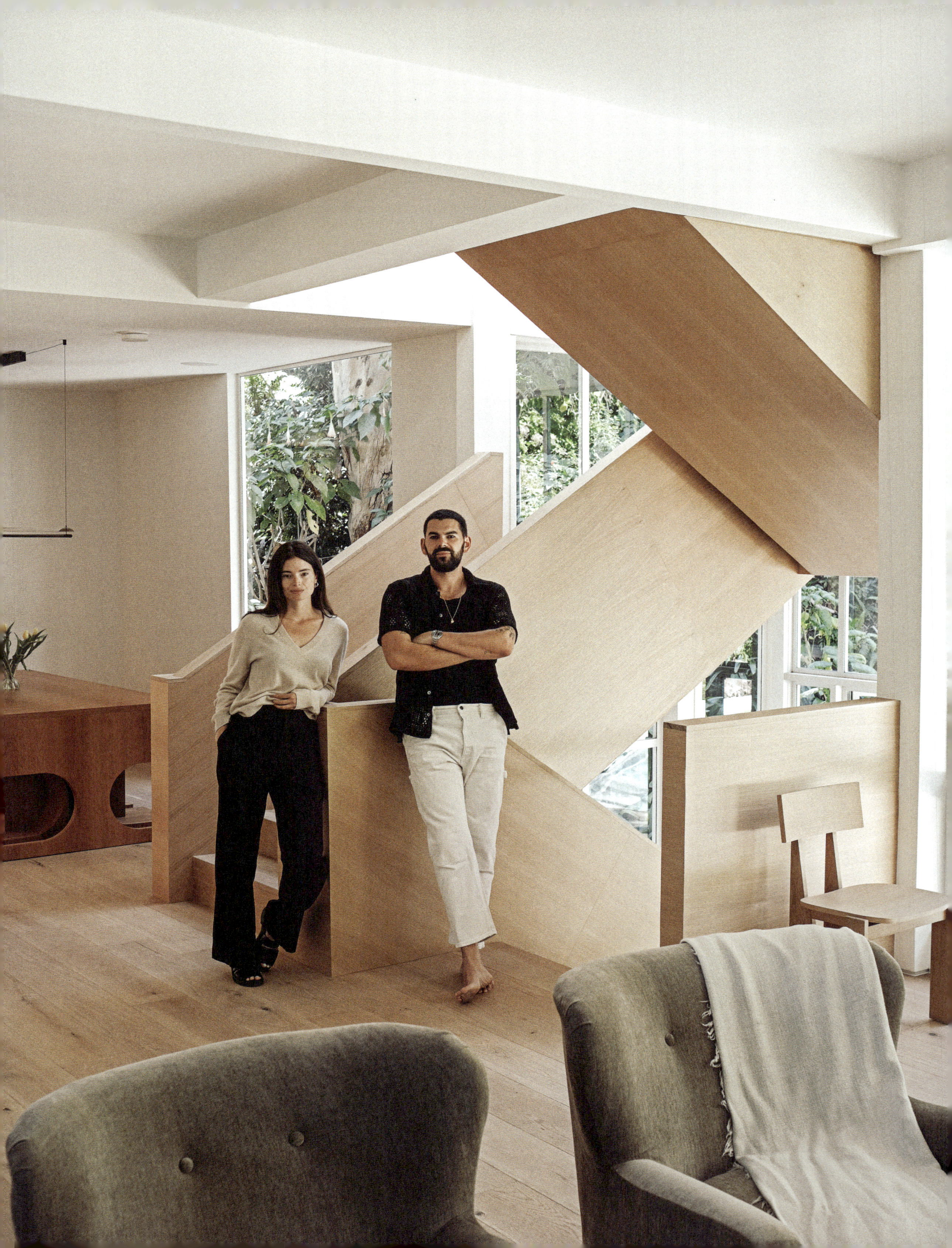

# Meet the design duo restoring LA's most glamorous homes.

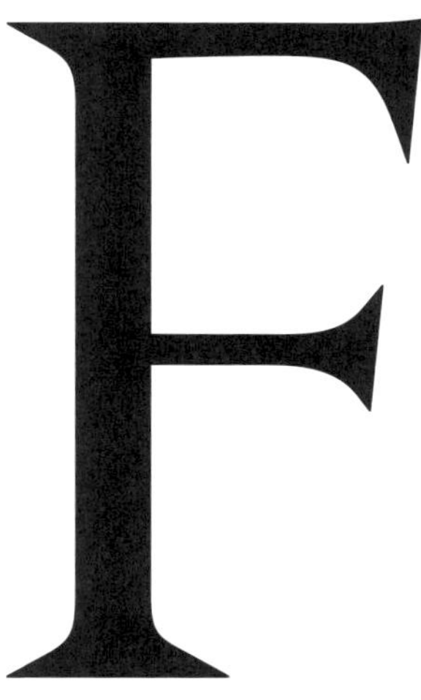

or many years, Los Angeles–based interior design studio Ome Dezin worked wherever their projects took them.[1] That means that since launching their practice in 2021, Joelle Kutner and Jesse Rudolph have spent most of their days on-site, communicating their vision with references and mood boards, troubleshooting with the millworker or the tile setter and adjusting details in real time.

It's a hands-on approach to residential restoration—the duo's focus—that allows for a fusion of research and intuition, conversation and craftsmanship; an art of constant adaptation that evolved out of their previous experiences. Rudolph, who grew up "surrounded by old buildings" in Pittsburgh, spent his early career in construction and development. He met Kutner when she moved from Toronto to LA to study film; before Ome Dezin, she worked at Acne Studios and across interiors, stage design, packaging and branding.

Then, in 2020, the friends came together when one of Rudolph's contacts— a contractor at O'Connor Estates—trusted them enough to refurbish a Beverly Hills condominium and some townhouses in Santa Monica without needing plans to understand what they wanted to do. "The final design was in our heads. We would say, This goes there and that goes there," Kutner recalls. "We would go from house to house to house all day because if you're not on-site, you're on the phone or texting with someone who is."

The finished projects exude a glamorous serenity—a calm and clarity that belies the peripatetic nature of their practice's development. Amplified on Instagram, the work quickly attracted investors and private clients, but the bulk of their focus today remains on restoration, and in particular on LA's mix of California Craftsman, Spanish Revival, Tudor, Deco and midcentury modern architecture.[2]

Not that they would describe themselves as preservationists: "We're editing the noise," says Kutner. "When we walk into a historic home for the first time, we're looking for the spine—the proportion of rooms, the rhythm of light, the materials that give it soul. Those are nonnegotiable. What can change are the elements that don't belong to that story: bad additions, awkward circulation, cosmetic fixes that flattened its character. We just clear a path for the original design to breathe again."

One of their most notable projects was the restoration of a midcentury Brentwood house designed by modernist architect A. Quincy Jones. They leaned into the home's virtues, including its modernist openness and circulation that decants visitors outward from the living spaces, a process that involved emphasizing light and organic materials, simplifying spaces and using windows to build "walls" of nature, bringing the outdoors inside.

"We aim for a harmony that feels inevitable," explains Rudolph, picking up from



*Words*
Shonquis Moreno

( previous )    Kutner and Rudolph in the A. Quincy Jones–designed house they restored in Brentwood.
( below &    A 1960s home in Laurel Canyon that required extensive restoration. Ome Dezin used black flagstone inside and out, blending the interior with the patio.
  opposite )

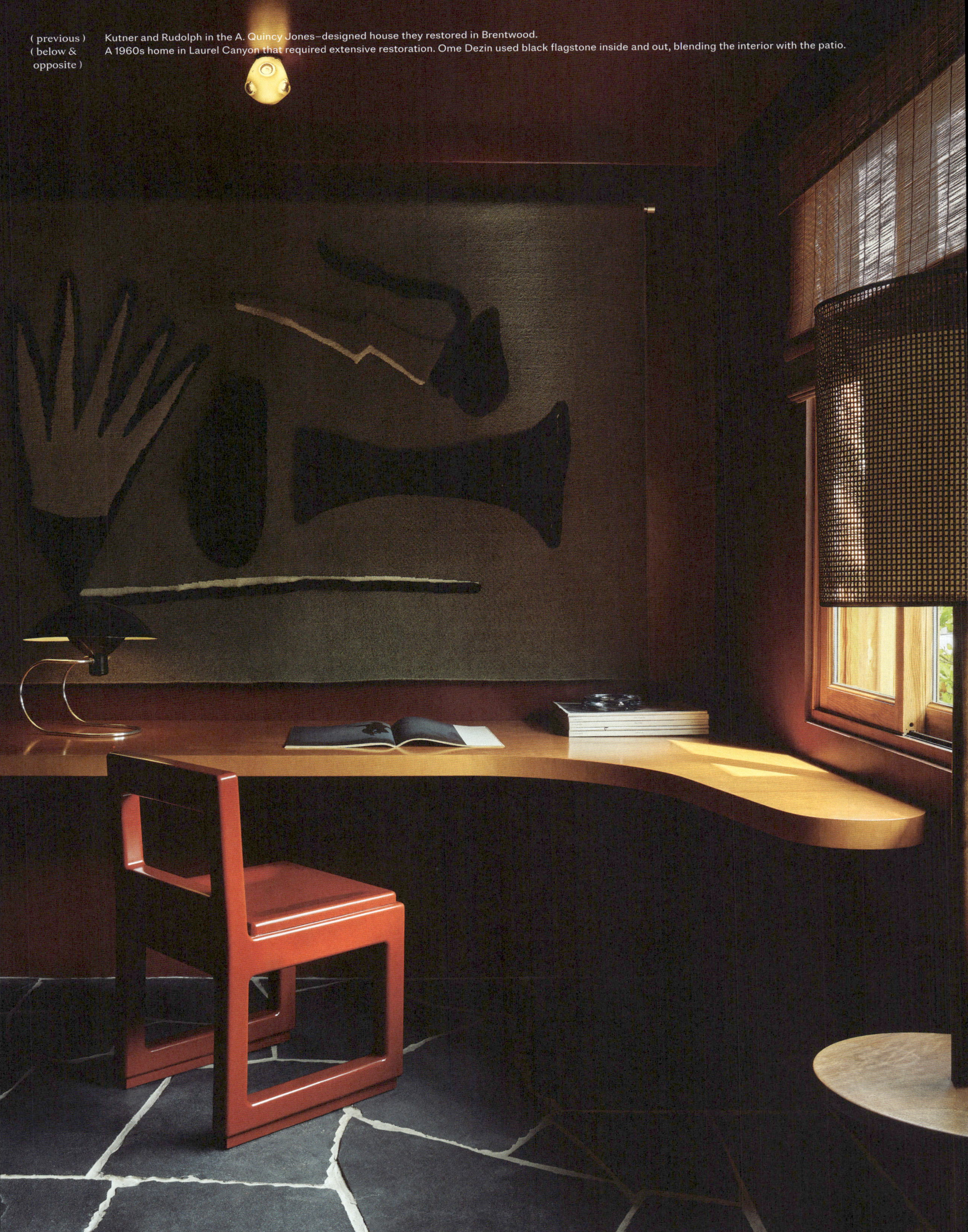

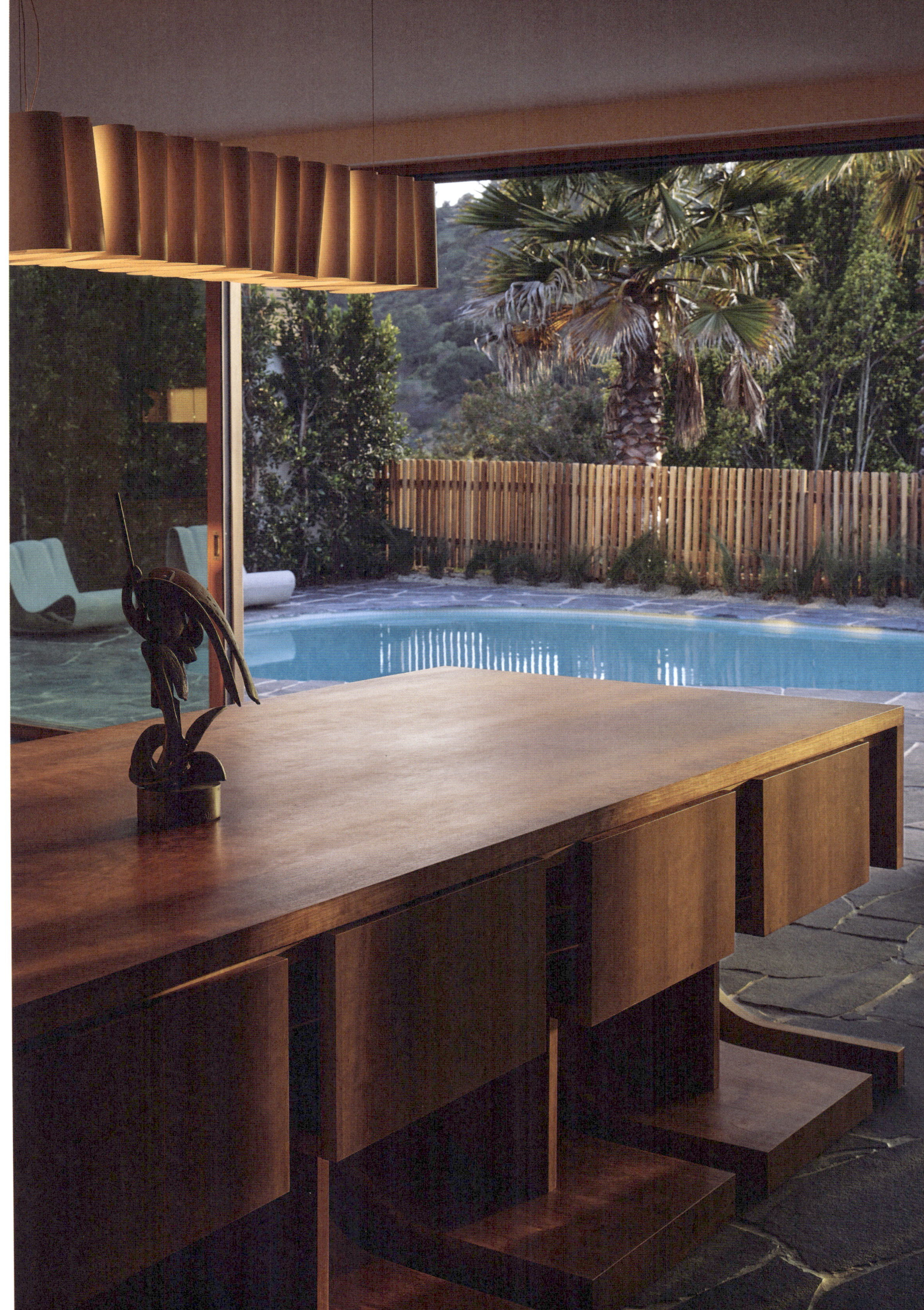

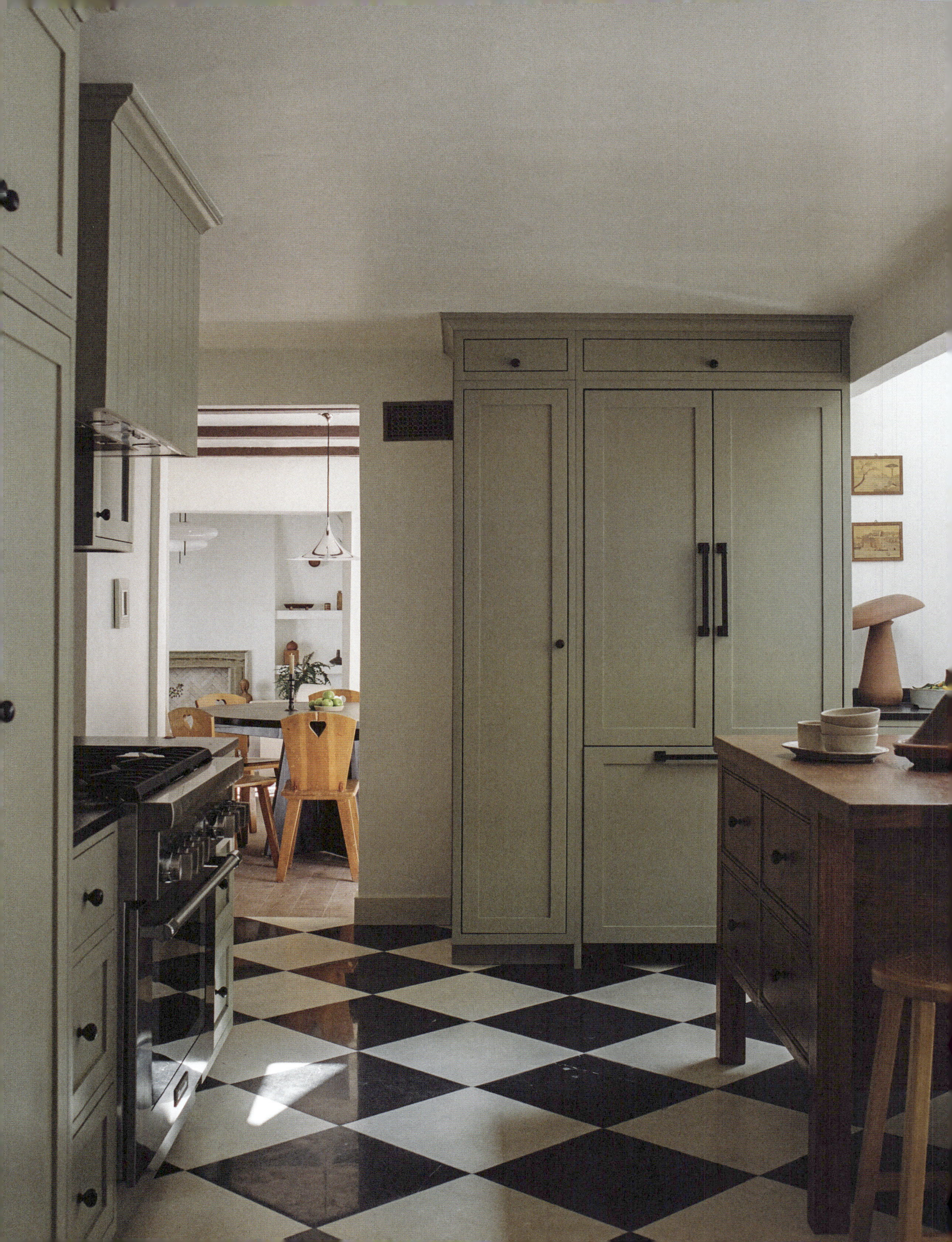

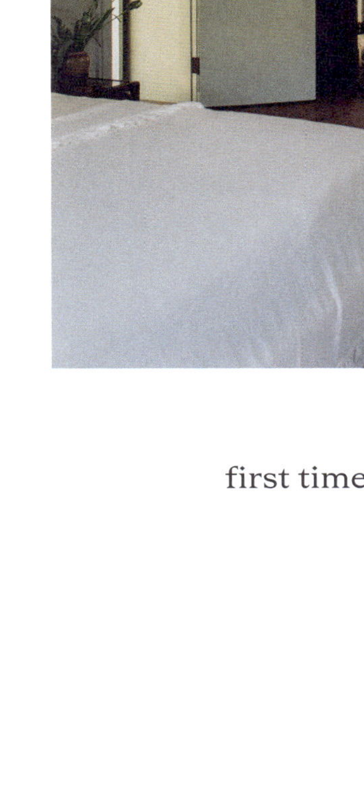

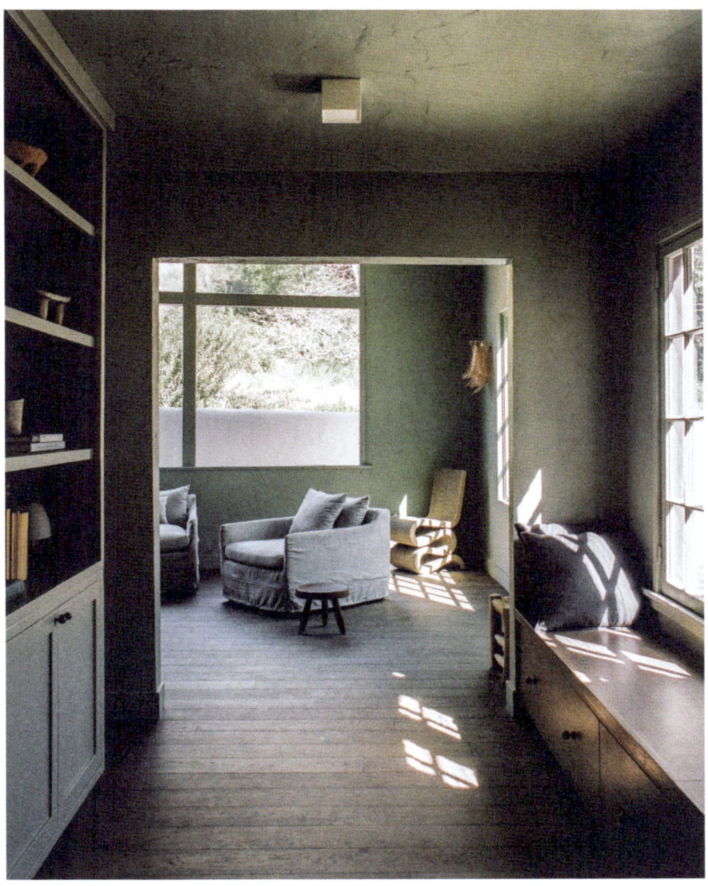

"When we walk into a historic home for the
first time, we're looking for the spine—the proportion of rooms, the rhythm
of light, the materials that give it soul."

( above &
opposite )

A 1927 Tudor-style cottage in Beachwood Canyon, once owned by burlesque star Lili St. Cyr, whom Marilyn Monroe was said to have patterned herself on.
As Liza Dawson, an editor at William Morrow, who published a biography of St. Cyr, put it in 1989: "Norma Jean was a mousy, brown-haired girl with a high
squeaky voice, and it was from Lili St. Cyr that she learned how to become a sex goddess."

Kutner. "We'll echo an arch radius, replicate a plaster texture or match a wood tone—but we'll simplify it so it reads as contemporary workmanship. When you're done, it should feel like the new and old have always been in conversation."

This preoccupation with context is a driving force in all their projects. But while the original designer's intention, the character and history of the architecture and the neighborhood all provide them with a starting point, the designers also look outside those references to art, film and fashion.

Two markedly different projects showcase just how varied these influences can be: In a postwar Brentwood home, they borrowed from the Bauhaus, introducing stained-glass elements to honor the original dyed-glass half walls. Meanwhile, in the Hollywood Hills, another historic home indulges moments of intensity. While its Spanish Revival architecture inspired the look and feel of most of the house, a stand-alone room is saturated with color and texture, taking its cues from surrealist director David Lynch and one of the client's own Prada handbags. Shag carpet, plush drapes and

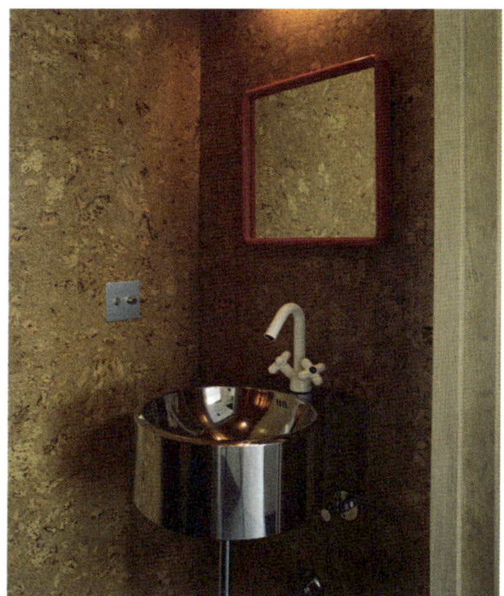

walls painted in "Dinner Party" cocoon the space in a soothing claret, punctuated with yellow leather de Sede sofa and chairs and wooden speakers.

Ome Dezin's reputation for sophisticated, considered design owes as much to its communication as to its deft styling. The properties they worked on in the early years had to be lushly photographed for sale, and the pair learned how to promote themselves, grow the business and build community. "Instagram has been our primary platform because it's immediate," says Kutner, who writes the captions. "We can share the story in progress, not just the reveal." Posts go beyond project portfolios to feature travel guides, playlists and stop-motion process carousels where white boxes blossom into layered interiors.

Kutner and Rudolph have also launched a Substack newsletter where they discuss context and process in more detail, and even if a private client nixes publication of their space, the team still documents everything internally. "It helps us track decisions, preserve details and deliver a more thoughtful final result," says Kutner. "It also creates a record that clients appreciate, like an archive of their home."

Key to the pair's success is the community of collaborators they have built. They return to the same contractor (who is still willing to build from mood boards, not renderings) and plasterer (who has an understanding of texture and imperfection crucial to restoration). They also revisit ceramicists, photographers, vintage dealers and salvage sources.

"Building community, for us, is about repeat collaborators," says Rudolph, "people we trust creatively and personally and who bring a different point of view." They tapped designer Marco Zamora for one project because he was mid-restoration on his own Spanish Revival home. Designer Ben Willett's skill in designing built-ins was well-suited to a midcentury modern home for which he sculpted custom pieces. These partnerships add texture, variation and

authenticity and have become part of Ome Dezin's identity.

But push and pull between the friends also generates richness and distinction. For the most part, there are no rules, except for one: If they disagree, they take note of the idea, move on, let it percolate and revisit it later. Then, if one feels strongly enough, they'll adopt or veto it. "It's a whole house of a thousand subjective decisions, just one opinion versus the other and they're both right and wrong," Kutner pauses, "or right and right."

"Or wrong and wrong," Rudolph adds.

"There you go," Kutner concludes.

In six years, growth has brought change. "We now have better documentation, clearer systems and a team, so we don't have to be on-site as constantly as we once were," Kutner says. "At the same time, the company has expanded—we work with architects who spend a lot of time on laptops and benefit from having a consistent physical workspace."

This summer, the firm will move into a Silver Lake building they're renovating from the studs up to provide the growing team with desktops, storage and electrical outlets. But flexibility is embedded in their ethos: "We still like to leave certain decisions to the last minute," Kutner says. "We want to see how things feel as they come together. We wait to see what the floors look like before we make other decisions. There are layers to it. I'd just say, never buy all the furniture all at once."

( 1 )  Ome Dezin's name was inspired by the way Kutner's husband, who is French, pronounced the word "home." "Jesse and I grew to love the sound, especially its natural connection to 'Om,' the meditative chant that symbolizes a deep connection to something higher," she told *House Beautiful* in 2025.

( 2 )  The British architecture critic Reyner Banham attributed Los Angeles' "large body of first-class and highly original architecture" to what he called "a sympathetic ecology for architectural design," citing its mild climate, relative lack of historical constraints and a culture of clients open to architectural experimentation.

"When you're done, it should feel like the new and old have always been in conversation."

( above &
opposite )

For a midcentury home in Brentwood, Ome Dezin's vision was shaped by a shared fondness for the Bauhaus movement. The roof, foundation and windows of this 1956 home had to be upgraded while preserving its midcentury character.

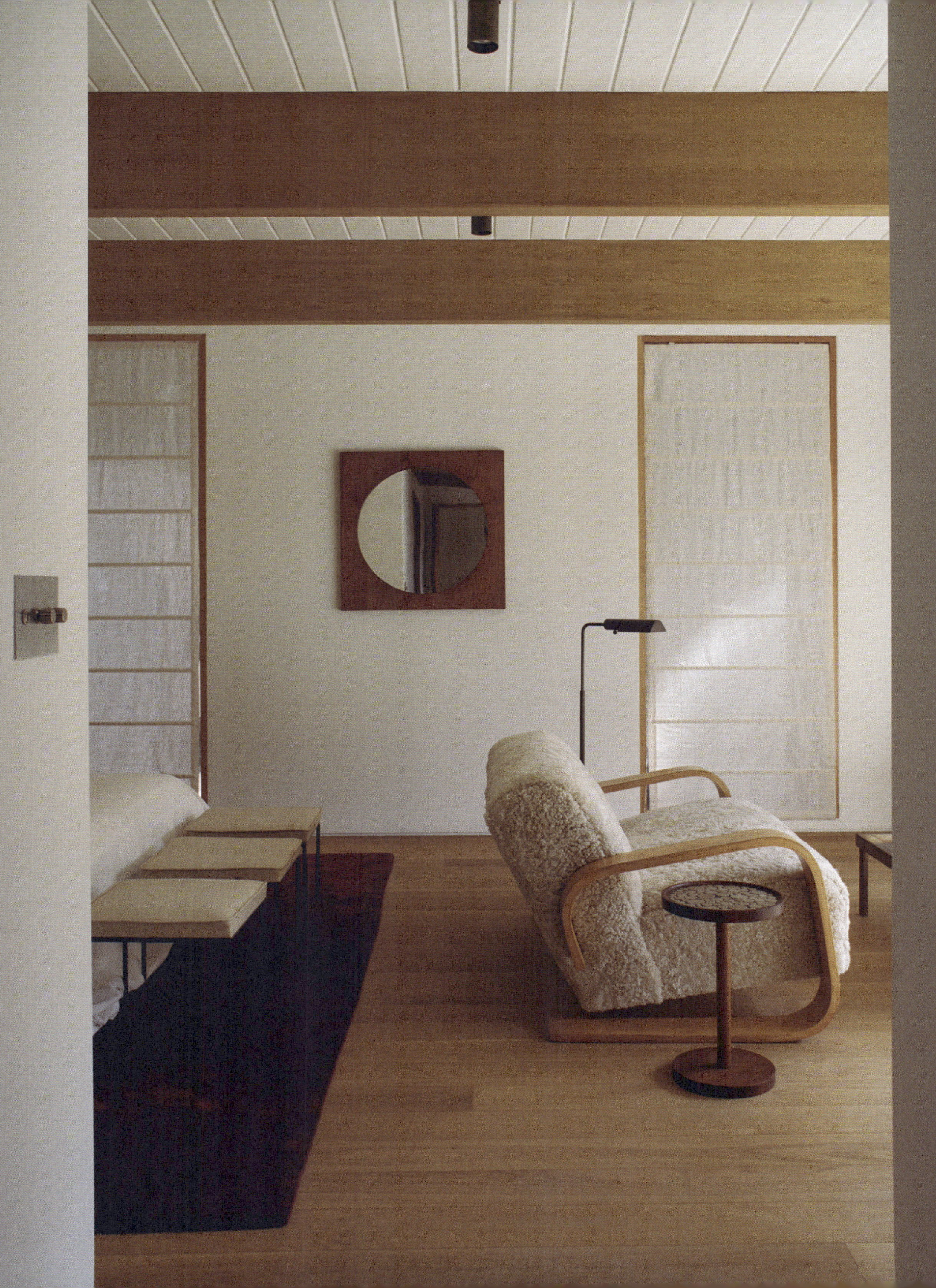

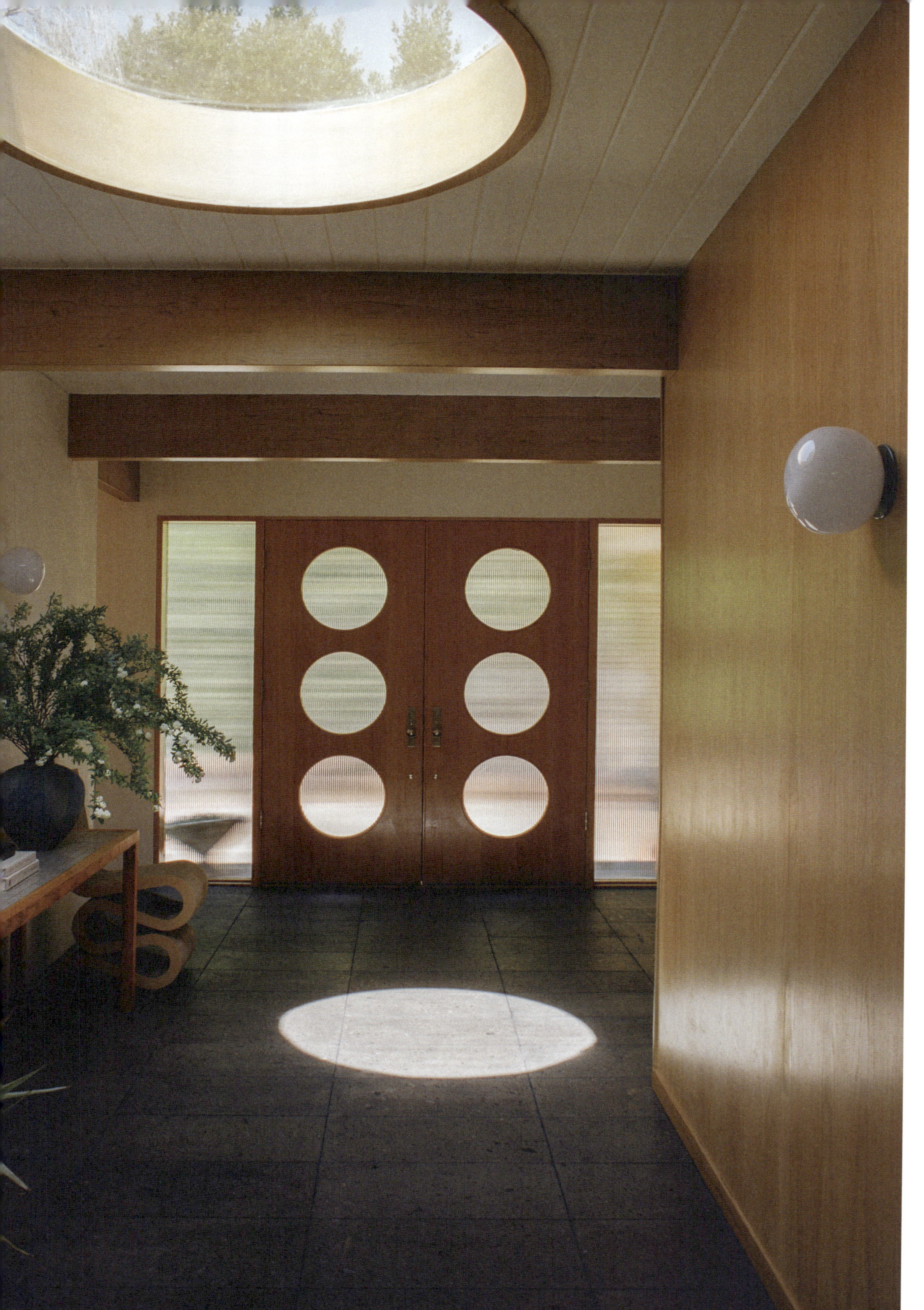

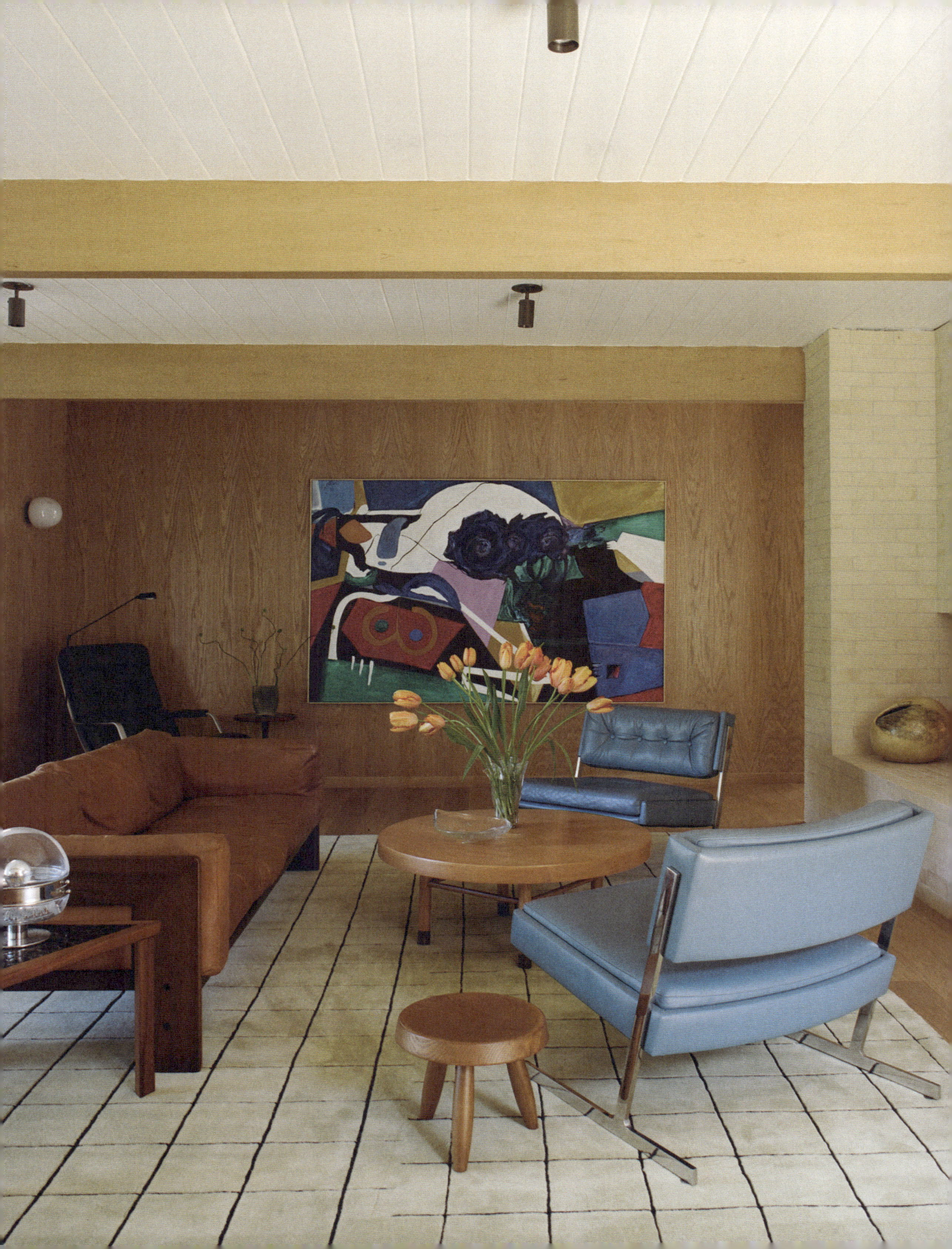

# TIME LESS

*Photos*
Gregory Chong

*Styling*
Una Ho

Enduring ensembles that never go out of style.

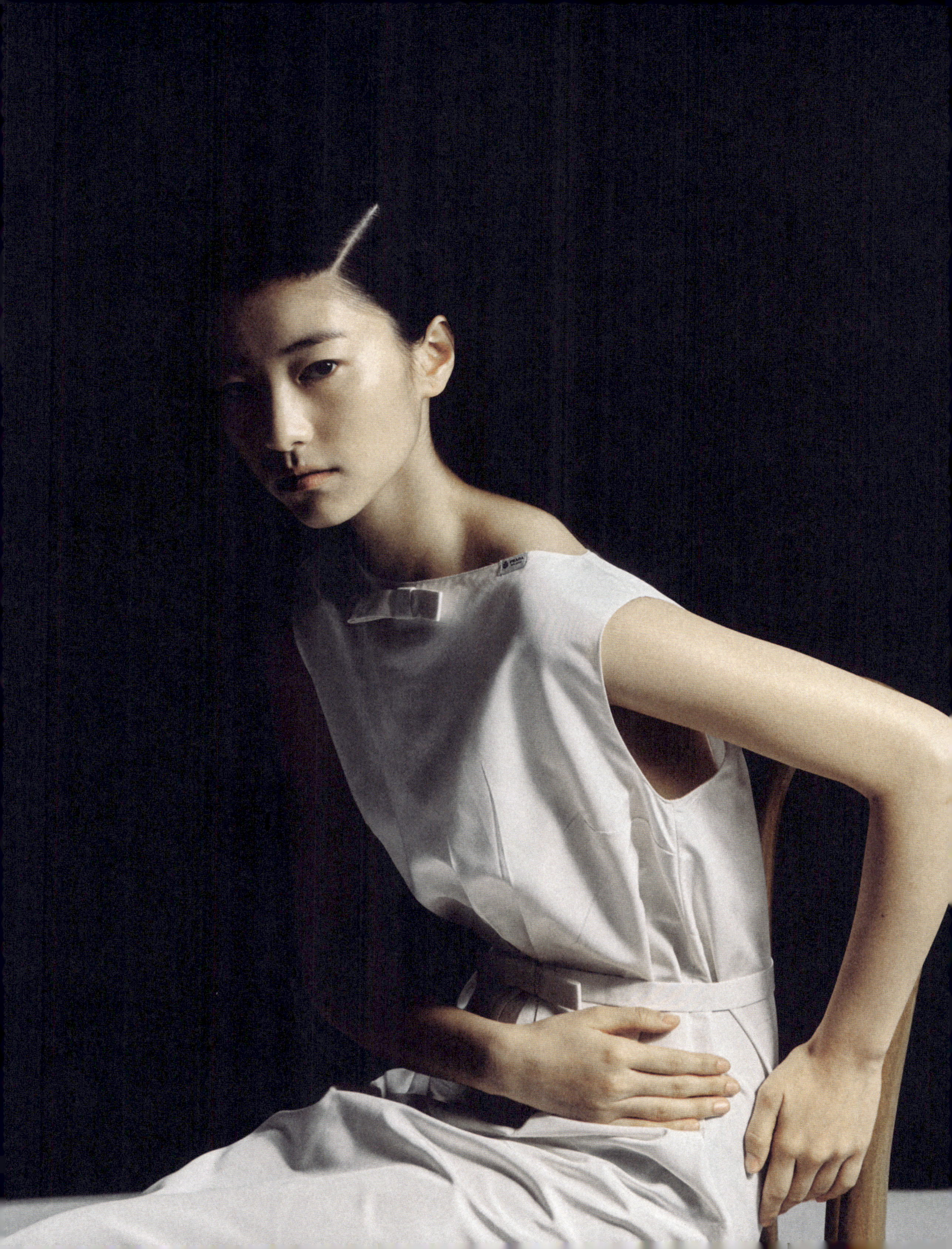

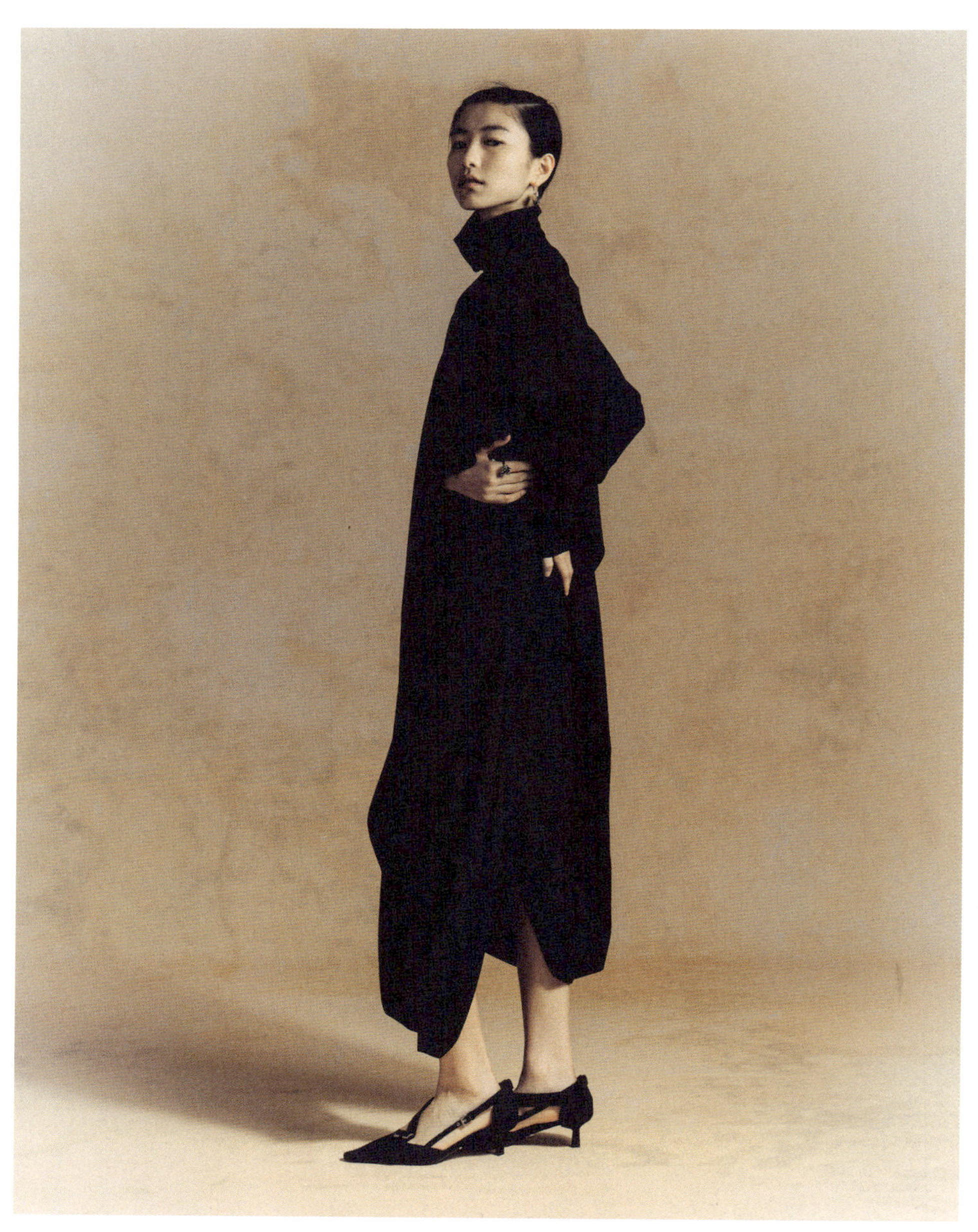

Set Design: Owen Lo Yuk Chi. Hair: Cooney Lai. Makeup: Jenny Shih. Production: Una Ho.

( above )    Tong wears a dress by MUGLER, shoes by PRADA and jewelry by LE MANDORLE.
( opposite ) Benji wears a look by KARMUEL YOUNG.
( previous ) Tong wears a dress by PRADA.

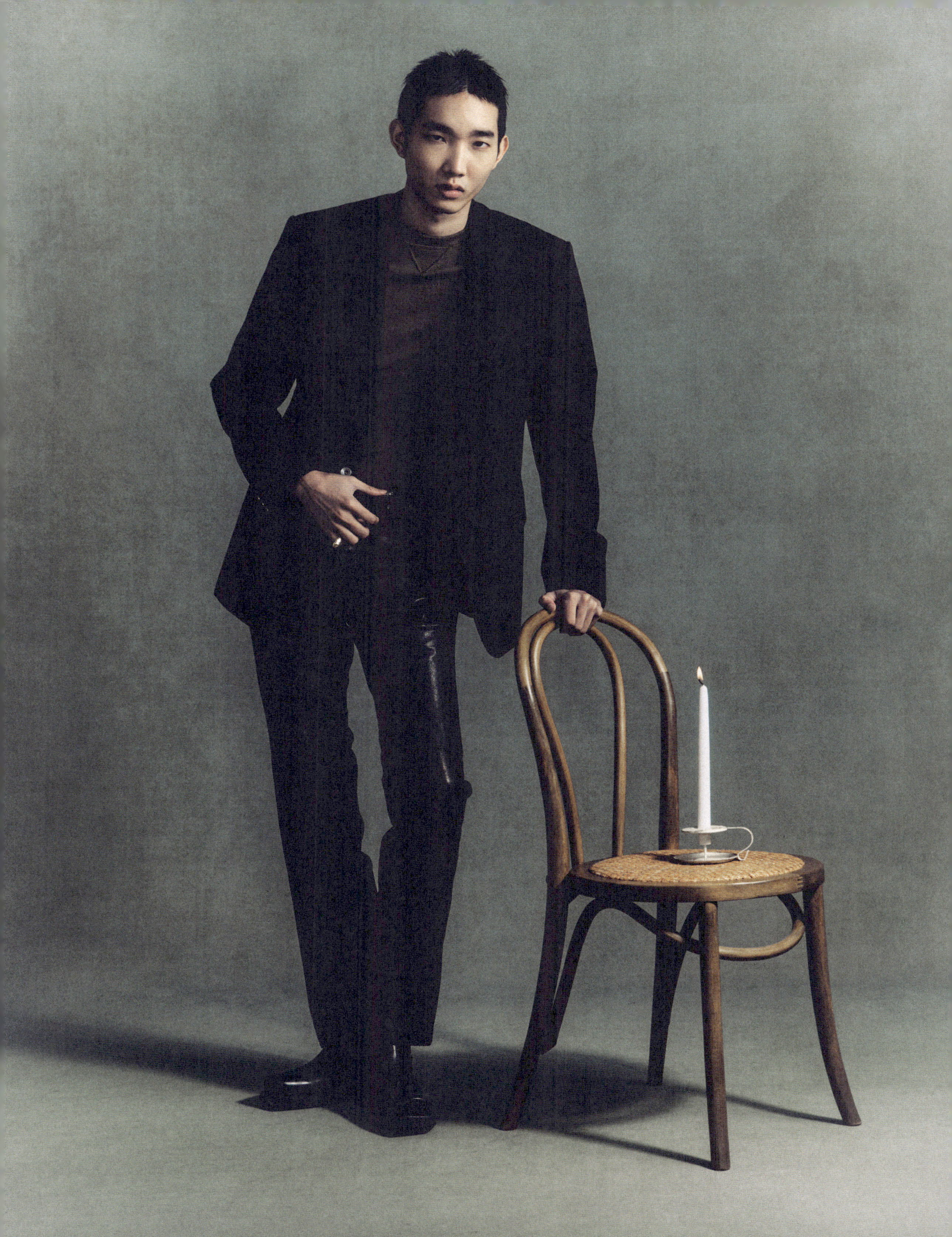

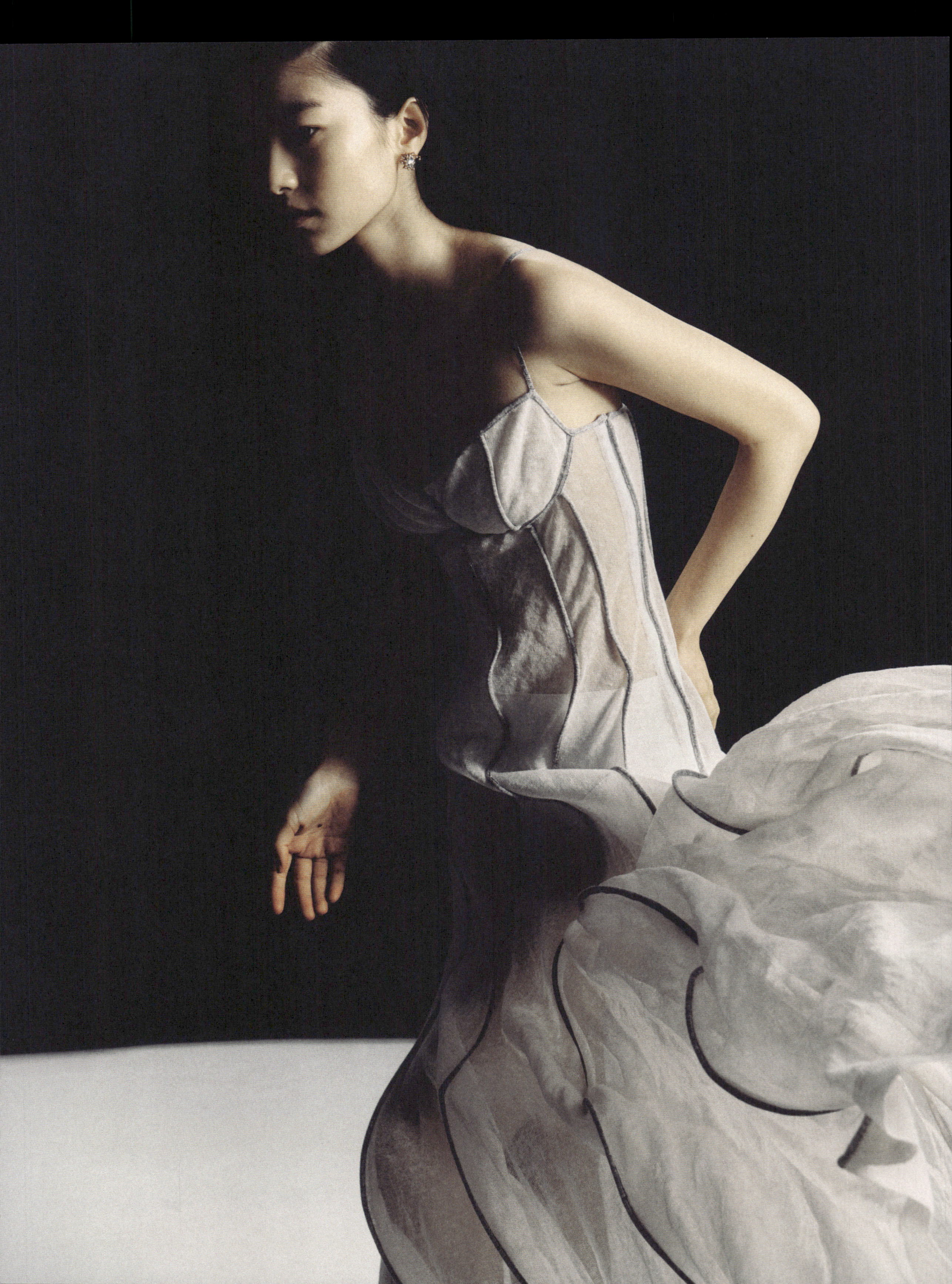

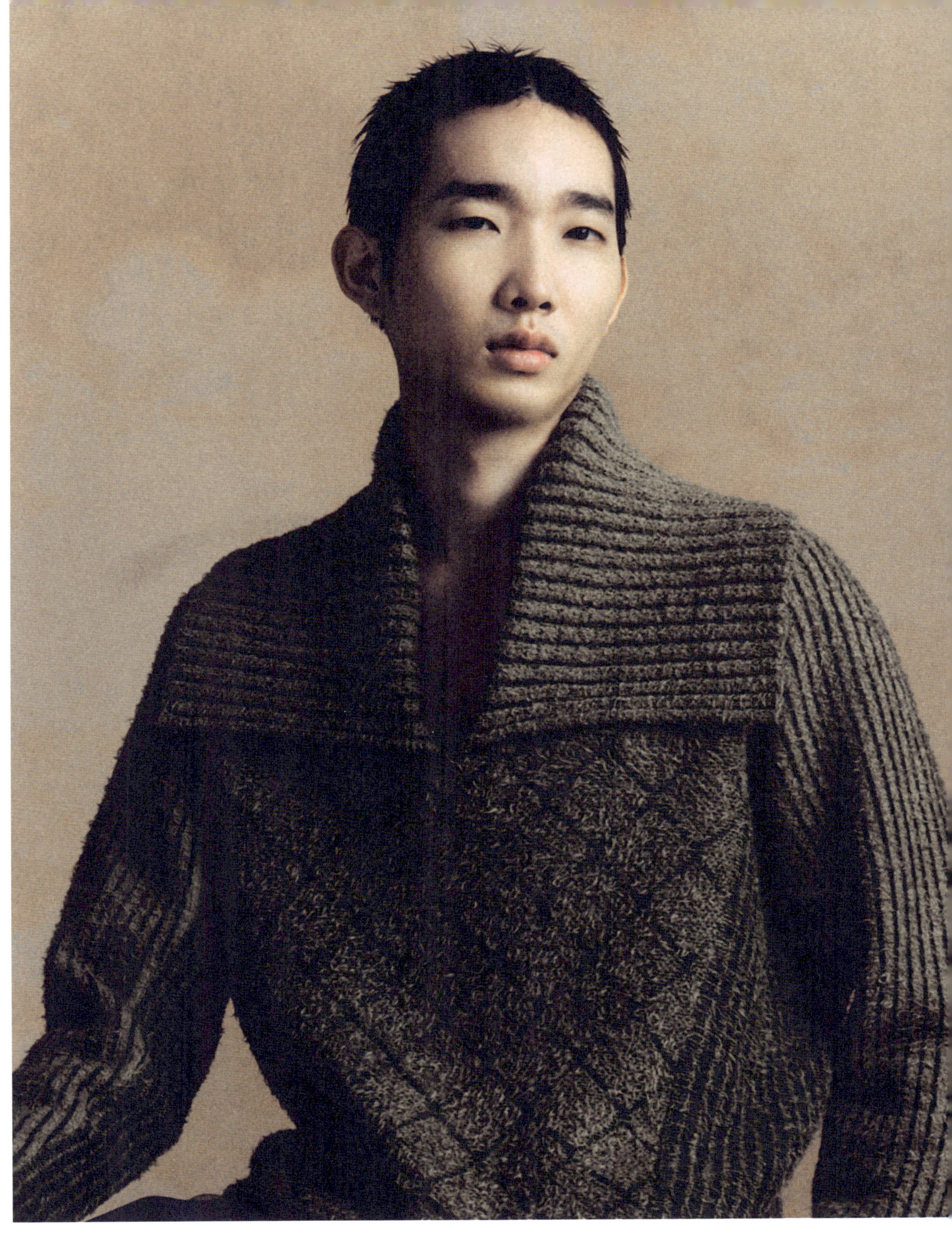



( above )     Benji wears a sweater by MATT HUI.
( opposite )     Tong wears a look by LOUIS VUITTON.

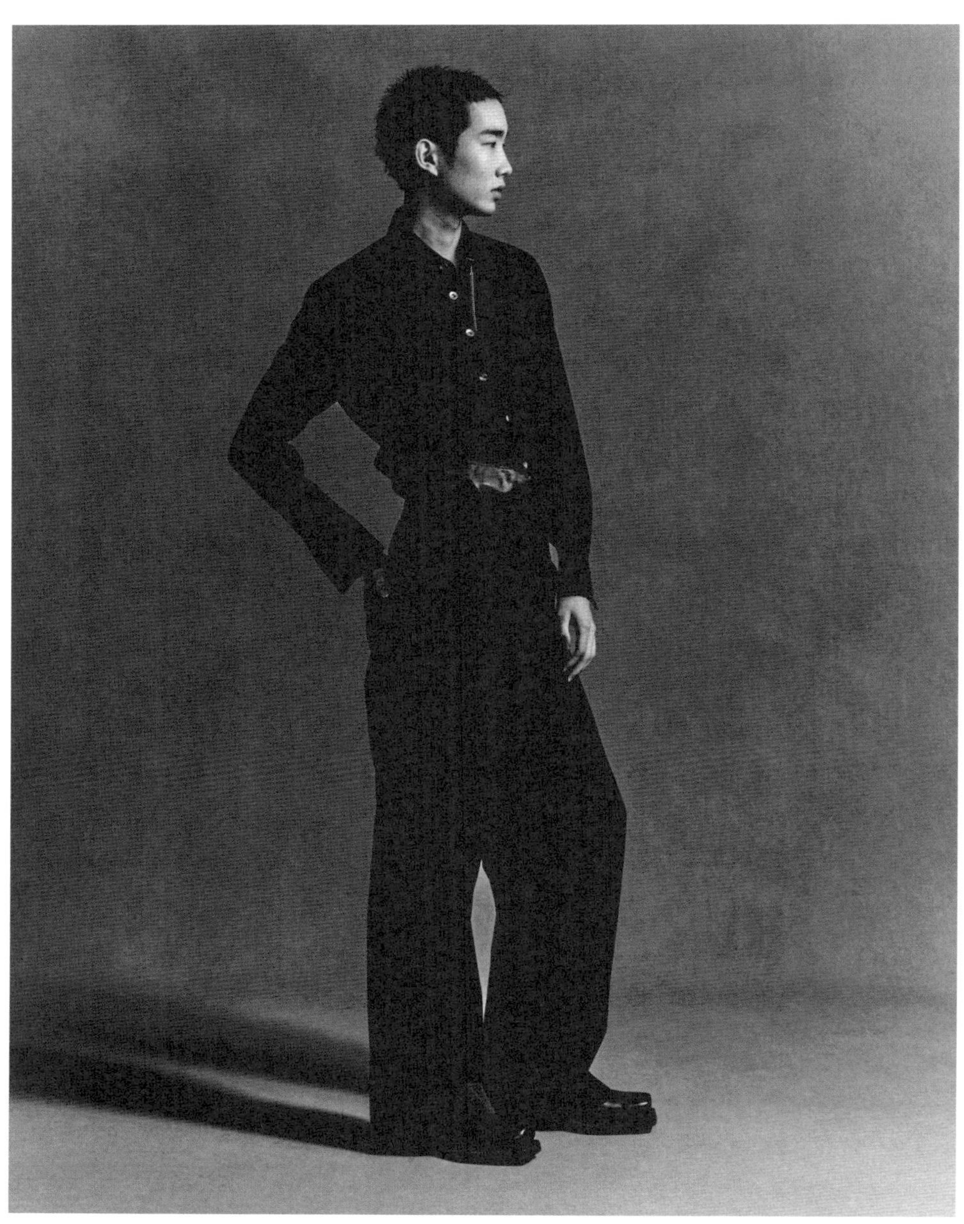

( above )    Benji wears a look by KARMUEL YOUNG.
( opposite )    Tong wears a look by LOUIS VUITTON.

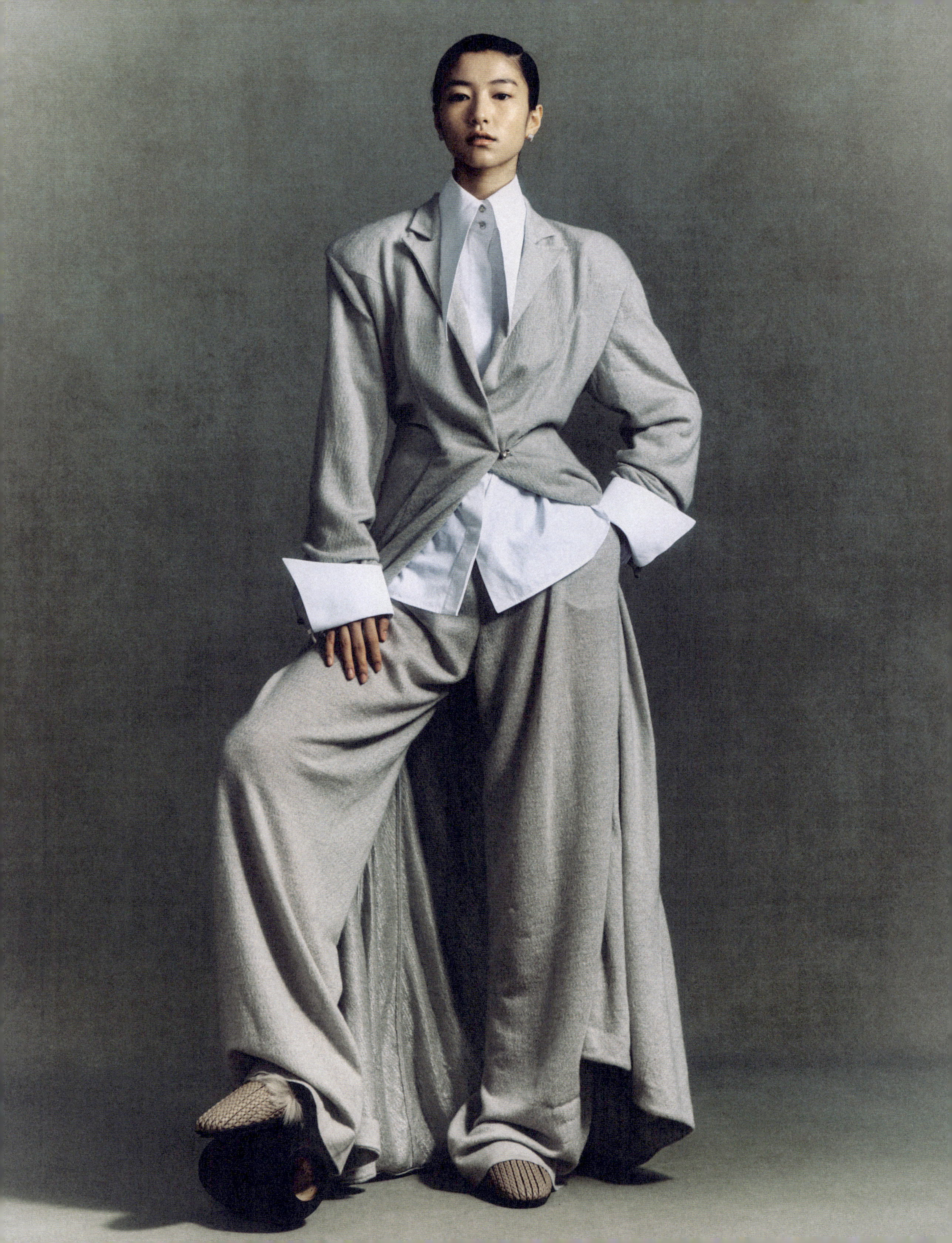

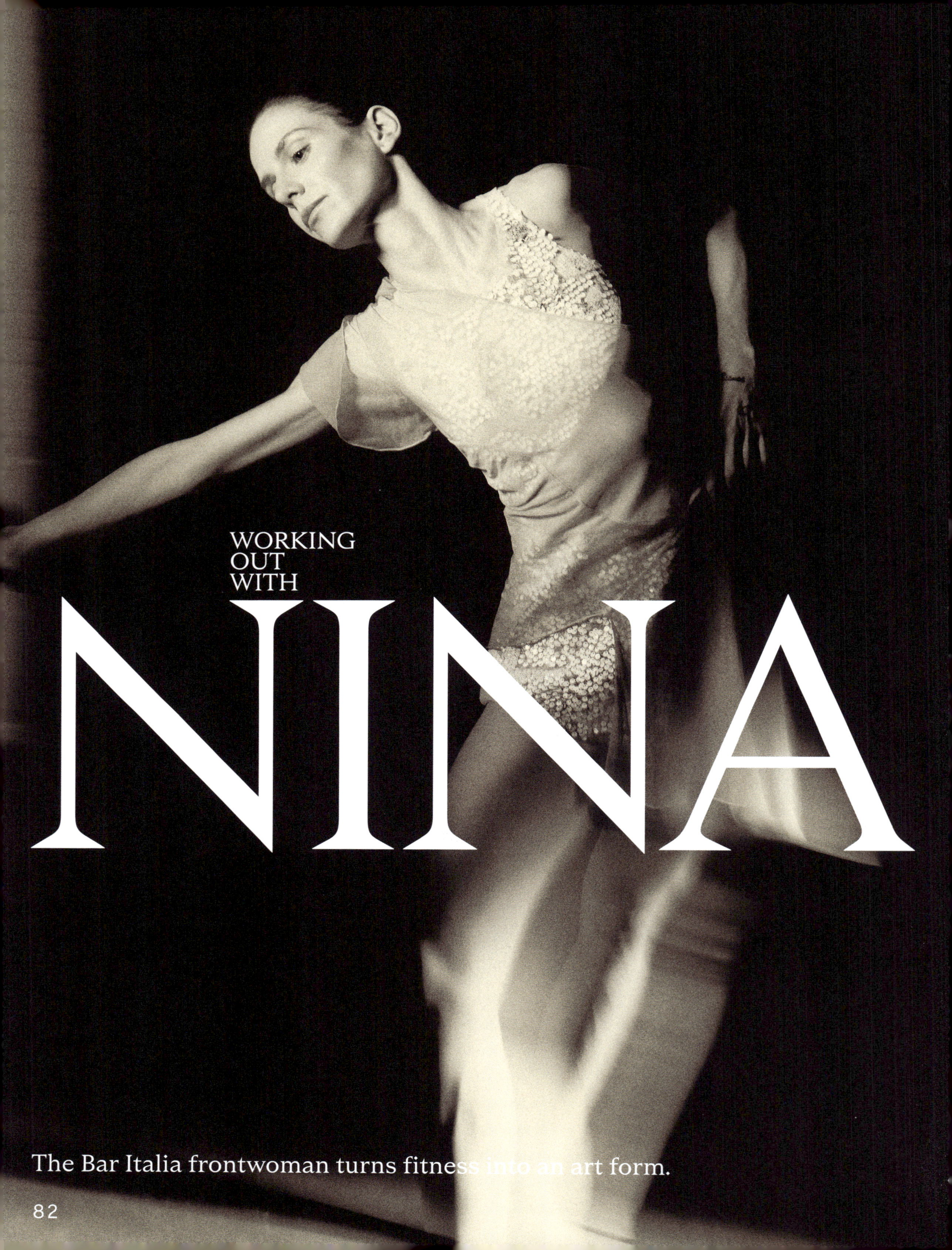

# NINA

The Bar Italia frontwoman turns fitness into an art form.

# CRISTANTE

*Words*
Kitty Grady
*Photos*
Joe Whitmore
*Styling*
Partthie Mahakuperan

Nina Cristante is on top of the world. When she joins the video call, she floats across a backdrop of Earth as seen from outer space, her navy blue sweatshirt blending into the inky blackness. Her brown hair is tied up in a high ponytail and throughout the conversation she moves around the frame, changing her position with the casual precision of a ballerina.

Cristante is not in outer space, of course, but in London, where she is preparing to go on a 20-show tour across Europe with Bar Italia, the post-punk band she formed in 2020 with Sam Fenton and Jezmi Fehmi. "It's hyperfocused," she says about the experience of being on tour. "You're basically on the road and you're geared up towards this one hour and a half. I meditate a lot and do a lot of breathing. You really need to shift mode."

This mindful approach makes sense for Cristante, who, beyond her career as a musician, is a Pilates instructor and has an art practice integrating fitness and movement. It's also a necessity at this time of particular momentum for the band. Since its formation, Bar Italia, named after a scuzzy, neon-lit café in London's Soho, has released five albums. With the moody *Quarrel* (2020) and *Tracey Denim* (2023), the group quickly became associated with the "indie sleaze" revival of the early 2020s—a nostalgic resurgence of aesthetics based on the hedonism of the aughts—though it's an association that Cristante rejects.[1] "The references I have when I'm singing are not indie sleaze," she says. "I don't smoke or drink or do drugs."

With a more monumental rock- and even pop-inflected sound, 2025's *Some Like It Hot*—whose standout tracks include "Fundraiser" and "rooster"—is helping to create distance from the indie sleaze appellation. It also sees the band maturing. "It wasn't conscious, but you play 200 shows and massive festivals and you get a more refined ear," says Cristante, who sings in a naïf and breathy timbre, and moves onstage in a free but coquettish manner. "You naturally shed any awkwardness."

Cristante came to music late, in 2014, via her ex-boyfriend, the musician Dean Blunt, founder of the label World Music to which Bar Italia, as well as her solo act, NINA, are signed.[2] "He sent me a loop of a sample, and he didn't ask me to, but I just put words to it, and that's kind of the first song with lyrics I ever made." The track was "Romance," a dark exploration of domestic violence. Despite the subject matter, Cristante found the process liberating. "It just felt right and really fun. When you don't even question it, it means you are in a flow state. It's nice how intuitive the process is."

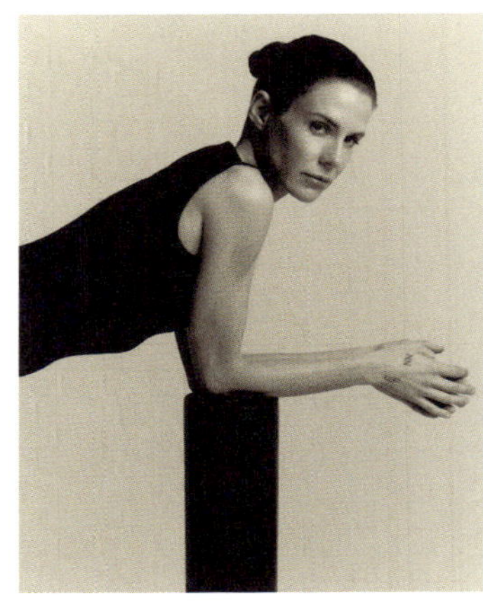

( above )
Cristante wears a dress by MALOA.

( opposite )
She wears a bodysuit by
INTERMEZZO and boots by KALDA.

( previous )
She wears a dress by JOHANNES
WARNKE.

( 1 )    "Indie sleaze" was coined around 2021 to describe a wave of new music that seemed to draw inspiration from 2000s indie bands such as the Strokes and the Yeah Yeah Yeahs. Other bands have also rejected the label, including the LA duo the Hellp, who called it "insipid."

( 2 )    Dean Blunt is a musician and producer who has been described as "an art-pop provocateur." In addition to running the World Music label, he has released music with Inga Copeland as Hype Williams, through his hip-hop project Babyfather and in collaboration with rapper A$AP Rocky.

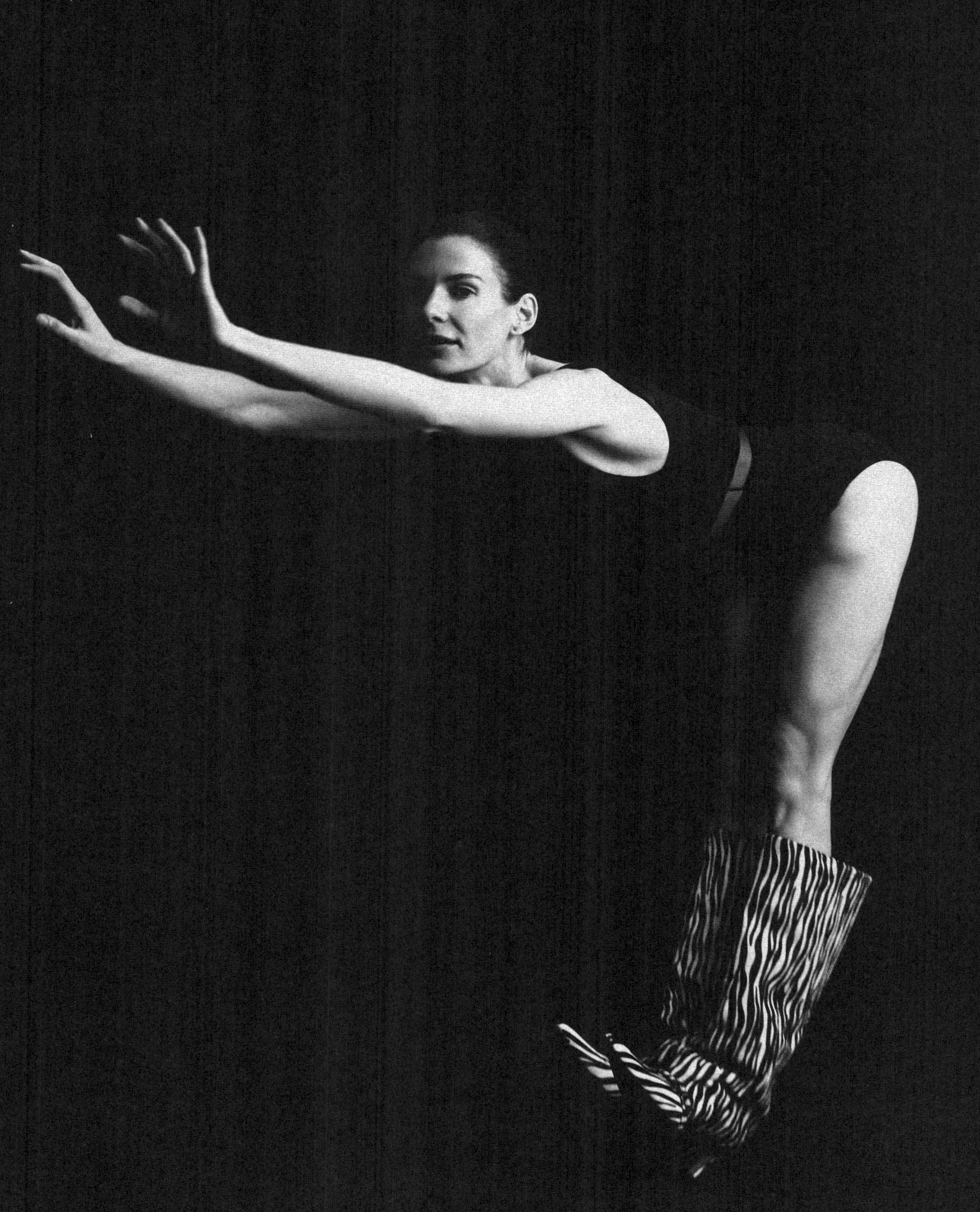

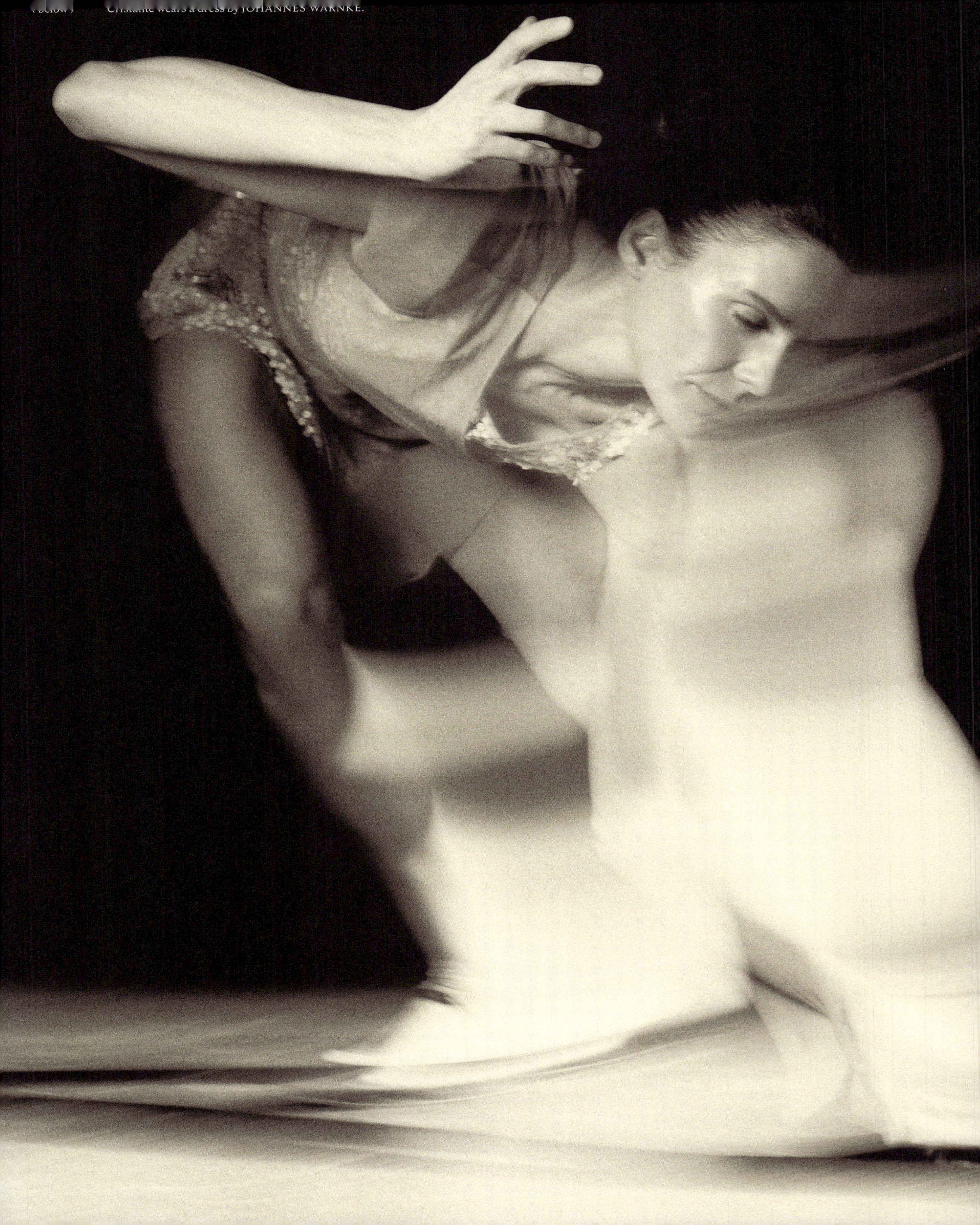
( below )     Cristante wears a dress by JOHANNES WARNKE.

Bar Italia came together in an unusual case of neighborly connection: Fenton and Fehmi heard Cristante, who was then training as a Pilates instructor, playing music in the apartment upstairs. The three soon formed the band and built a devoted following. "My performances at the beginning were very bedroom pop, using this very low range of my voice," she says. "[Now] I'm interested in female performances that have extreme dynamics and which are quite strong, but also ephemeral and angelic."

Written by all three members separately, Bar Italia's lyrics—whose broader themes include boredom, urban life and anxiety—have a certain ironic detachment. "But for me there is no irony," says Cristante, who was born and raised in Rome and speaks English with an Italian-inflected London accent. "I sing in English, which brings a natural distance to the meaning of words. I always think about [Irish playwright Samuel] Beckett, who wrote in French to achieve that, because the words in English were so immediate. I started singing in Italian recently, and it's so much harder, I just get cringed out by things way easier."

Arriving in the British capital at 19 ("or 20"—Cristante prefers not to be specific about her age), she enrolled at Goldsmiths to study art history. After interning at galleries, she landed on a new interest: health. "I got really into training and exercise—but rather than thinking about exercising to lose weight—that very boring, toxic health trope—this was movement that I could approach as a growing person."

Her own struggles with nutrition and diet culture led her to create the Zao Dha Diet (ZZD),[3] which is designed to encourage intuitive eating, and "Fitness Povero," which parodies the strange demands of exercise culture through a series of no-equipment workouts designed to be accessible to everyone during times of austerity ("povero" is Italian for "poor").[4] "Images of fitness are all quite pornographic," Cristante says. "I became obsessed with [videos of] moms working out with their kids, this idea that you should work out while cleaning the floor." In lo-fi video tutorials, Cristante, dressed in simple white exercise outfits, repeats basic movements. "I love the repetition of discipline, and the ritualistic experience of that," she says. "There's something monastic and spiritual about it. I'm obsessed with athleticism in general."

( 3 )   The Zao Dha Diet rejects the rules of mainstream diet culture—there are no banned foods, no trending superfoods—in favor of teaching individuals to read their own body's responses to what they eat.

( 4 )   Fitness Povero takes its name from Arte Povera, the radical Italian art movement of the late 1960s in which artists such as Mario Merz and Michelangelo Pistoletto used everyday materials—rags, soil, twigs and neon tubes—to challenge the commercialization of art. The term, coined by the critic Germano Celant in 1967, translates literally as "poor art."

Cristante is somewhat aloof when talking about Bar Italia: The band's formation? "All of this is already online." Lyrical inspirations? "Just life as it is happening." She opens up however, when discussing the fitness side of her artistic practice, explaining, in long and intricate sentences, her current passion for myofascial training—a form of exercise that focuses on the connective tissues surrounding muscles, organs, nerves and bones. In 2024, Cristante also released *The Richest Man in Babylon*, a short film based on her own experience, which follows a personal trainer with rich clients who endures existential malaise. "The money chasing is relentless, but it was an incredible experience," she says of making the film. She hopes that it will become a trilogy.

When it comes to the future, Cristante has the world ahead of her—and she'll be traveling far and wide. After the tour, she'll head to Mexico City for a solo gig, followed by a period spent recording a new solo album. Having released "We Don't Count," a collaborative single with Yves Tumor last year, the two are set to share more music. For now, though, she's staying grounded, thinking about where she'll go for a run when the tour begins in Istanbul tomorrow. "I hate the idea of just living in the hotel," she says. "I find nature wherever I go."

She admits, however, that this period of momentum has coincided with a creative block—at least in her visual art practice: "Art is always what I've been drawn to more than music," she says. "I just haven't found my freedom in art-making yet, it always feels like condensing, whereas in music there is this freedom which feels quite healthy in a vulnerable way."

Still, the constant is the body. A deepening focus on movement has shaped not only her art projects but her performances onstage. "I've become better at singing since I've started dancing," she says. "My body has an intelligence that my psyche doesn't."

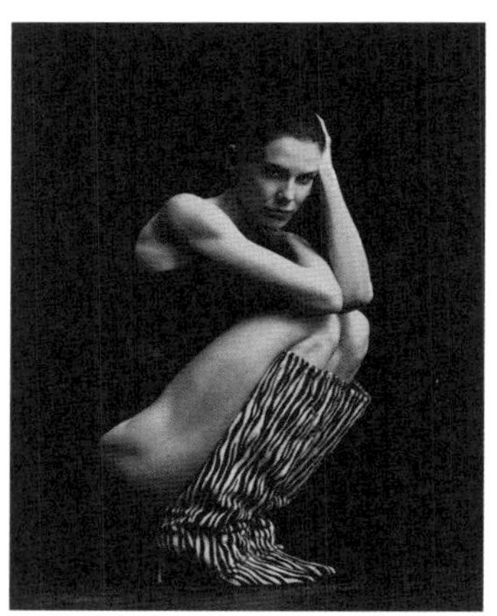

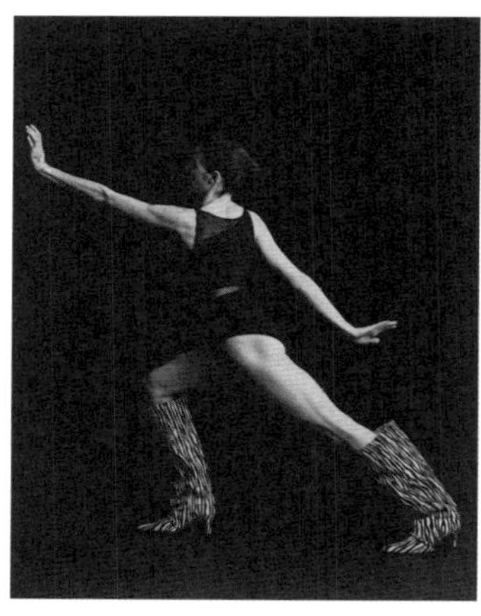

( above )
Cristante wears a bodysuit by
INTERMEZZO and boots by KALDA.

( opposite )
Cristante wears a dress by MALOA.

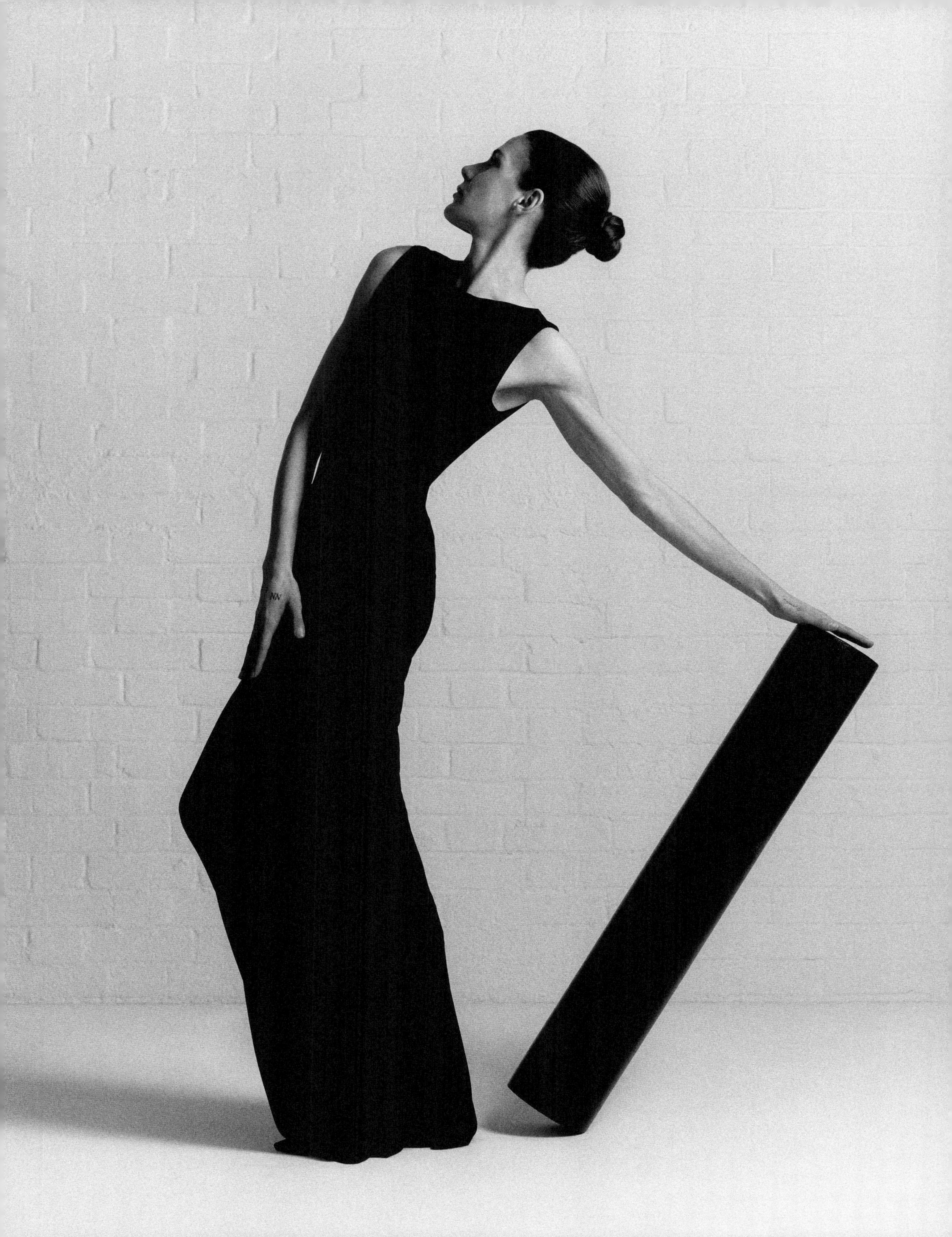

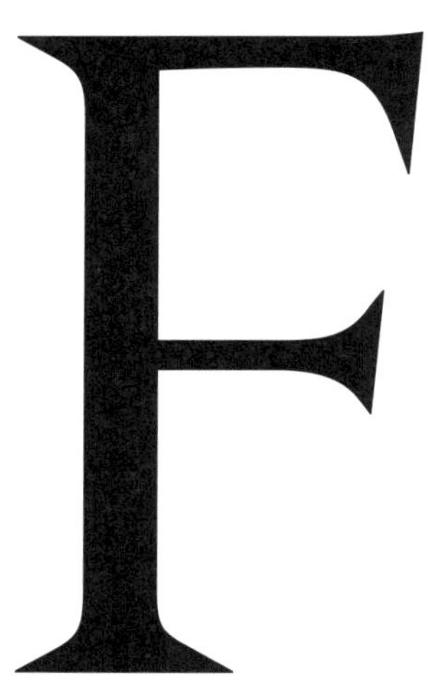

# AU NATUREL:
## Flamingo Estate—the house that became a brand, and the brand that became a phenomenon.

*Words*
Jean Trinh
*Photos*
Hugh Davison

lamingo Estate is the "home of radical pleasure." In just a few short years, the LA lifestyle brand's aspirational offerings, which include a farm box of organic artisanal mushrooms, an heirloom tomato–scented candle and creamed manuka honey, have garnered a cult following among A-listers and the Angeleno elite, championed by everyone from Oprah to Gwyneth Paltrow; Martha Stewart says its olive oil is the only one she uses at home.

The verdant estate from which the brand takes its name belongs to its charismatic founder, Richard Christiansen, and sits atop a hill in the Eagle Rock neighborhood of Los Angeles, with views across the city. "It is a radical act to put our phones down, make a meal, have a hot bath, or just walk in the garden, and get in your own body again," Christiansen says of the pleasures celebrated by Flamingo Estate. It's a philosophy that he tries to embody himself, having bought the property in 2013, back when he was the burned-out head of a creative agency.

It's a stormy Monday afternoon in February when Christiansen gets on a Zoom call, not from his idyllic grounds, but from what he calls a "terrible dungeon room" above his warehouse down the street. (Our in-person interview was canceled due to excessive rain; Christiansen had to rush to the office to deal with a leak in the ceiling.) He's wearing a cozy, dark green teddy fleece jacket and sits in front of a wall painted in olive green. "Oh my God, it's so wet," he says of the home that he shares with his partner, Aaron Harvey (Flamingo Estate's head of creative), and their two English cocker spaniels. "Everything's soaking. The goats are unhappy."

"Can a garden mobilize you to live a more robust, joyful life?"

Christiansen has a lot going on, but it's still a world away from the fast-paced, hyper-connected life he used to lead in New York. He's just finished writing his next book for the brand, *Pleasure Principles: An Almanac from the Garden*, which will be published in September. Both an encyclopedia and workbook of sorts, it serves as a guide to planting 12 gardens—one for each month of the year—and includes ideas on what to make and cook with the produce. The garden at Flamingo Estate inspires the brand's products, and Christiansen's team has brokered partnerships with 150 local farms to ensure they are all produced locally. "I really got excited about this idea of actively getting into the garden," he says of the book. "Can a garden mobilize you to live a more robust, joyful life?"

It's certainly prompted Christiansen to practice what he's preaching, partly because he says he doesn't want to be called out for writing about marvelous spice gardens when he doesn't have one himself. His team has planted 130 varieties of sage, a massive camellia garden and is currently building a

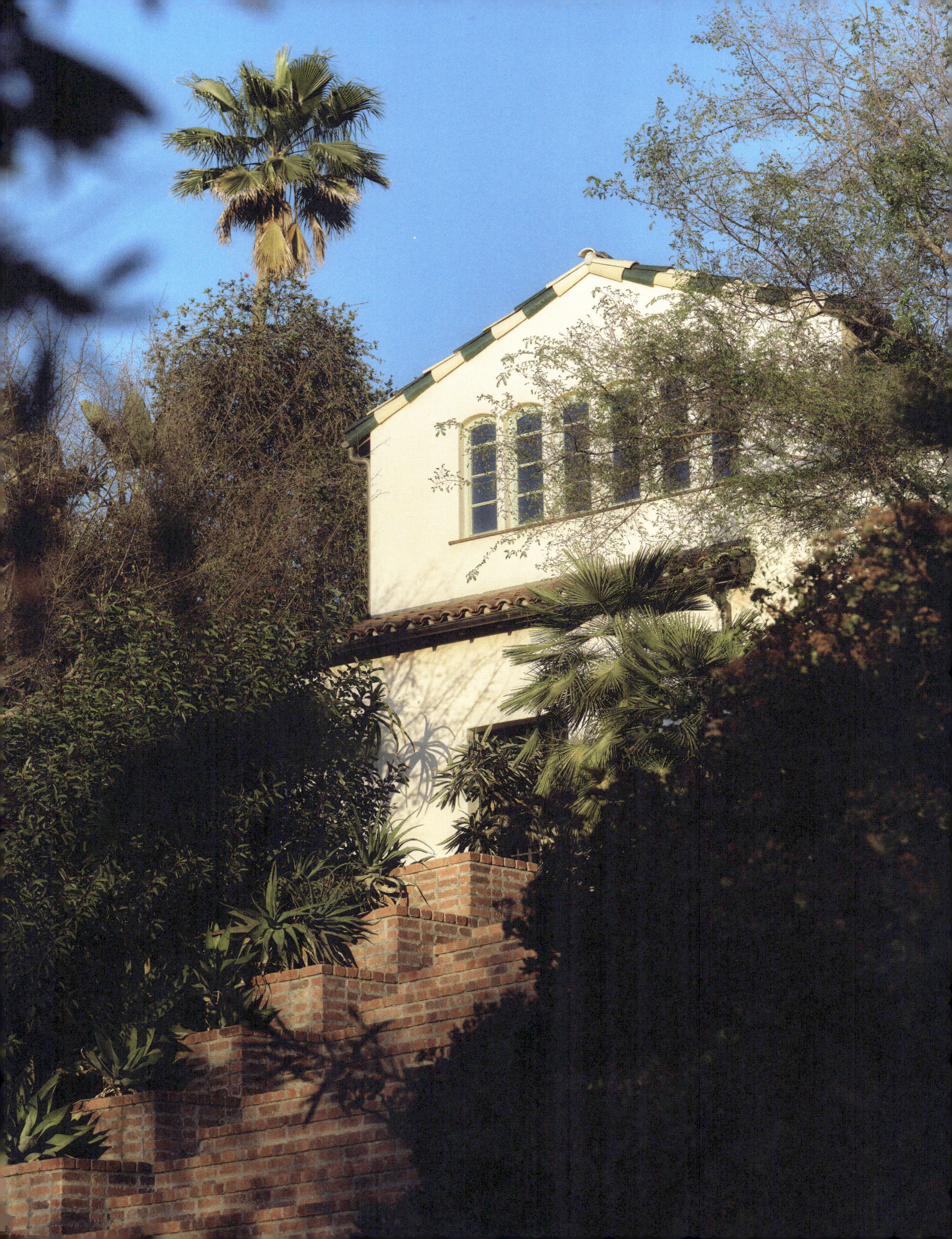

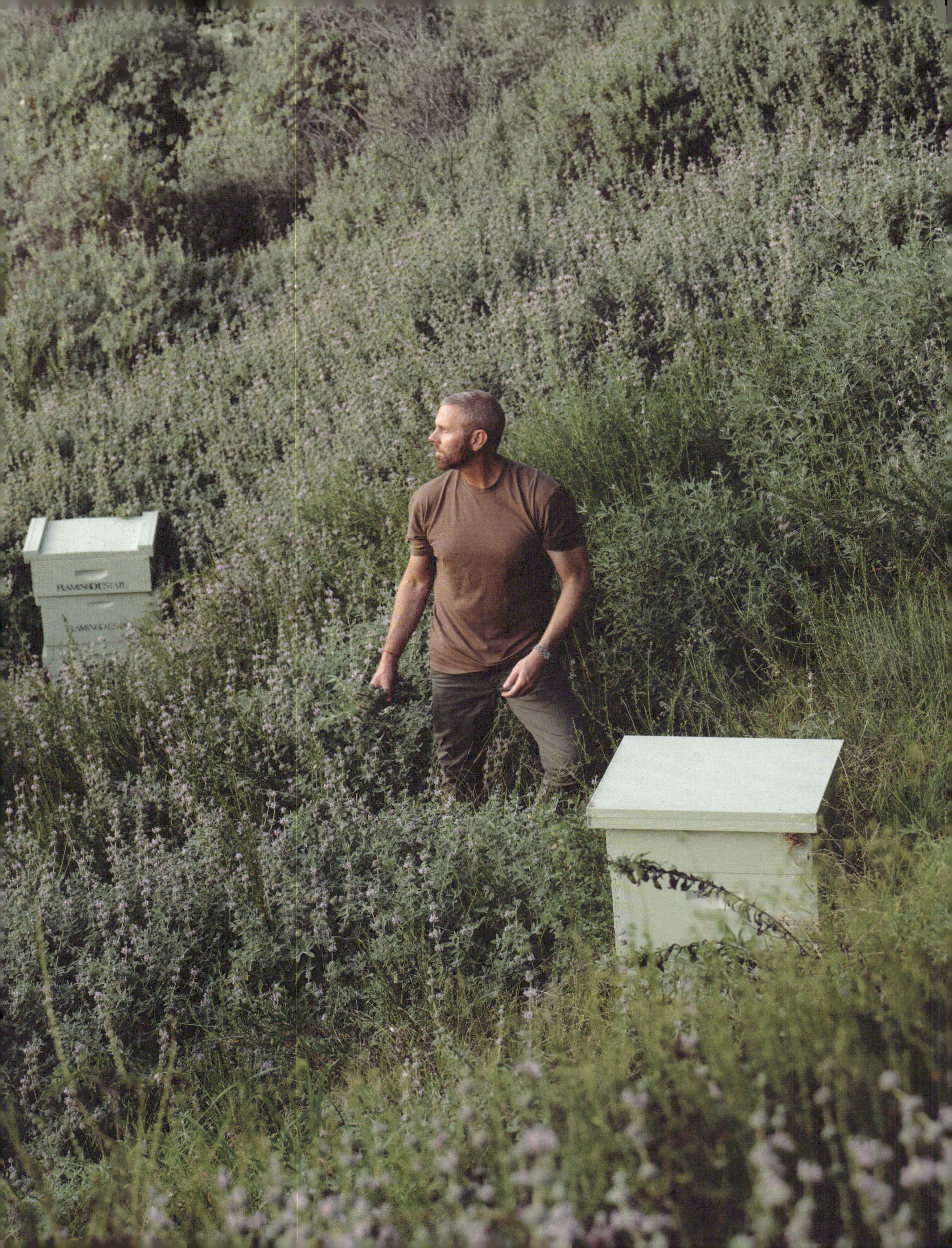

greenhouse out of glass bricks. Christiansen also recently bought the properties on either side of Flamingo Estate, expanding the grounds to nearly 8 acres. "My mother thinks I'm crazy," he says. "She can't believe how much money I'm spending on plants."

Christiansen grew up on a farm in Duranbah, a tiny town close to the famously idyllic Byron Bay in New South Wales, Australia. His parents, who he describes as modest and hard-working, grew avocado, sugarcane and tea trees, but he remembers desperately wanting to get away from his rural upbringing. At 17, he left for London to study law and eventually landed in Italy, working in fashion publishing. In 2005, he founded Chandelier Creative, a creative agency in New York, where he worked with luxury brands including Hermès and Cartier. "It was so thrilling until I sort of collapsed from exhaustion after 16 years of doing it," says Christiansen, who left his day-to-day leadership role at Chandelier in 2021.

When COVID hit, Christiansen was introduced to a farmer who needed help selling his produce. His photographer friends were out of work, so he asked them to shoot the farmer's fruit and vegetables like luxury goods. "The one differentiator for us was that we took this thing that was otherwise quite earnest—farming and vegetables—and put a design filter onto that," he says, adding how, soon after, he had 50 delivery trucks transporting CSA-style boxes of produce throughout LA.

Word of mouth spread and other farmers soon approached Christiansen. He got



creative. If a farmer wanted to sell sage, for instance, his team would turn it into shampoo, learning through Google and finding people to help with the process. He says their naivete in doing things the old-fashioned way—like making natural castile soap—set them apart. Christiansen ended up with 150 products that first year, everything from shampoo to hot sauce, though has since scaled back to around 100 products.

When he first bought Flamingo Estate, the 1940s Spanish-style house had, at various times, been an adult film studio, a pirate radio station and a goat farm. In 2013, Paris-based architecture and design firm Studio KO helped transform the home, drawing on a medley of influences from around the world. The house has roof tiles from Mexico, burgundy marble from Iran and a space lacquered in striking cobalt blue, taking inspiration from Yves Saint Laurent and Pierre Bergé's former home in Marrakech. The once overgrown and neglected garden now has over 150 botanical species, including mango and plum trees, and California natives including poppies and mugwort.

While the revenue is expected to hit $50 million at the end of this year, they're still operating in some ways like a small business. The company has grown to almost 100 employees, but maintains a core creative team of five, and Christiansen estimates they make 80% of their products, with the rest coming from farmers and artisans who make special-edition collaborations for the brand. He says they don't use third-party logistics, and continue to tie every bow and

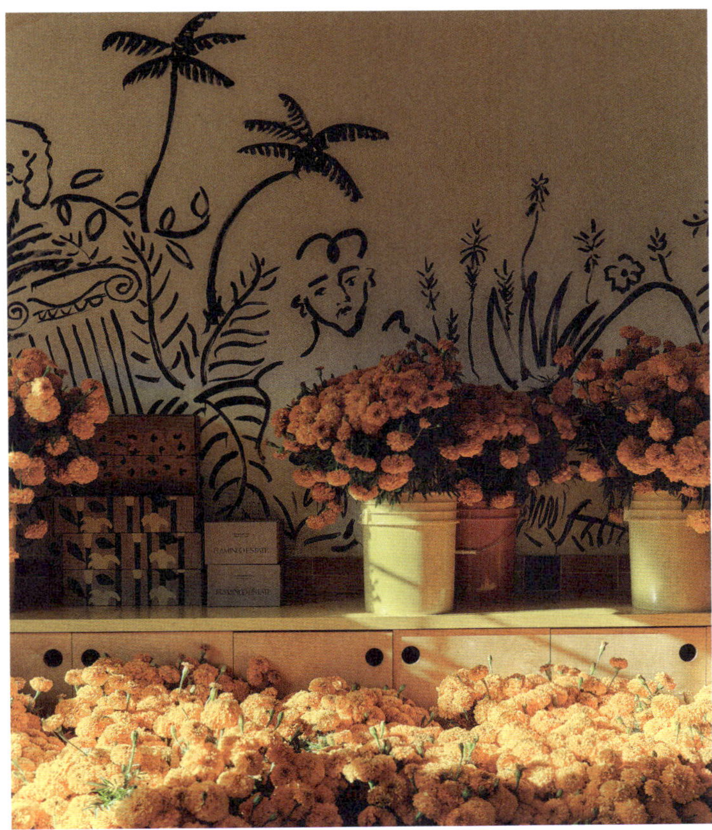

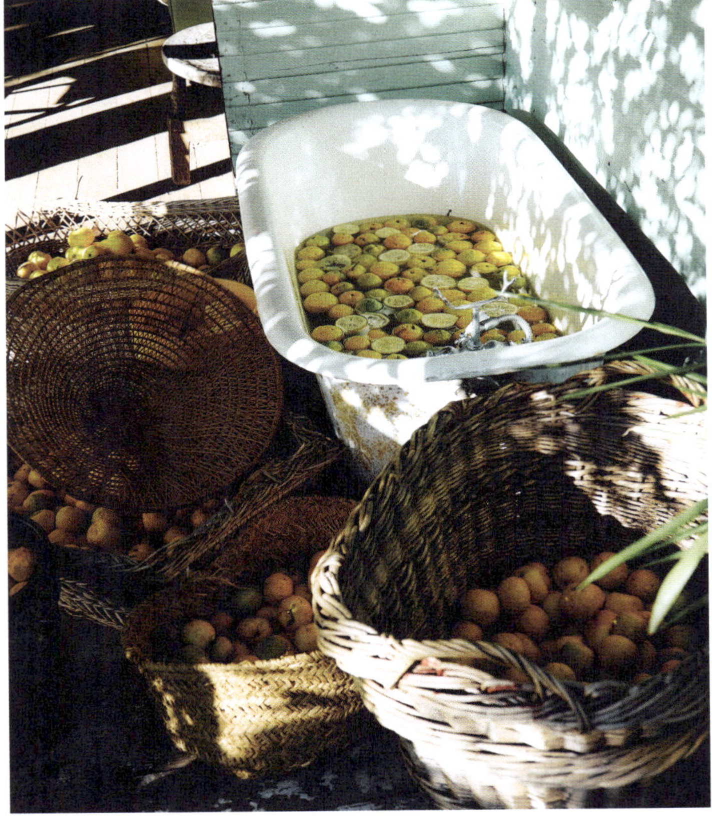

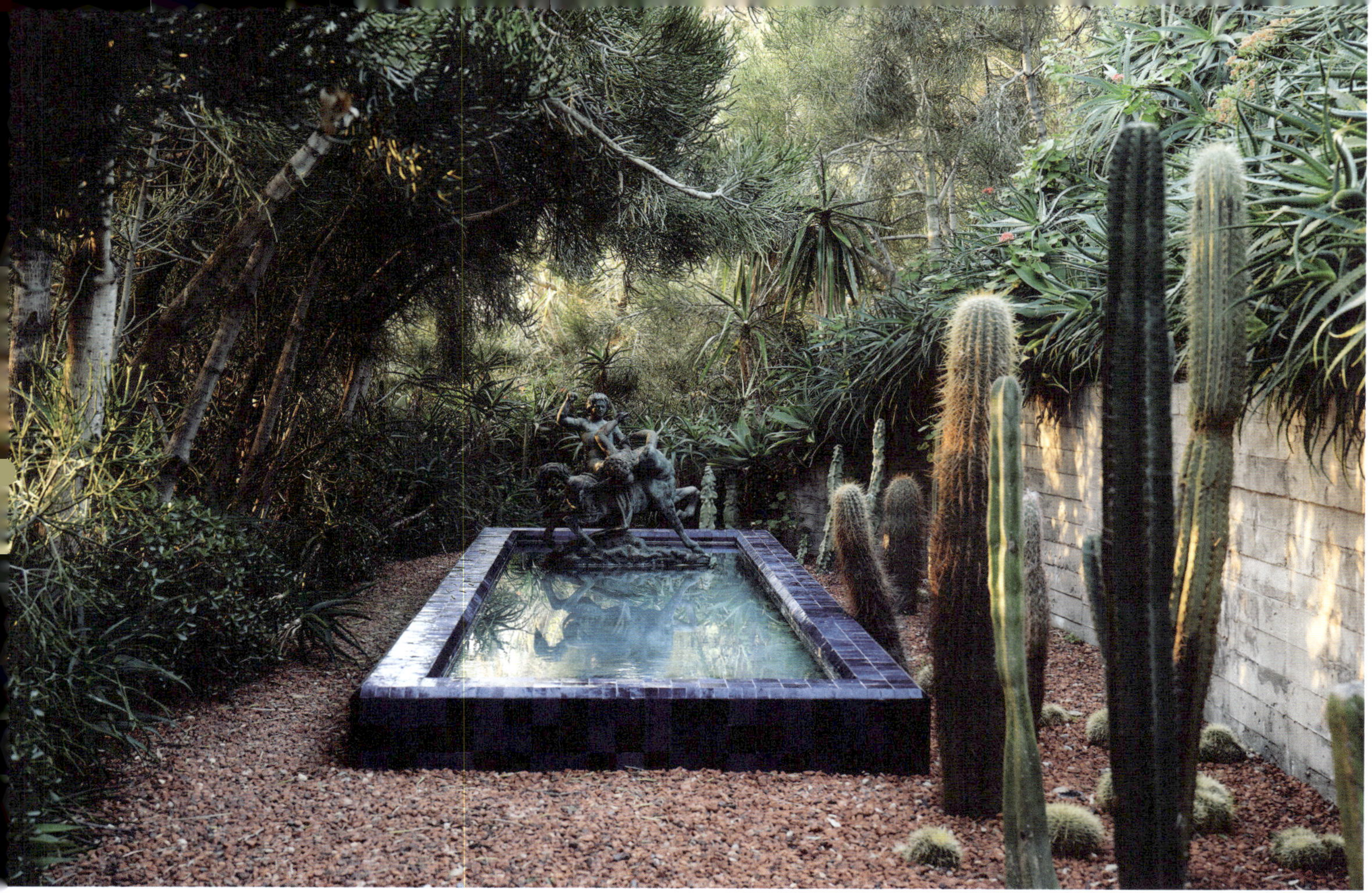



write every gift card: "I'm trying really, really hard not to outsource, and I want to control it as long as we can until we get too big."

Even while trying to keep the business intimate, the brand's celebrity collaborations through the The Flamingo Estate Fund, its charity arm, demonstrate its star appeal. Christiansen, who keeps beehives on his estate, has transported the apiaries to the homes of celebrities such as Julianne Moore in Montauk, New York, and artist Ai Weiwei in Portugal.

The honey produced from their gardens sold for $250 a jar, with proceeds going to charities chosen by the celebrities. Christiansen explains that celebrities are not paid for the partnerships, and that they happen organically without agents involved. "The business is really healthy," he says. "We're making money. We're not greedy. We're so happy to give some of that away."

Christiansen mentions that everyone's favorite criticism of Flamingo Estate is that it charged $82 for a 6.5-ounce jar of dehydrated strawberries. But he argues that the fruit comes from Harry's Berries—the "greatest strawberry farm in America." The popular Southern California organic farm has a devout following, with folks willing to pay up to $25 a pound at supermarkets; Flamingo Estate uses three pounds of them for each jar, along with premium ingredients like dried Guajillo chile peppers grown by Boonville Barn Collective in Northern California. He admits that they didn't make a lot of money from it.

"I have said many times, food in America doesn't need to get cheaper, it needs to get more expensive," he says. "This idea of race-to-the-bottom supermarket prices is killing farmers. People get horrified when I say that, but we can't keep asking people to cut corners and then use pesticides and not pay people a living wage."

Christiansen is working on securing a location for the brand's first flagship store, following a pop-up shop in Highland Park, and will launch a fragrance line next year, inspired by the tropical plants he'll be growing in his greenhouse. However, he has learned there are limits to the brand's growth.

He says they'll never expand into fashion, for example, or employ a creative agency. And he says he no longer wants to collaborate with hospitality companies, criticizing a model that requires brands to cut corners and adjust their formulas and ingredients to lower costs. "I won't do hospitality in the way that it's currently done," he says.

Christiansen—who turns 50 in August—says that he's evolved since starting Flamingo Estate: "I really do love this business so much. It's my whole life. It's my home, my dogs, it's my every minute of every day. It doesn't really feel like work, which I know sounds cheesy, but we're so blessed that we get to smell, taste and make things, and meet new people all the time."

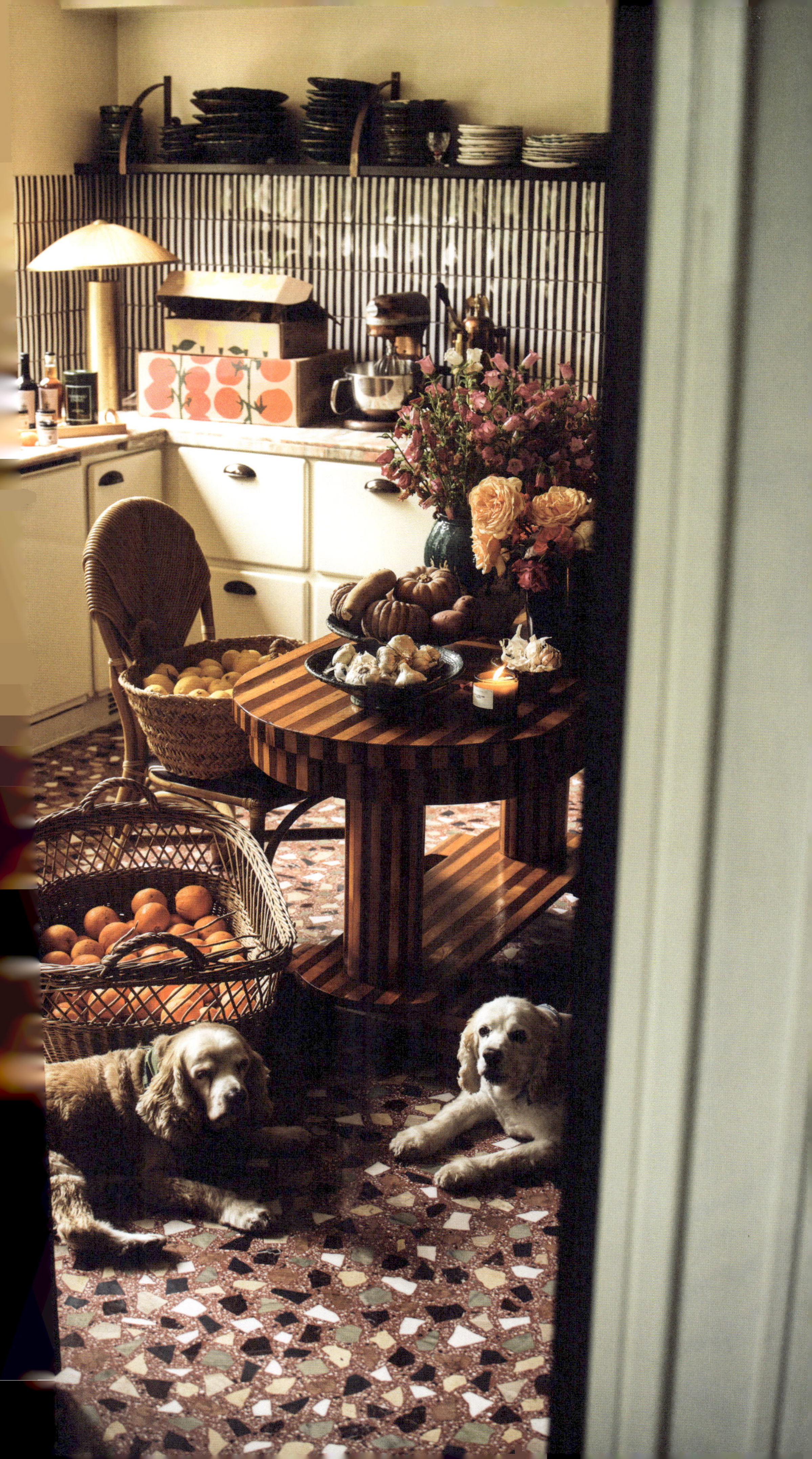

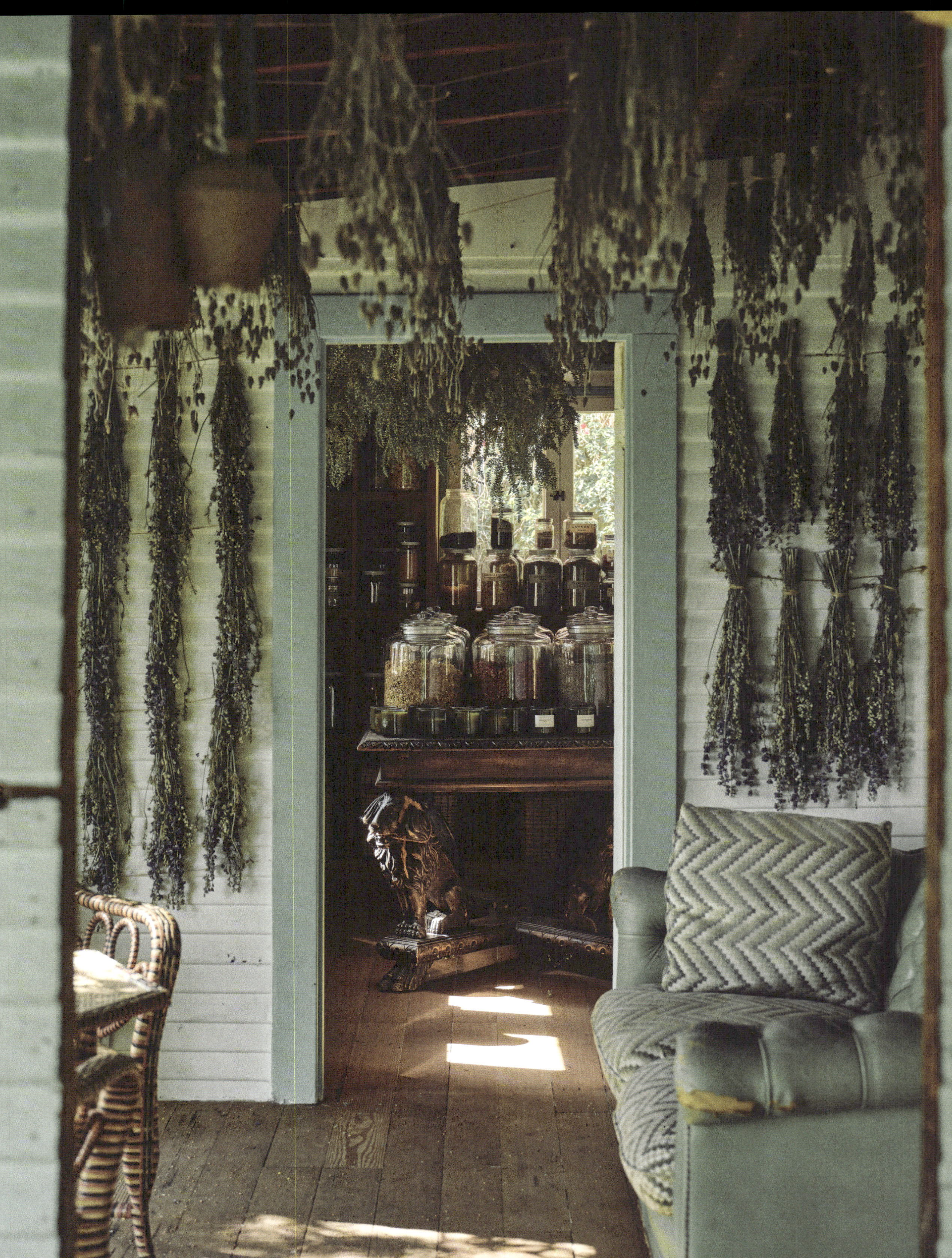

# History.

I

# FINDING ALBION
## The writer, broadcaster and DJ *Zakia Sewell* is on a quest through the history and folklore of the British Isles.

*Words*
Tom Faber

*Photos*
Alixe Lay

Ten years ago, Zakia Sewell had an encounter that changed her life. She was 23 years old and working at Honest Jon's, a record shop in West London. One day she was at a cheap Malaysian restaurant, her usual lunch spot, when she overheard a group at the next table talking about spirituality. "I was in quite a difficult chapter of my life," she recalls. "It was before I'd started therapy and I was feeling lost and unhappy, and they were having this fascinating conversation and I thought: Oh my God, I need to know who these people are." It turned out that they were Sufis, belonging to a mystic branch of Islam. One of them began to talk to Sewell about life's core spiritual quest, which he described as "using the natural tools we're given, like intuition, empathy and logic, to learn more about ourselves and the world around us." She found herself strangely moved by the conversation. Outside the café, tears sprang to her eyes.

The man's words would stay with her, and she credits that moment with prompting her to start therapy, question her religious beliefs and embark on her professional path. When she started her own show on alternative radio station NTS three months later, she knew exactly what to call it: *Questing*.

It's a decade later almost to the day, on a gray afternoon in South London, and Sewell is sitting in a cozy café in an orange sweater, picking at a blueberry muffin. She's clearly still moved by this pivotal moment in her life, and she starts explaining how it kick-started a winding path through the media, making audio documentaries, hosting a radio show on the BBC and now to the publication of her first book, *Finding Albion*: an exploration of the history of her family and her country, and a search for new narratives to heal a broken Britain.

Speaking with Sewell, it's immediately obvious why she makes such a good radio presenter; she has a gentle, soothing voice and

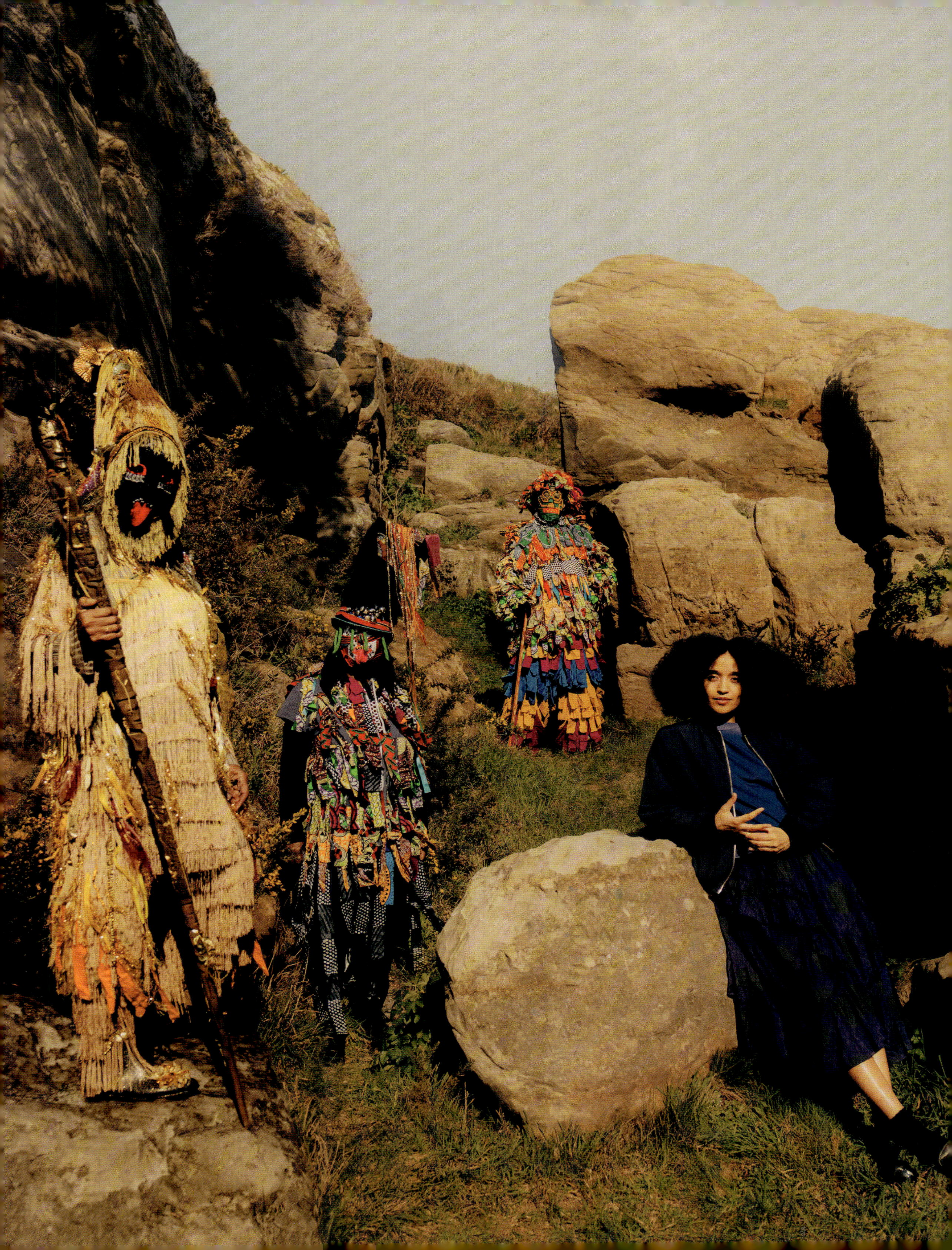

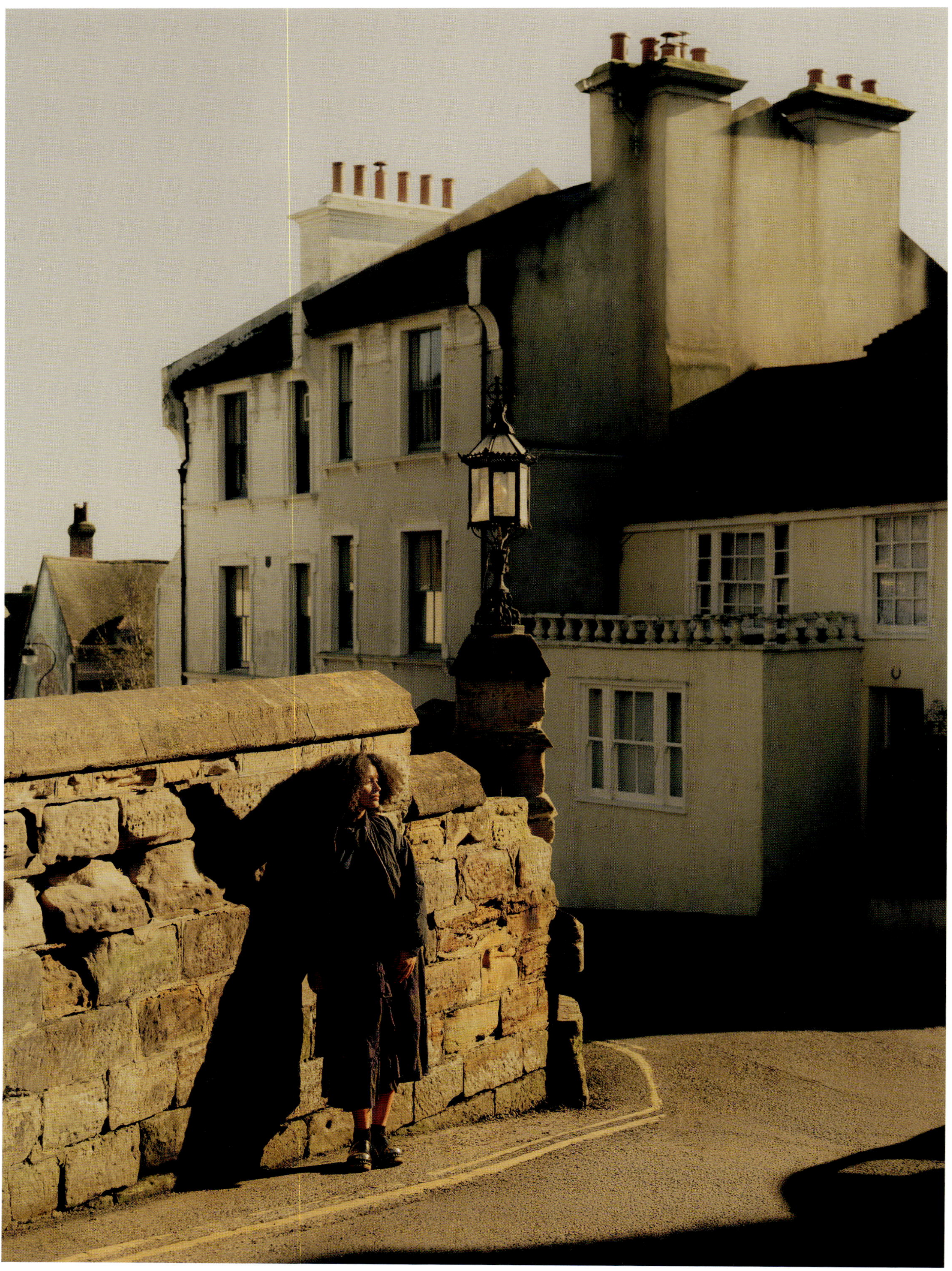

is formidably articulate. When she's discussing a subject she's passionate about, her eyes light up and she sweeps her long braids, woven with golden threads, behind her shoulder. You can't help but be drawn in, even when she's talking about something stale, pale and male, such as the topic of her book: British folk culture.

Mention "British folk" to a random passerby in the UK and it would conjure a variety of eccentric traditions, none of them remotely cool: dancing men in socks and sandals, hopping about gently on the village green; centuries-old ballads picked out on acoustic guitars; druids tracking ley lines at ancient stone circles. Yet Sewell has loved and been part of this culture since she was a child, when her father was in a folk band and took her to see jazz-folk pioneers Pentangle in concert, and from spending time with her grandparents in the Welsh town of Laugharne (pronounced "Larn"), "exploring ruined castles, hearing whispers of Merlin in the wind, and absorbing the magic and mysticism in the landscape."

Her mother's family is from the Caribbean island of Carriacou, and Sewell says she didn't often see other non-white people in folk circles. Despite loving the music, she sometimes wondered if British folk culture really belonged to her. When Sewell wasn't in misty Wales, she was in a distinctly urban foil: Hounslow, West London, right under the flight path of Heathrow Airport. While she played folk music at home, Sewell was listening to R&B and grime with her friends. She couldn't quite articulate it at the time, but there was a tension between these facets of her identity: two halves, each pulling her in a different direction.

> "Folk connects us to all these radicals throughout history who tried to fight to make Britain a fairer place."

As she learned more about British history, the dissonance grew stronger. "Even though my ancestors were most likely enslaved in the Caribbean, living here in Britain today I'm benefiting from all that was extracted by colonial exploitation. I went to Oxford, I got free school meals. Can I make my peace with that?"

Sewell is not alone wrestling with the idea of Britishness. As the political landscape becomes increasingly more polarized—with surging support for smaller parties on both the left and right threatening to topple the country's long-established two-party system—the idea of what it means to *belong* in Britain has become increasingly fraught. As part of the discourse, history is being reshaped and weaponized: On the left, there are calls from the Green Party to reckon with the country's imperial past and confront the racism and systemic inequality embedded in its legacy; on the right, anti-immigration rhetoric from populist parties such as Reform recast Britain—falsely—as a nation that has always belonged to white people. The conflict reached a new peak last summer when fierce debate erupted over whether Operation Raise the Colours, a grassroots campaign encouraging people to hoist the St George's Cross—the flag of England—signaled pride or prejudice. Some framed the act as harmless patriotism; others regarded it as a menacing display of far-right xenophobia.

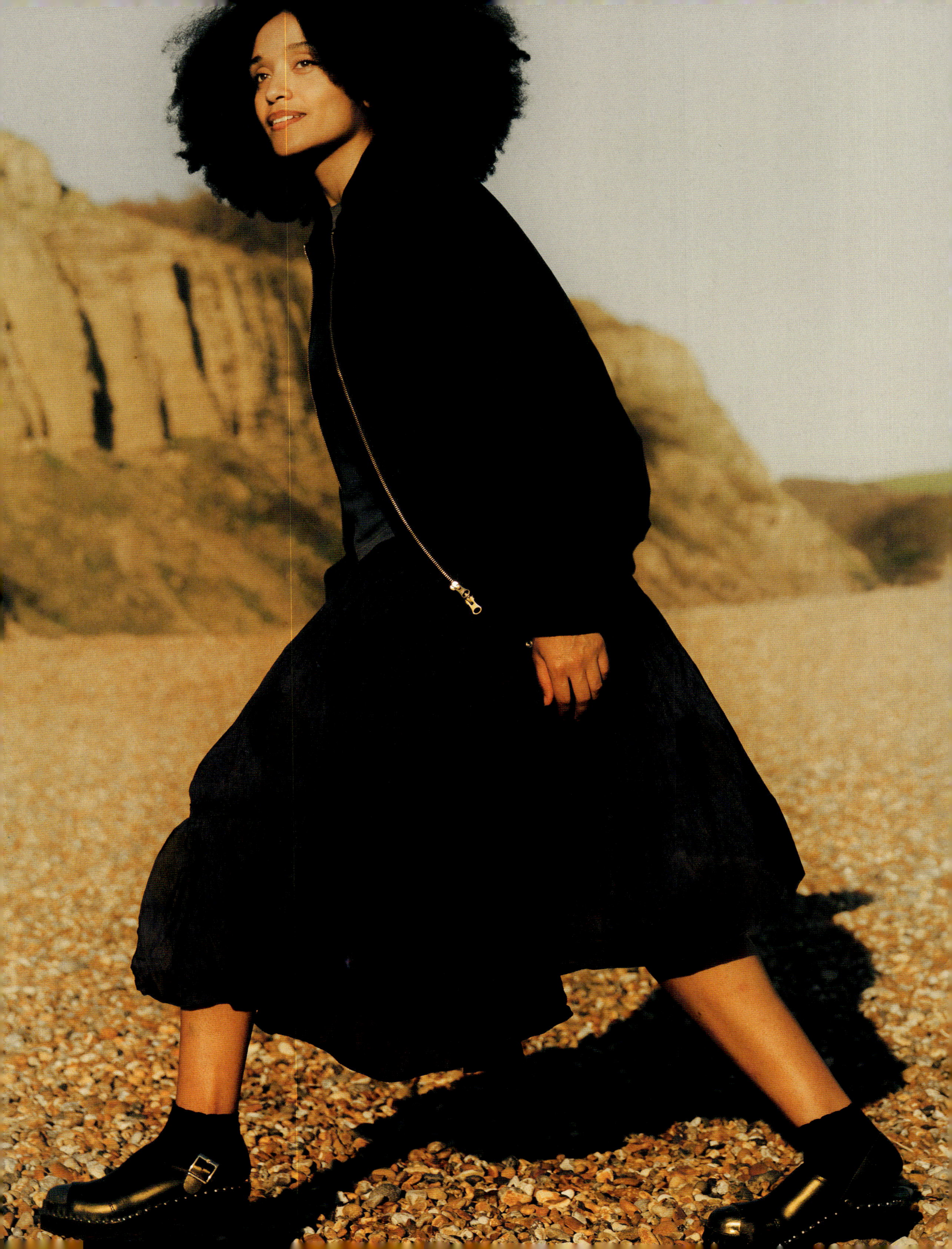

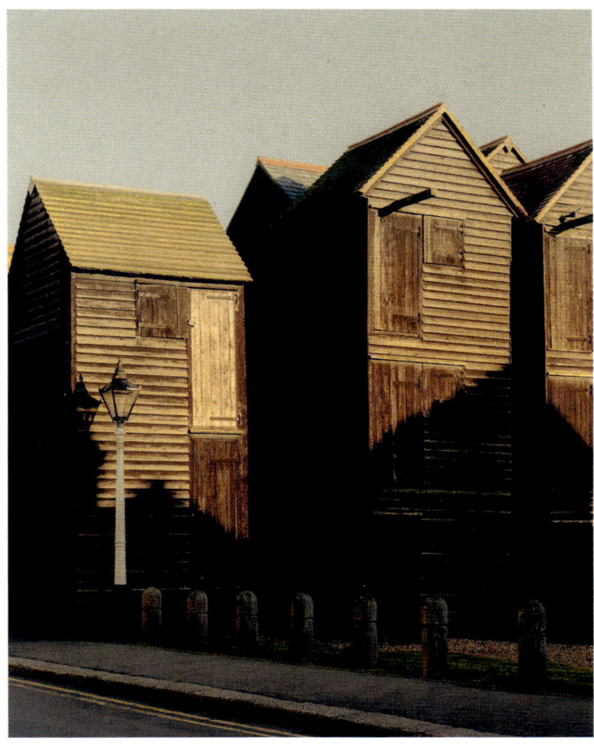

Sewell believes that folk culture may provide a balm and a way forward. Having first explored her own knotty feelings as a mixed-race person in the folk scene on *My Albion*, a four-part radio series for the BBC, she is now broadening the lens. In her book, she asks: "Can we conjure more progressive and inclusive visions of national identity through looking at our folk heritage?"

*Finding Albion* follows the course of a year as Sewell travels around the UK visiting neo-pagan events that mark the passing seasons, from the spring equinox at Stonehenge to All Hallows' Eve in the ancient city of York. Her interpretation of what constitutes "folk" is broad, defined as stories or culture that are not created by the establishment. This means there is space for her to include London's Notting Hill Carnival, a massive celebration of Caribbean culture and an essential date in London's summer calendar.

Sewell wants to embrace readers who—like herself—do not necessarily relate to traditional symbols of Britishness. "Some people think: Oh God, the Union Jack, the monarchy, red phone boxes, policemen's hats. What has that got to do with me?" she says. "But in saying you don't want to have anything to do with Britishness, you're ultimately rejecting a part of yourself. When we can find alternative stories and see ourselves reflected in them, we're able to reclaim an aspect of ourselves and ultimately become a little more whole."

Her research often starts with music, as in the case of a song she chronicles called "Rufford Park Poachers," which in 1908 was one of the first folk songs to be recorded commercially. "It's an incredible, crackling old recording with this old man's voice, singing out to you like a ghost," Sewell says. "And if you sit and listen again and again, you realize there's more behind what he's saying. Pulling threads, you discover a radical history that underpins the song."

The lyrics tell of a clash between poachers and gamekeepers in the 1850s—a time when poaching laws forbade the working classes from hunting animals, such as pheasants or hares—and of the pain of starvation, imprisonment and being exiled. What sounds like a lovely old folk song is actually a fierce revolt against social injustice. Sewell connects this example to other moments of antiestablishment resistance in British history, such as the Luddites smashing up machines in protest against factory owners in the early 19th century,



or the leaders of the Pentrich Rising who tried to topple the government in 1817 and were beheaded. "Folk connects us to all these moments and radicals throughout history who tried to fight to make Britain a fairer place," she says, "and history is the tool that helps us to unpick and decode and reveal those messages."

She looks out of the window of the café, as if debating with herself internally for a moment, before turning back. "Okay, as a person of color, some people might feel that's not their history. But it's an alternative vision of British people throughout the ages. It shows they weren't all complicit with the colonial machine or slave owners, but that there were also people who lost their lives to fight injustice. We can see that as a fertile strain of Britishness, and incorporate that into our own sense of what it means to belong to this land."

While Sewell's quest began with the hope of finding a radical utopia buried in Britain's past, in some preindustrial time untainted by Britain's colonial legacy, she soon realized that such a place did not exist. Dig deep enough into any folkloric history and you will also find problematic people. Percy Grainger, for example, the man who recorded "Rufford Park Poachers," was a virulent anti-Semite.

Another example can be found in Morris dancing, a 15th-century British folk custom, often mocked, which involves dancing through square formations waving colored handkerchiefs.

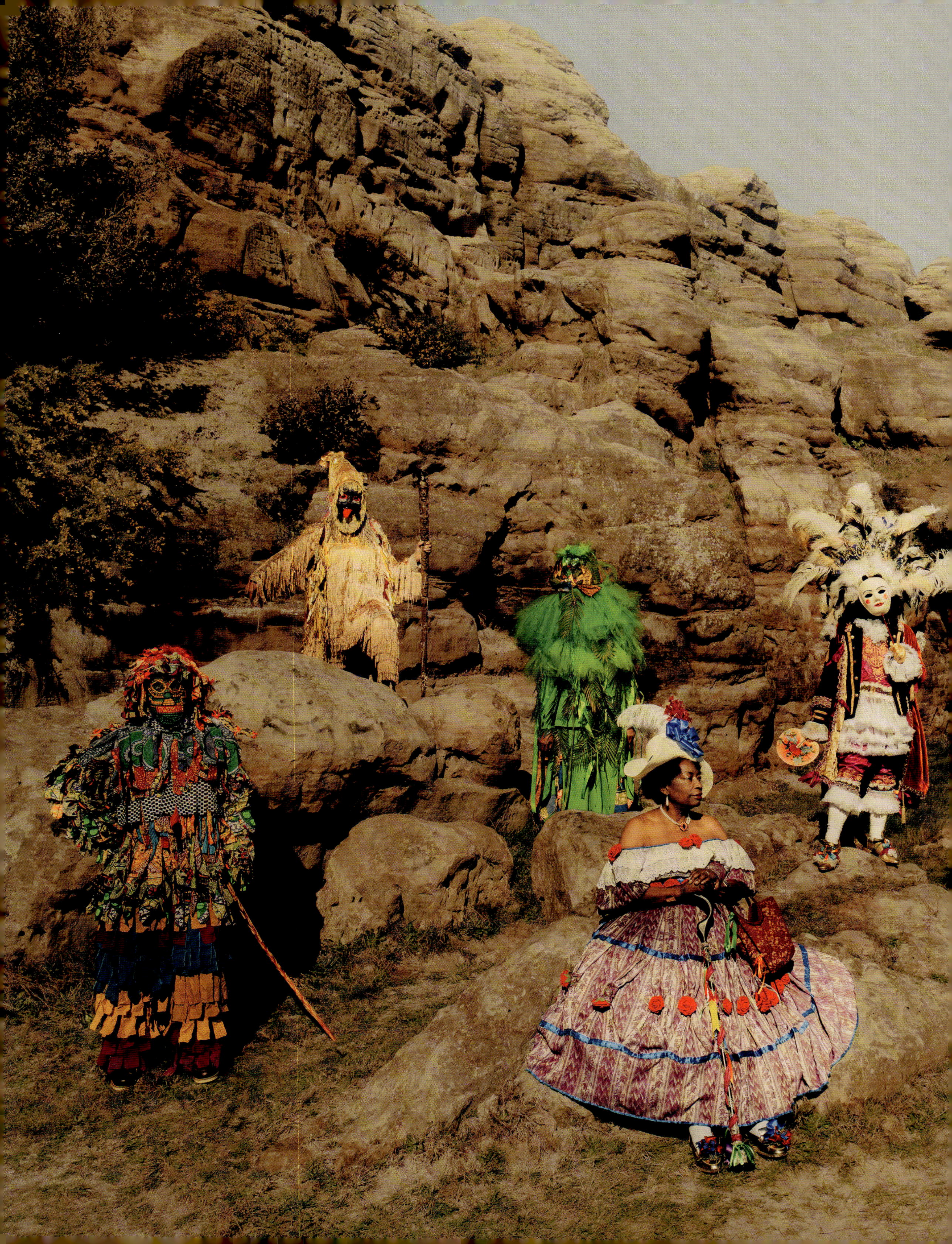

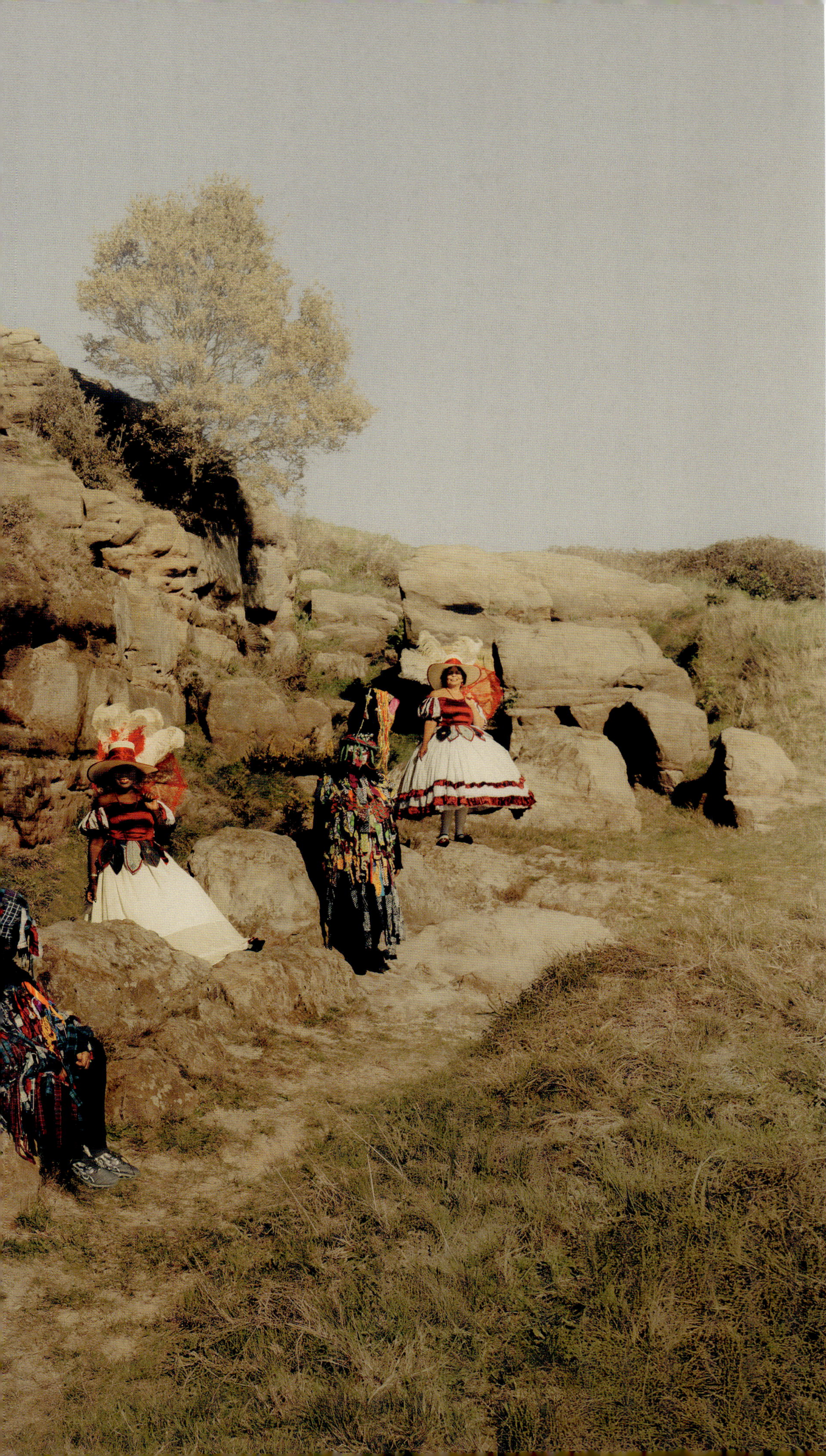

( left )
Sewell is photographed with members of the Hastings-based community arts organization Playing the Race Card, founded by Claudine Eccleston, whom Sewell met while writing *Finding Albion*. One of the organization's ongoing initiatives is the Jonkunnu project, which revives a traditional Caribbean masquerade in the UK. Eccleston (fourth from left) appears here as the Queen of the Sets, a prominent character representing European royalty.

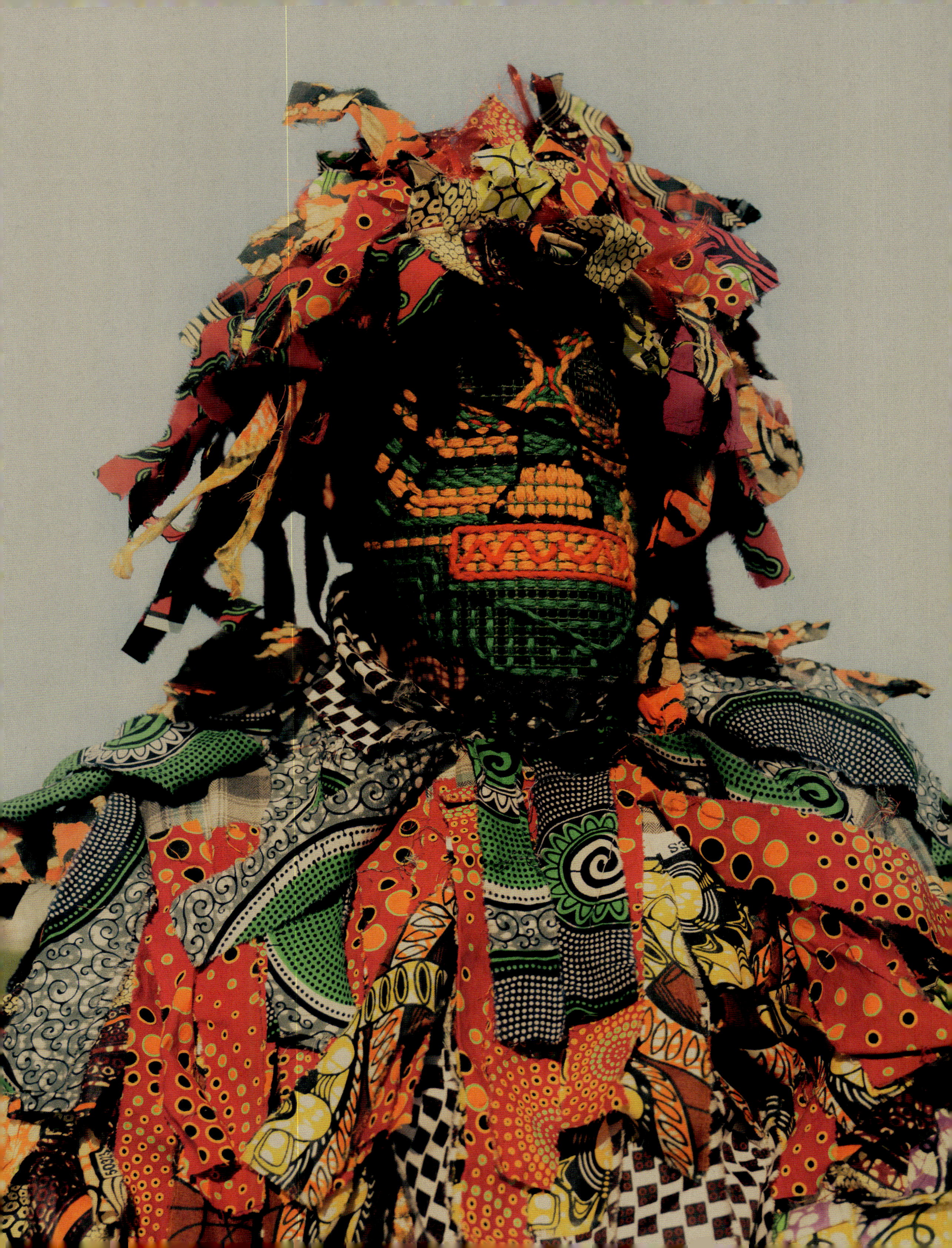

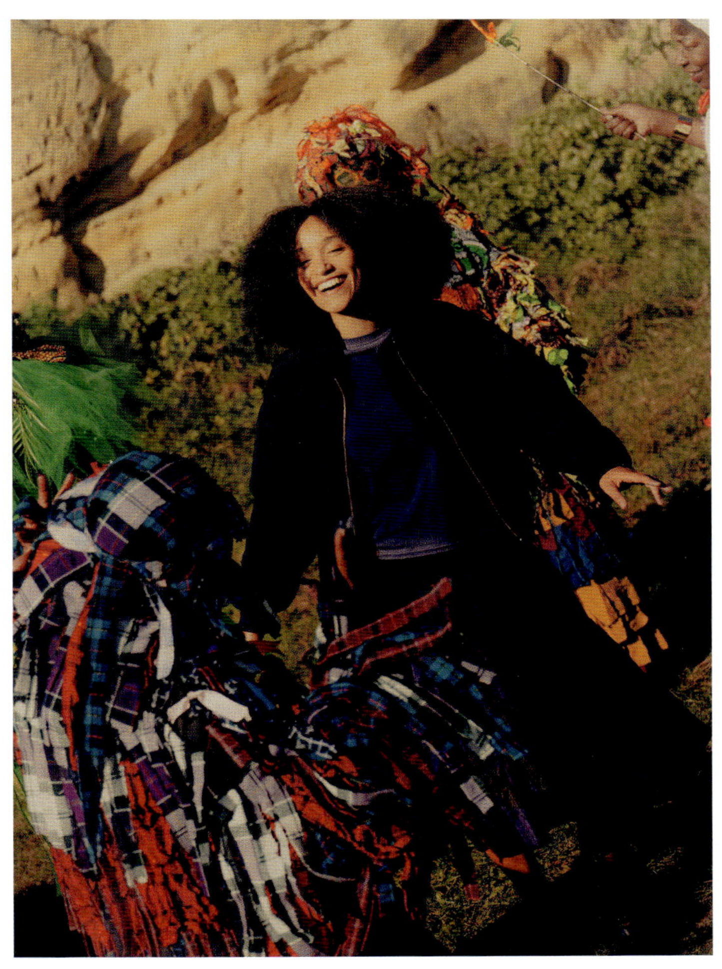

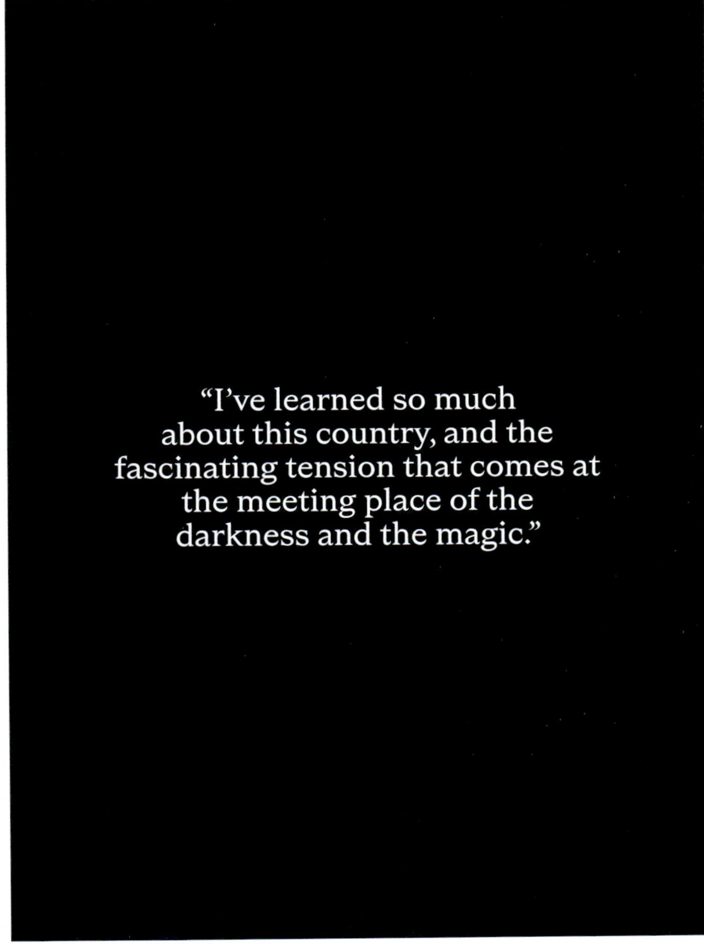
"I've learned so much
about this country, and the
fascinating tension that comes at
the meeting place of the
darkness and the magic."

When Sewell first saw it, she thought it was "so silly, eccentric, fun, merry and ridiculous, full of hope and possibility." But during her research, she learned that there is a long history of Morris dancers wearing blackface, and that some still do it today.

"That was a moment where I really thought: Maybe this folk culture stuff isn't for me," she says. But time and again throughout her work, Sewell chooses to grapple with thorny histories rather than turn away. She does not excuse racism or anti-Semitism, but instead reckons with them as a fundamental part of the story. "If we're looking for stories about who we've been as a nation, the complex, contradictory history of Morris dancing reveals a truthful story about who we are," she says. "Blackface has to be part of it. We can't not include it."

"I've learned so much about this country, and the fascinating tension that comes at the meeting place of the darkness and the magic," she continues. "That's the aspect of British culture I find most interesting—where the two meet."

Sewell's book lands at a time when there is a growing interest in esoteric and alternative forms of knowledge, ranging from astrology to crystals to holistic medicines. She feels that this trend is the result of modern society not delivering on its promises. She also believes that while we've lived in an age of scientific empiricism since the enlightenment, this ideology has not brought peace, happiness or prosperity to the majority of the population. "The world is falling apart," she says. "We've reached this hideous crescendo of our hyperrational, materialistic culture and people are not happy. We're living in such a disenchanted age that there's a real yearning for magic and mystery."

Her journey has also shed light on the role that history plays in forming our personal and national identities. Sewell feels empowered by her journey through the UK, its past and present. "I feel like I just know the country better now," she says. "Learning more about colonialism, enslavement and working class struggles in Britain, I feel really well equipped to fight off anyone who says I don't belong here because I've studied and I know the truth. I know there's this deep, dark history of exploitation, this pile of bodies on which Britain is built. And there's so much work that needs to be done to really excavate that history, to come to terms with it and integrate it into our story." Grueling as it may appear, facing the realities of our troubled histories can also be an act of hope for the future. In her book, Sewell quotes the Nigerian British author Ben Okri, who writes: "Nations and peoples are largely the stories they feed themselves. Change

> "There's a new landscape unfolding, a new quest is beginning, but I don't know yet what the grail is at the end."

the stories individuals and nations live by and tell themselves and you can change the individuals and nations.... If they tell themselves stories that face their own truths, they will free their histories for future flowerings."

After a couple of hours talking about folk culture and her new book, Sewell finishes the last of her coffee. "The latest quest was to finish the book, and now I'm back at the zero space," she says. "There's a new landscape unfolding, a new quest is beginning, but I don't know yet what the grail is at the end."

She knows better than to try and predict the next step before it's ready to reveal itself. Her life has always been like this: "There's never been a grand plan," she says. "I never thought I'd write a book or be a radio broadcaster. All these things just sort of happened as a result of me following my passions and seizing the opportunities that came up."

It might be all the therapy, or just life experience, but Sewell has learned something that many medieval knights of folklore never quite grasped. "I have to accept that I'm not really in control of my quest," she says, shrugging on a plush blue puffer jacket. "I step out onto the path, I pack my bag, I have my map, but I can't control which old sage will meet me by the bridge, or when the path suddenly becomes overgrown. I can do what I can do, but some elements are totally out of control. And with that, magic can happen."

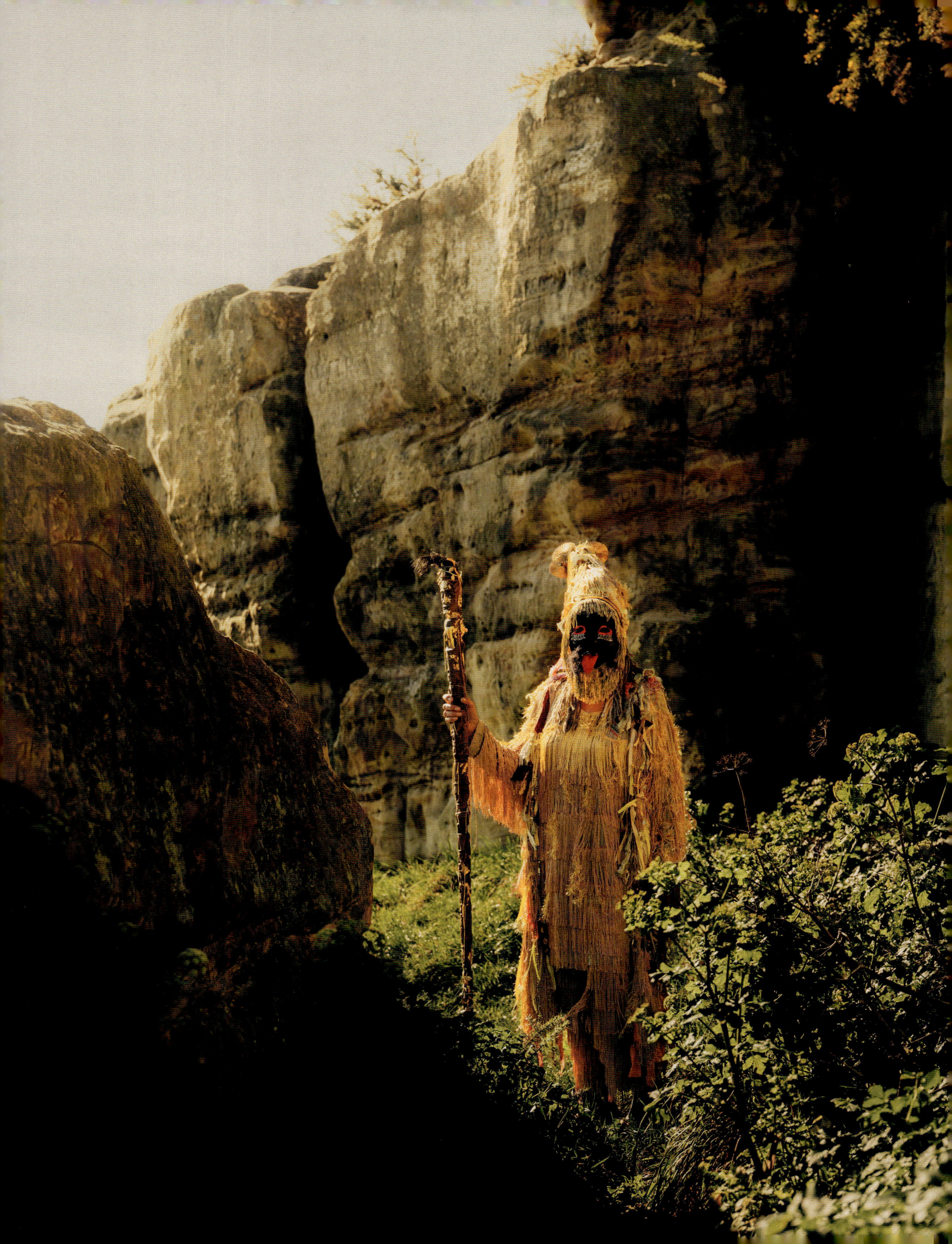

# II

# A SHORT HISTORY OF A LONG TIME:
## How to make sense of the past.

*Words*
Francis Martin

How do you warn future inhabitants of Earth of the presence of radioactive waste? This was the question that, in the 1980s, a group of physicists, sociologists, psychologists and semioticians attempted to answer in relation to a proposed nuclear waste repository in Nevada. Their task was to design a system that would be capable of warning inhabitants ten thousand years into the future—a stretch of time which, in the other direction, reaches back to the Neolithic age, when humans were just beginning to develop agriculture. The Human Interference Task Force, as the group was known, could not assume that any contemporary language or writing system would be intelligible; it couldn't even assume that the audience would be human.

In conceiving a way to communicate with a culture, civilization or even species distinct from our own, the task force had to consider how our conception of the world is informed by our vantage point in the present; how language, culture, knowledge and reason act as a lens through which we understand the world. Having stripped away nearly every convention we normally use to produce meaning, the task force was left with an array of increasingly eccentric solutions, ranging from a system of symbols and diagrams to hostile architecture, such as a field of giant granite spikes. Semiotician Thomas Sebeok suggested creating an "atomic priesthood," which would transmit knowledge of the site through ritual and folklore; philosophers Françoise Bastide and Paolo Fabbri proposed genetically engineering a cat that would change color in the presence of radiation.

None of the more radical proposals were considered feasible, but their creativity—and improbability—reveal the scale of the challenge: how to see beyond the limits of our own time. And just as those limits make it difficult to imagine communicating with the far-distant future, they also distort our view of the deep past, warping our understanding of history.

The most famous, but perhaps still most startling, example of this is that the time between Cleopatra's life and our own is shorter than the span separating her from the construction of the Great Pyramid of Giza. The way in which we collapse the millennia between the pyramids and the last pharaoh of ancient Egypt and stretch out the millennia between her reign and the present day—"far-shortening," as it were, the more distant past—is partly due to our greater familiarity with more recent history.

However, the dramatic acceleration of modern history also makes it easy to assume that a pre-internet 1980 feels further from today than, say, 1480 would have felt to someone living in 1526. Yet that half-century saw Columbus land in the Americas, Vasco da Gama sail to India and Ferdinand Magellan circumnavigate the globe.[1] It was a stretch of time in which technological advancements meant that the number of books in existence rose from the tens of thousands to perhaps over ten million—a transformation that, at least for some of the world's population, must have felt as radical as the proliferation of the internet or AI feels to us now.

*"It is the privilege of modern man to have a full awareness of the historicity of everything present and the relativity of all opinions."*

In the 20th century, Hans-Georg Gadamer was one of the theorists who helped to popularize this idea of "historical consciousness." He argued that we can only ever interpret the past through our own prejudices and traditions, and that meaning emerges through a fusion of past and present "horizons." Appreciation for the subjectivity of our historical consciousness was, he suggested, a relatively new phenomenon. He believed it was "the privilege of modern man to have a full awareness of the historicity of everything present and the relativity of all opinions."

An awareness of this privilege is important: We can't avoid all bias, but at least we can be conscious of its impact. For example, Trump's injunction to "make America great again" presumes a lost era of greatness without specifying which moment should be restored. In such appeals, history becomes malleable—shaped by individual understanding, or misunderstanding, and projected onto a very real collective present. In time, that collective present hardens into the history future generations will struggle to interpret.

> *"The human understanding of history will only ever be partial: We use the past to interpret the present, even as the present shapes how we remember the past."*

Systems that shape our understanding of the past therefore shape the present and the future as well. The calendar is the most literal expression of this dynamic. The cultural theorist Walter Benjamin wrote that calendars "do not measure time as clocks do; they are monuments of a historical consciousness." Despite the ubiquity of the Gregorian calendar, now standard around the world, it has not usurped other conceptions of the past: The Taiwanese and Coptic calendars, for instance, take as their first year a formative event in the life of the people. In Taiwan, it is currently year 115 since the overthrow of the Qing dynasty and the birth of the Republic of China. For Coptic Christians, it is now 1742 *Anno Martyrum*, which reflects the accession of the Roman Emperor Diocletian and his violent persecution of Christians.

Among the First Peoples of Australia, the foundational event is the "Dreaming," in which the land is brought to life by ancestral beings. But the Dreaming is less a moment in time, and more an eternal reality: "as much a part of the present and the future as it is of the past," according to the anthropologist Howard Morphy.

The Dreaming, Aboriginal cultural leader Karl Telfer says, is "happening now." He rejects the term "dreamtime," which has often been used for the concept, on the basis that it implies an equivalence to a sequential chronology.[2] "Whereas Western conceptualizations of time are heavily influenced by ideas of 'progression' and 'development,' Aboriginal concepts of time are essentially atelic (purposeless). Or, rather, purpose lies in the Dreaming, which is in many respects infinite and timeless," Morphy writes.

Key to the Aboriginal conception is the relationship with the land, known as Country. "Time and place are infinite and everywhere. Everything is part of a continuum, an endless flow of life and ideas emanating from Country," according to the Aboriginal historian Margo Neale. This relationship, she writes, "gives rise to the expression 'Our history is written in the land,'" and she uses the terms "enduring present" and "eternal time" to articulate the concept.[3]

Benjamin, in a gnomic essay, describes "an angel of history" facing toward the past and watching history unfold as he is propelled forward through time. "Where we perceive a chain of events, he sees one single catastrophe which keeps piling wreckage and hurls it in front of his feet," Benjamin writes. "This storm is what we call progress," he concludes, implying that our careful ordering of historical events is an illusion.

Unlike the angel's vantage point, the human understanding of history will only ever be partial: We use the past to interpret the present, even as the present shapes how we remember the past. We are not gods and cannot, to borrow the words of William Blake, "hold infinity in the palm of your hand, and eternity in an hour." History exceeds our ability to grasp it whole. What always remains is the present—imperfect and incomplete.

( 1 ) Technically, it was Magellan's expedition that first circumnavigated the globe rather than Magellan himself, who was killed in the Philippines in 1521. Some historians have hypothesized that the first person to travel around the world was Magellan's enslaved interpreter, Enrique of Malacca, who had been taken from present-day Malaysia a decade earlier.

( 2 ) Neither "Dreaming" nor "Dreamtime" offers a perfect translation, as there are many words across different Aboriginal languages that refer to the idea, only a few of which translate directly as "dreaming." The English terms, Morphy writes, "should not be understood in their ordinary English sense but, rather, as terms for a unique and complex religious concept."

( 3 ) There are conceptions of time in Western thought that resemble this notion of an "everywhen." The medieval scholar Thomas Aquinas described God as existing in *nunc stans*, a kind of suspended "everywhen," while Walter Benjamin coined the term *Jetztzeit* for, in the words of Ronald Beiner, the "now-time... in which the present and the past are drawn into a messianic relation."

# HISTORY EXCEEDS OUR ABILITY TO GRASP IT WHOLE. WHAT ALWAYS REMAINS IS TE PRESENT.

# III

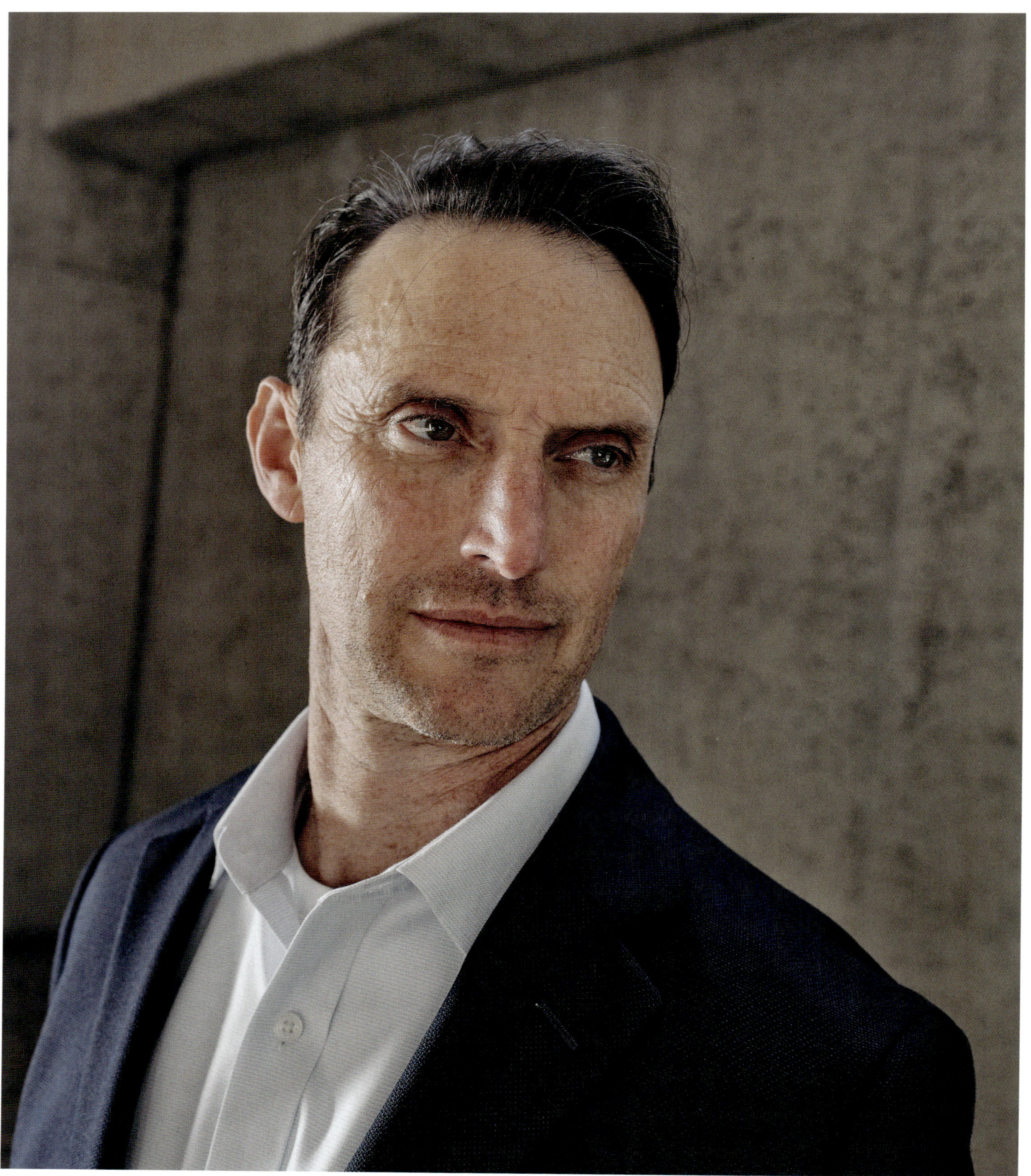

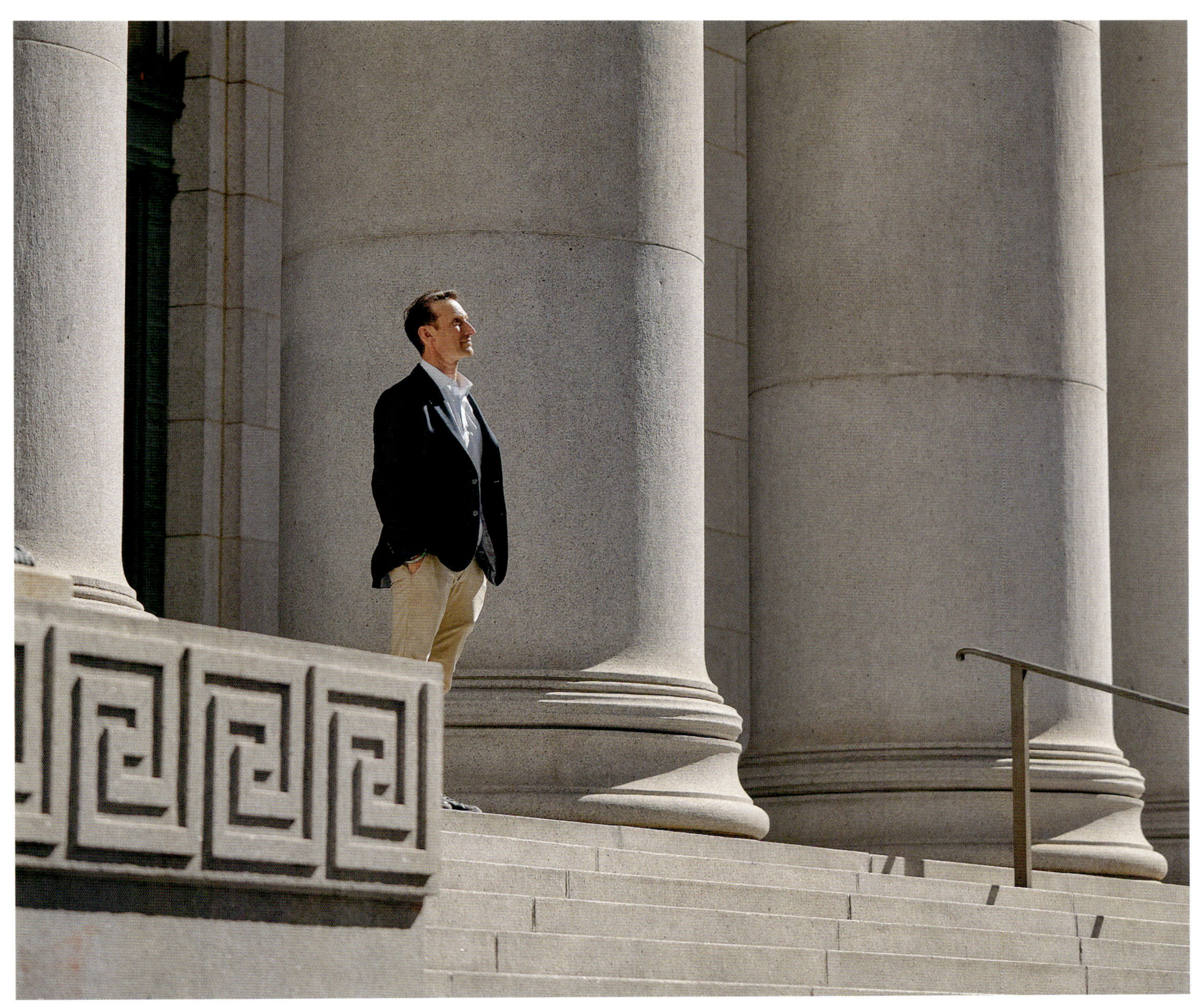


THE DESCENDANTS
What does it mean to live in the
shadow of a family member who
reshaped history? Three relatives
discuss the weight of greatness.

*Words*
Robert Ito

# 1.  CHARLES OPPENHEIMER

*The atomic bombs which were dropped on Hiroshima on August 6, 1945, and on Nagasaki three days later forever changed the nature of war and peace. The architect of the Manhattan Project was the American physicist J. Robert Oppenheimer, whose grandson, Charles Oppenheimer, is now an entrepreneur and advocate for nuclear energy.*

Charles Oppenheimer can't remember the first time he heard what his grandfather did during World War II. He can't recall how old he was, or precisely where, but he does remember being in the family truck, and his parents telling him that his grandfather had been in a war, and he did what he had to do, like a soldier, but he was a scientist, so he used science as his tool in the big struggle.

It wasn't until years later that he discovered that his grandfather, J. Robert Oppenheimer, was the leader of the Manhattan Project and the so-called "father of the atomic bomb." Before that, he says, "I remember playing with some kids in an arroyo and they were like, 'Oh, this is a giant bomb. You would know all about that, Oppenheimer!' And I remember *not* knowing what they were talking about."

Even after he began to learn more about his grandfather's story, much of it still remained a mystery to him, like his grandfather's loss of security clearance in 1954 after questions arose about his past affiliation with members of the Communist Party, as well as the efforts of Presidents Kennedy and Johnson to rehabilitate his reputation in later years. "I remember one time when I was a freshman in high school, my history teacher said, 'Wow, that was so terrible what happened to your grandfather; I always really respected Kennedy and Johnson for what they did,'" he remembers. "And I was like, 'Yeah, yeah, totally!'"

Moments like those inspired Oppenheimer to research his grandfather. "I ended up reading everything I could get my hands on and became an amateur Oppenheimer historian, which, as it turns out, is a whole profession." He discovered that his grandfather became the first chair of the Board of Sponsors for the Bulletin of the Atomic Scientists, keepers of the Doomsday Clock (the symbolic timepiece that measures the Earth's proximity to human-created global catastrophe), and how J. Robert Oppenheimer worked for international control of nuclear weapons and against the development of the hydrogen bomb. People still wrestle with his legacy today. Is he the man who brought us closer to doomsday, or the one who worked for years to pull us back from the brink?

As famous figures go, Oppenheimer says, "My grandfather is not just famous. He's kind of iconically famous." And it's different, he explains, than having a relative who was a big movie star in the '40s, say, or who performed at Woodstock. Even if he had done something less controversial within the world of science, it would have still been a mixed blessing for his descendants. "There's no upside in being associated with a famous scientist," Oppenheimer says. "You have some raised expectations at first, and then people realize, Oh, you're not a genius."

Oppenheimer worked for years in the tech industry in Silicon Valley, and while he never hid the family connection if anybody asked, he also wouldn't bring it up. In 2015, the US Department of Energy reached out to his family and asked if they could name one of their leadership training programs after his grandfather. Oppenheimer gave his approval, and the experience got him wondering: "If the Energy Department is going to create an Oppenheimer Science and Energy Leadership Program, why don't we do something?"

In 2019, Oppenheimer began working in earnest on the Oppenheimer Project, a nonprofit grounded in his grandfather's vision of reducing the risk of nuclear Armageddon through international dialogue and cooperation, while promoting peaceful uses of nuclear energy to combat the climate crisis. The foundation was formally established in 2023. "We look at any element of science and say, We can use that to make bombs and destroy the world, or we can use it to create unlimited energy," Oppenheimer explains.

With the release of *Oppenheimer*, Christopher Nolan's Academy Award–winning biopic, also in 2023, J. Robert Oppenheimer became a household name once again. The film was a box office sensation, grossing nearly a billion dollars in ticket sales. "I think they did a good job with the material and told a story that people really liked," Oppenheimer says. "But it's always a strange experience to be outside a business entity that's using your name and your family members to make something. They were an entity that owns the

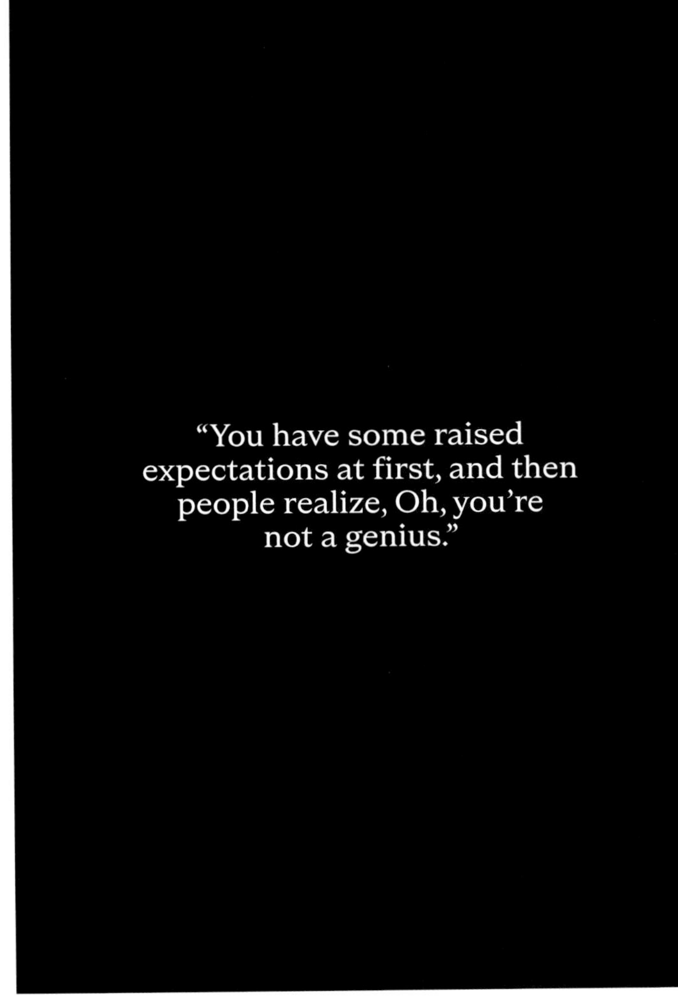


Oppenheimer story. They're representing how Oppenheimer is perceived and controlling every part of it, and you have no voice in that." For Oppenheimer, part of the problem in telling the family's version of events is that, for years, few of them felt comfortable talking about his grandfather with outsiders. "My father, in particular, is a very private person, and the way he lived his life and dealt with his father's place in history was to try to not be involved in any of that." There was one exception, however. "Literally the advice I was given was that if you can use your name to deal with the problems of nuclear weapons, you should do it," he says. "And I saw my father do that a little bit."

Because of his grandfather's enormous place in history, Oppenheimer's family has relatively few of his writings or personal mementos. Most of his papers are in the Library of Congress and the Smithsonian Institution. Oppenheimer says he is always asked about his grandfather's hat, a brown porkpie immortalized in a portrait taken by the photographer Alfred Eisenstaedt for *Life* magazine in 1947, and later on the poster for Nolan's film. "My dad says that we had it at some time, but we didn't think it was that important," Oppenheimer says. "So that has been lost to history."

Not lost to time is J. Robert Oppenheimer's belief that the atom bomb had ushered in a new and hopefully better era in world history, a belief now promoted by the Oppenheimer Project in much of what they do. "He knew the world had changed, and believed that a world with nuclear weapons was not compatible with peace," Oppenheimer says. "He and other scientists hoped we were going through a period where we were transcending war, and going into a non–zero sum period of humanity's existence. And I think we're actually in that world, 80 years later."

Part of the Oppenheimer Project's mission is to transform the ways that J. Robert Oppenheimer's scientific discoveries are used. "There's 12,000 nuclear weapons in the world and 440 nuclear power plants," Oppenheimer says. "We'd like to reverse that, for a start. What if we had abundant, clean, carbon-free energy for everybody in the world? It would reduce conflict, and the cooperation you would have to build to get there would mean you weren't out there making bombs. That's what we see as our path forward for humanity."

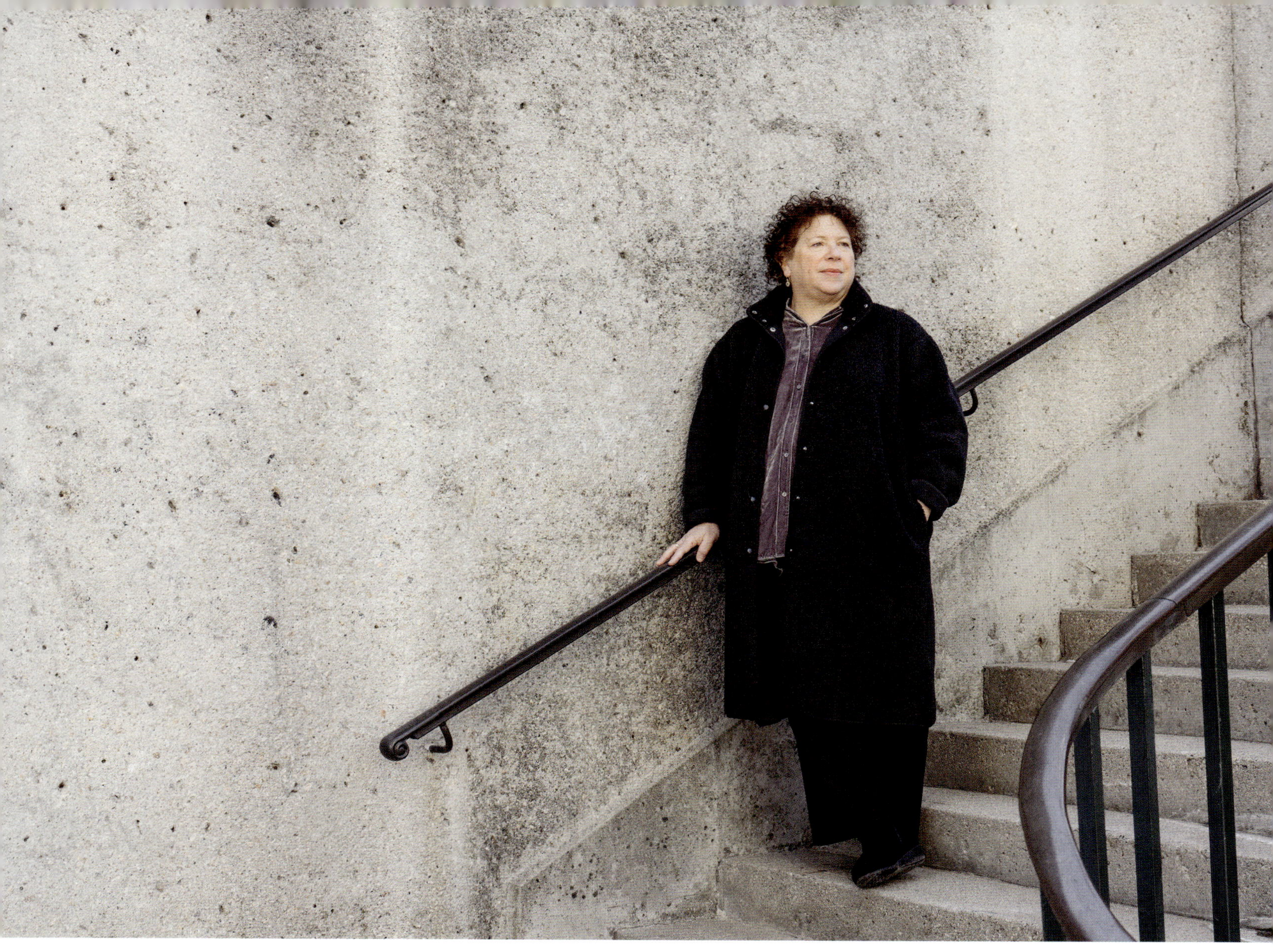

## 2.   HESTER KAPLAN

*Edward Bernays is widely credited as the father of public relations. Over a career spanning much of the 20th century, he manipulated public opinion on behalf of corporations and governments, and laid the foundations for modern advertising, political spin and the influencer age. His granddaughter is Hester Kaplan, a celebrated novelist and memoirist.*

When the writer Hester Kaplan was growing up in Cambridge, Massachusetts, her family would often visit her maternal grandfather, Edward Bernays, who lived nearby. Short and round and a lover of sweets, Bernays would regale her and the other grandkids with funny stories, then send them off with a fancy box of chocolates, purchased at a candy store in nearby Harvard Square.

To Kaplan, Bernays was simply Eddie, or Grandpa, but for as long as she can remember, she also knew of her grandfather as "the father of public relations." "I certainly didn't know what that meant," she says. "It was just a title, and it sounded good, and he used it, and other people called him that." While others may have given him the title, it was Bernays himself who coined the term "public relations." Before that, people simply called it propaganda.

Among Bernays' most famous PR stunts was the 1929 "Torches of Freedom" campaign, in which he encouraged women to smoke by equating the practice with female liberation and gender equality. For an Easter Sunday Parade in New York, he hired women to march and smoke their "torches of freedom" as photographers, also hired by him, sent their images around the world. In other campaigns, Bernays promoted cigarettes to women as slimming, stylish and "kind to your throat."

"His legacy falls on me in a very complicated and weighty way," Kaplan says. "I'm constantly navigating between the feeling I had about him as a grandchild, and ones I have about him as a person in the world, seeing some of the work that he did." This includes convincing folks that fluoridated water was good for you (turns out, it is), as is bacon (not so much) and that disposable Dixie water cups (clean!) were better than the drinking glasses you had around the house (filthy!). He helped the CIA overthrow the Guatemalan government in the 1950s on behalf of the United Fruit Company, and warmed up the previously dour image of President Calvin Coolidge, aka "Silent Cal." In his 1928 book, *Propaganda*, Bernays promoted "the conscious and intelligent manipulation" of the masses, an idea that caught the attention of Joseph Goebbels, Hitler's minister of propaganda.

"Eddie talked a lot about 'the masses,' who he saw as essentially unsophisticated and easily manipulated," Kaplan says. The nephew of Sigmund Freud, Bernays drew liberally from his famous uncle's ideas about hidden desires and the power of the unconscious to develop strategies of controlling human thought and behavior. In his essay "The Engineering of Consent," he argued that the strategic manipulation of popular opinion was not only desirable, but key, when done responsibly, to a modern democracy.

Looking at the impact of her grandfather's work has made Kaplan much more conscious of the interplay between what a writer puts out—be it novels or public relations campaigns—and what their audience takes in. "It made me very aware that there's an ethical responsibility in storytelling," she says. "You can't just put this stuff out there and not take responsibility for it, or not consider what the effects might be."

For much of her career, Kaplan has worked in fiction, publishing a series of celebrated novels and short stories over her four-decade career. In 1999, she won the Flannery O'Connor Award for Short Fiction for her critically acclaimed *The Edge of Marriage*, a collection of nine short stories. Last year, however, she moved into memoir with *Twice Born: Finding My Father in the Margins of Biography*, which was longlisted for the National Book Critics Circle Award for Autobiography. To write that book, Kaplan had to create a biography of sorts about her father, Justin Kaplan, himself a Pulitzer Prize–winning biographer. It meant reading his books—something she had never done while he was alive—and grappling with her sensitivity to the ethical responsibility of storytelling, magnified by the fact that she was writing nonfiction, and about her own family.

In many ways, Kaplan's father and grandfather could not have been more different. While Bernays was eager to let others know about his many accomplishments—a much-used room of his house "was filled with plaques and proclamations and awards, and he would show you this one and that one"—Kaplan's father was emotionally distant, a "cripplingly private" man. Not surprisingly, the two did not get on. "I think my father was very much on to him," Kaplan remembers. "He had this great line about my grandfather: 'His unconscious was nobody's business, not even his own.'"

Today it's possible to see the long shadow of Kaplan's grandfather everywhere, from the barrage of "fake news" to the rise of social media influencers. "It's so ubiquitous now that we don't really even stop to think about it all that much," she says. "This is just the way the world works now. We're always being sold a story. We're constantly being manipulated in some way."

"For my grandfather, he wasn't necessarily trying to prove that this one was right and this one was wrong, but he would try to plant some doubt in the public's mind," she continues. "This side says this and this side says that, so we don't necessarily know what's true. And you see that today, this degradation of a kind of truth that I find troubling."

For Kaplan, it's tough to square this side of her grandfather with the jovial fellow who handed out chocolates, gave her the cute ceramic animals she still keeps on her writing desk and who once bought an Egyptian mummy *because he could*.

There is one thing, however, that Kaplan is sure about her grandfather—how he would feel about her discussing him and his life and legacy now, three decades after he died. "He would have *loved* this," she says with a laugh. "For him, all publicity is good publicity. His push was to create this public persona and tout yourself as the best, or the expert, or whatever it was. And I think my reaction to that has been to go the other way. To be much more reticent, and not so comfortable about putting yourself out there."

> "His legacy falls
> on me in a very complicated
> and weighty way."

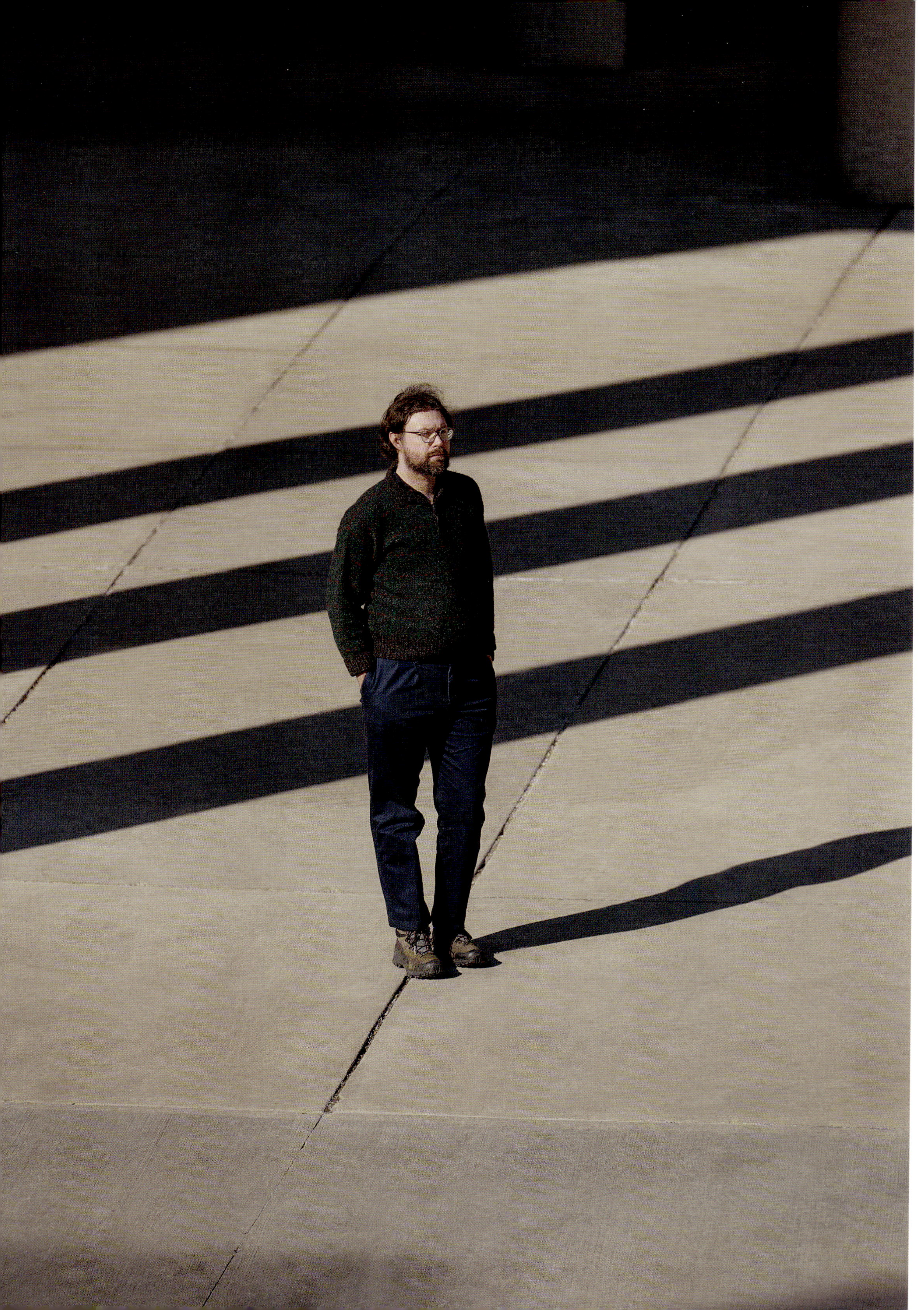

## 3.  MARSHALL JOHNSON

*The discovery of oil in Saudi Arabia in 1938 changed the course of the 20th century, contributing to the climate crisis and redrawing the balance of global power. The American geologist largely credited with first discovering oil was Max Steineke; his great-grandson is Marshall Johnson, an astronomer at Ohio State University.*

Max Steineke packed a lot of living into just 54 years: He found work at a lumber mill near the California/Oregon border at 13, became a skilled marksman in high school, graduated from Stanford with a degree in geology and traveled the world—from the Alaskan tundra to the jungles of Colombia—as a geologist for the Standard Oil Company of California. Today, however, Steineke is best known as the man who discovered oil in Saudi Arabia.

"I know now that it's a more complicated, nuanced picture than that," says Marshall Johnson, Steineke's great-grandson and a research scientist in the astronomy department of Ohio State University. "As so often happens in science, he was a leader of a huge team that made the discovery through their collective efforts."

Steineke had traveled to Saudi Arabia in 1934, joining a team of about a dozen American geologists searching for oil for the California Arabian Standard Oil Company (CASOC). In 1936, he was appointed their chief geologist. By 1938, however, CASOC wanted to nix the project, worried about the project's high costs and low returns. Steineke convinced the company to wait a bit longer, and pushed the team to drill much deeper. Within weeks, the well was producing more than 3,000 barrels a day.

Johnson is a descendant of a long line of scientists. His grandfather, Walter Goad, worked on the hydrogen bomb as a theoretical physicist at Los Alamos, and later was a founder of GenBank, the world's most widely used database of nucleotide sequences. His grandmother, Maxine Goad, authored New Mexico's first groundwater protection regulations, and became a powerful champion of those regulations.

And then there's Steineke, the oil man. Though his great-grandfather is a legend in the field of petroleum geology, Johnson came to learn about him more gradually: how he stayed behind in Saudi Arabia during World War II to help protect the oil fields for the Allies, and how he developed a deep respect for his Saudi colleagues and their culture while there. "He learned Arabic so he could speak with them, and dressed in Saudi dress when he was out in the field," he says.

Johnson also began to better comprehend Steineke's legacy and the impact of his world-changing find, for good and ill. "His discovery contributed to great things in the world," he says. "It helped contribute to the Allies' victory in World War II, as well as to a lot of the technologies that are the foundation of our modern life."

"But it also led to the current climate crisis, and is helping prop up the brutal Saudi regime," he adds. "So there's a lot to wrestle with in that legacy." Indeed, Steineke's discoveries brought great wealth and rapid development to the kingdom, but also transformed it into one of the world's largest oil producers and petro powers, giving the government a geopolitical weapon to wield against rivals—such as during the oil embargo launched during the Yom Kippur War in 1973. On a global scale, the abundance of cheap oil contributes to a continued reliance on fossil fuels, delaying investment in renewable alternatives.

After receiving his PhD in astronomy at the University of Texas at Austin in 2016, Johnson was awarded a Columbus Prize Postdoctoral Fellowship at Ohio State. He's currently studying exoplanets, the distant planets outside of our solar system that are so far away that most can only be detected by observing their effects on host stars. He's also helping to develop the iLocater, a state-of-the-art spectrograph designed to detect and study these far-flung bodies. In many ways, Johnson's search for exoplanets has parallels in Steineke's search for oil. "We've both made our careers studying the imprint of unseen things on what we *can* see," he says.

Besides his historical legacy, Steineke left his family a lode of physical artifacts from his travels: an archive of photos and letters; an Arabian tea set; jambiyas (Saudi ceremonial daggers); his Sidney Powers Memorial Award medal, the highest honor given by the American Association of Petroleum Geologists, which cited Steineke for developing exploratory techniques that "probably resulted in the discovery of greater reserves than any other geologist." Johnson, for his part, ended up with two rare cameras that his great-grandfather took on his travels.

Johnson also inherited Steineke's love for the sciences, although he balks at the idea that this is the sort of thing that is passed through the blood. "I think the biggest impact has been being in a family where I was supported and encouraged to be curious about the world and how it works," he says.

"I've built a career studying a field that I'm interested in, and managed to make it my living," Johnson adds. "I'm actually very nearly the same age that Max was when he arrived in Saudi Arabia for the first time. And while I may not be doing the types of things that would have nearly the same real-world impact that he did, I'd still like to think that he would have been proud of me.

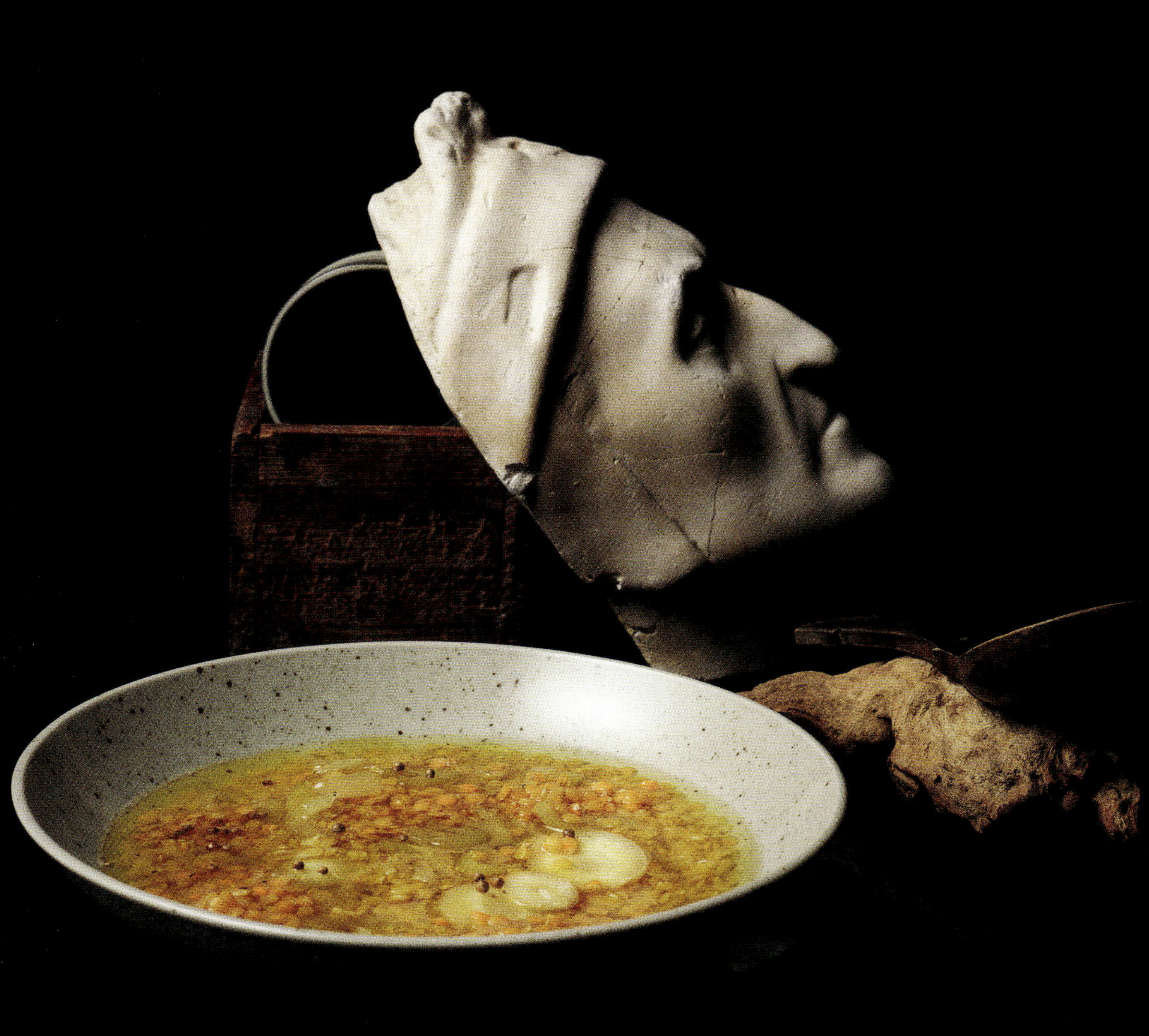

*Recipes*
Donnie Dodson

*Photos*
Gustav Almestål

*Food & Set Design*
Niklas Hansen

# IV

## SOUPES À L'ANCIENNE
## Recipes from the Eats History archive.

### 1.  ZENO STOIC LENTIL SOUP

This lentil soup draws from interpretations in Eugenia Salza Prina Ricotti's *Meals and Recipes from Ancient Greece*, a scholarly reconstruction of Greek foodways based on literary and archaeological sources. The Greeks did not leave cookbooks in the modern sense; much of what we know comes from writers such as Athenaeus in *Deipnosophistae*, where meals appear in philosophical dialogue. This preparation reflects the spirit of Zeno of Citium, founder of Stoicism in the 3rd century B.C.E.: simple ingredients, balanced flavors and nourishment rather than excess.

SERVES 4

1 pound (450g) lentils, rinsed
8 cups (2L) vegetable or light meat broth
1 large leek, minced
1 carrot, sliced
1 stalk celery, sliced
1 small onion, sliced
2 tablespoons red wine vinegar
1 teaspoon honey
Salt and ground black pepper, to taste
Extra-virgin olive oil, for serving
12 whole coriander seeds per bowl

INSTRUCTIONS

In a medium pot, combine the rinsed lentils with the broth. Bring to a boil, then reduce the heat to maintain a steady simmer. Cook for 25 to 30 minutes, skimming any foam that rises to the surface.

Add the leek, carrot, celery and onion. Continue simmering for 20 to 25 minutes, until the vegetables are tender. If a thicker texture is desired, mash a portion of the lentils directly in the pot or pass some through a sieve and return them to the soup. Stir in the vinegar and honey, and season with salt and pepper to taste.

Serve hot with a generous drizzle of olive oil and exactly 12 coriander seeds scattered over each bowl.

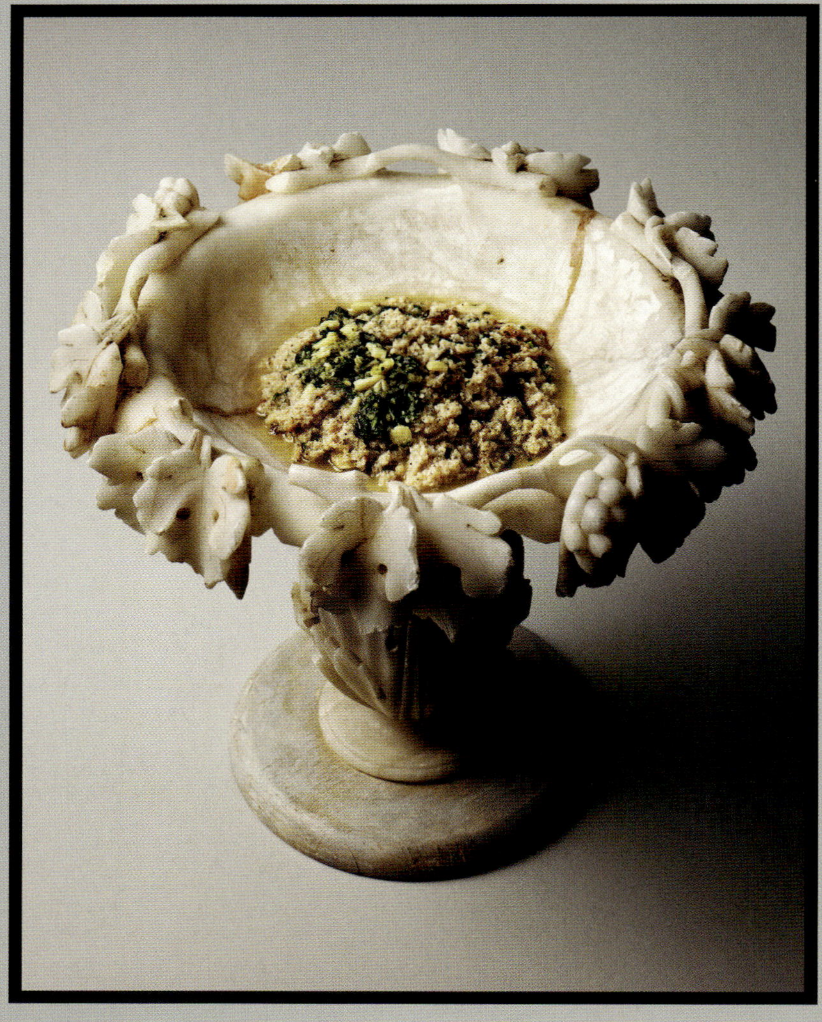

## 2.  ROMAN GAZPACHO

This chilled bread-based dish is adapted from *De Re Coquinaria*, the Roman culinary collection traditionally attributed to Apicius and compiled between the 1st and 4th centuries C.E. Though not a gazpacho in the modern Spanish sense, the recipe combines soaked bread, vinegar, herbs, olive oil and cheese into a cooling, restorative preparation. Roman cooks often revived stale bread with posca, a diluted vinegar drink common among soldiers and laborers. The result is tangy, herbal and surprisingly fresh, reflecting the Roman instinct for balancing acidity, sweetness and fat in even the simplest dishes.

SERVES 2 TO 3
1 small loaf rustic bread (about 3 thick slices)
½ cup water mixed with 2 tablespoons vinegar and 1 tablespoon white wine (a posca substitute)
1 clove garlic
1 tablespoon chopped mint, plus more for serving
1 tablespoon chopped cilantro, plus more for serving
Pinch of freshly ground black pepper (long pepper, if available)
1 tablespoon honey
¼ cup finely grated Parmesan or aged hard cheese, plus more for serving
2 tablespoons olive oil, plus more for serving
1 to 2 tablespoons white wine, for serving
Pinch of salt

INSTRUCTIONS
Tear the bread into pieces and place in a medium bowl. Pour the vinegar-water mixture over the bread until fully soaked. Let stand for about 5 minutes.

In a mortar and pestle, pound together the garlic, mint, cilantro, pepper, honey, cheese and olive oil into a thick paste. (A food processor may be used instead.)

Add the soaked bread and continue to grind or blend until the mixture becomes smooth and spoonable. Add a small splash of water if needed to loosen the texture.

Chill for 15 to 20 minutes before serving.

Spoon into bowls and finish with a drizzle of white wine, olive oil and a scattering of additional herbs or cheese. Salt to taste.

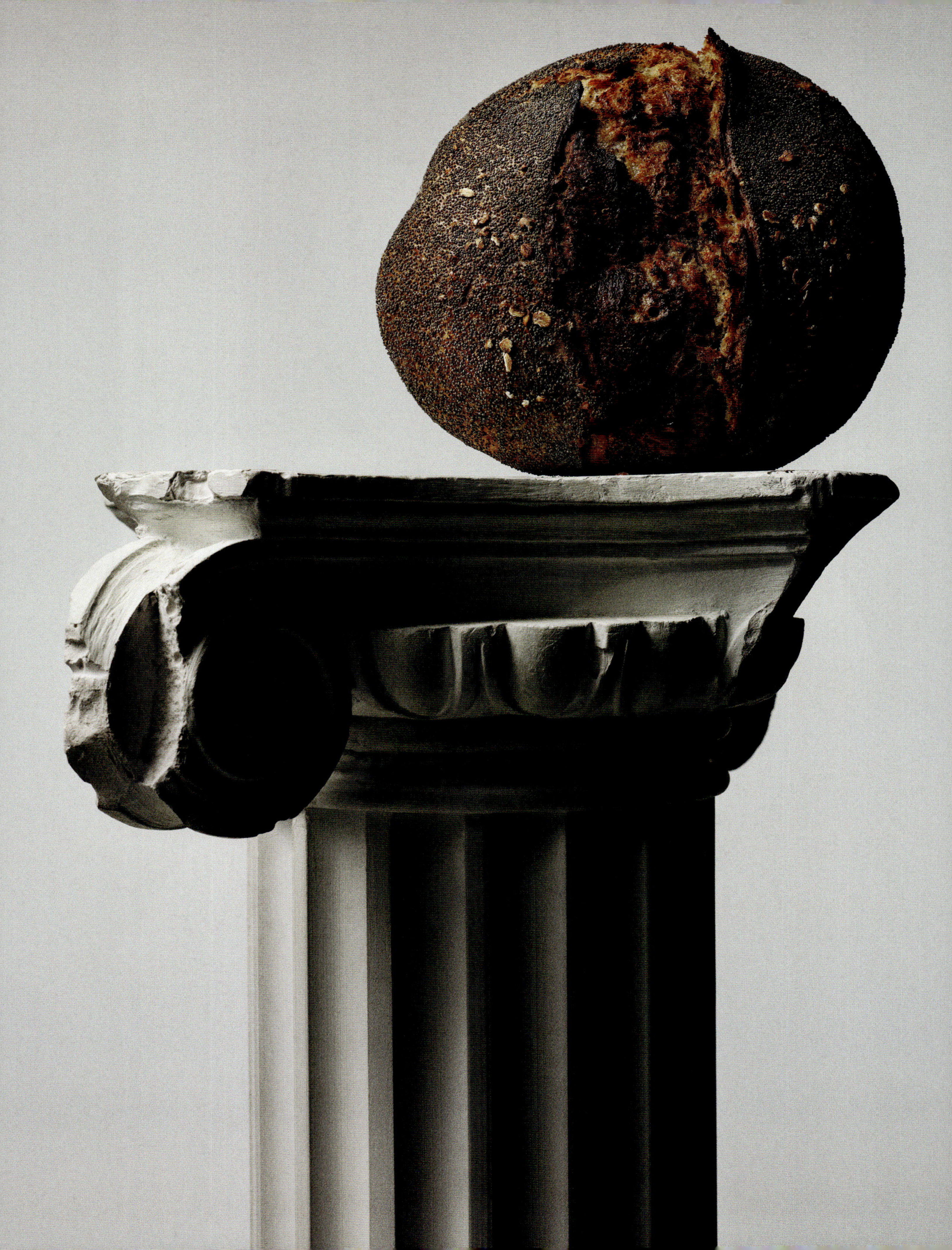

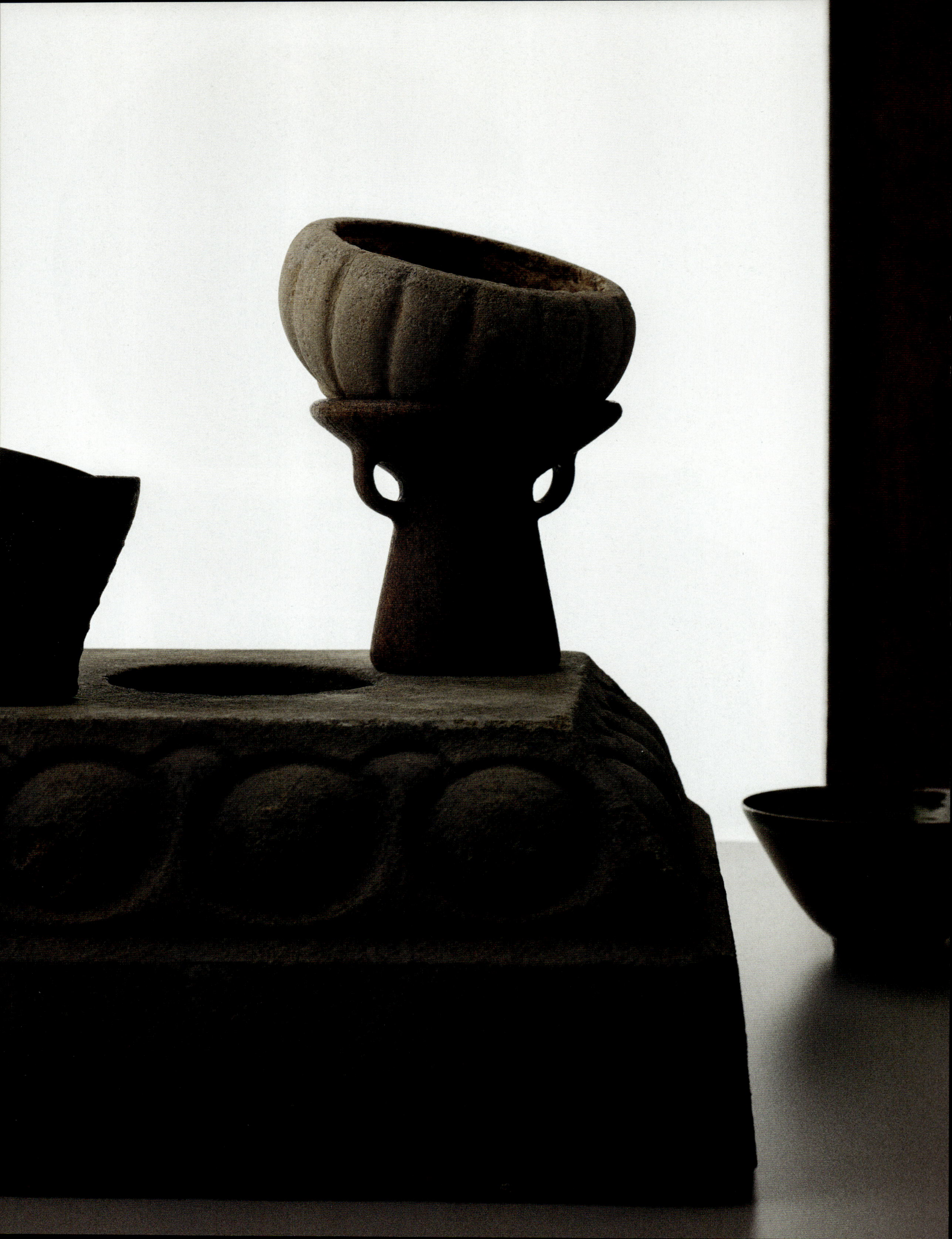

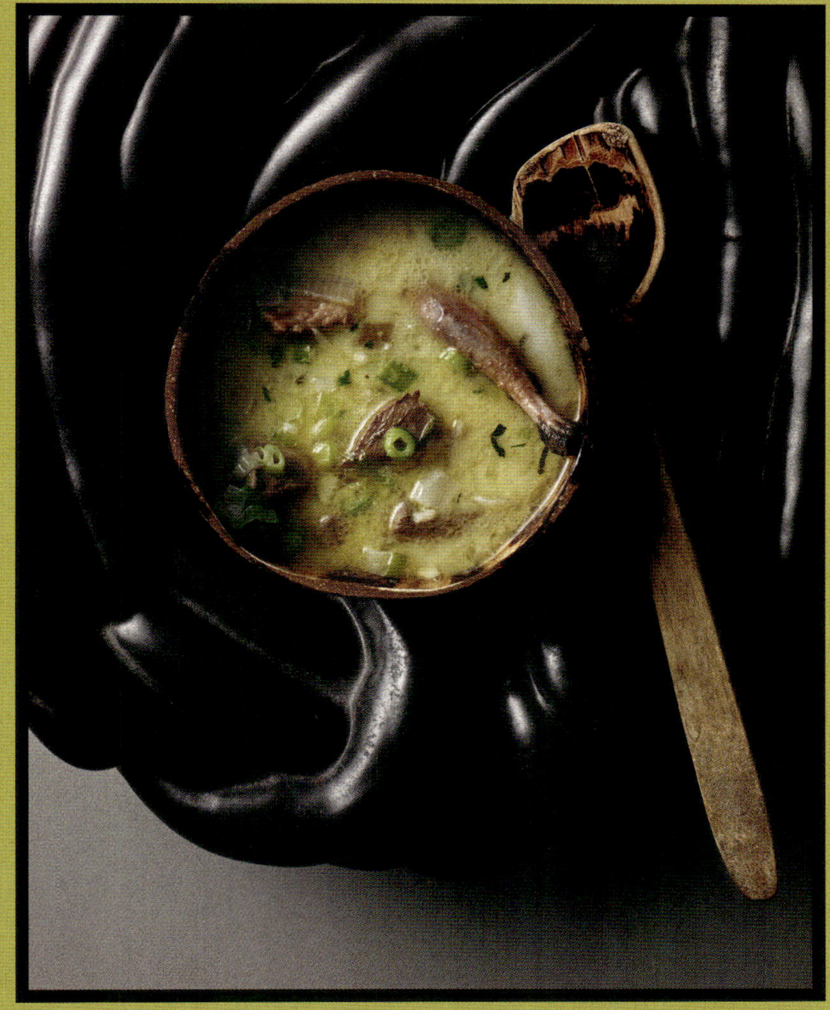

## 3.  BABYLONIAN PIGEON STEW

This recipe is adapted from one of the Yale Babylonian culinary tablets, clay inscriptions dating to around 1750 B.C.E. and often cited as the world's oldest recorded recipes. The original text, translated into English, reads with striking brevity: "Take a bird; prepare it; add water, salt, fat, onion, flour, milk, leek and garlic. Cook and serve." Scholars believe the bird was likely pigeon, a common and valued meat in ancient Mesopotamia. The result is a surprisingly delicate stew, enriched with milk and thickened with grain; a rare, tangible connection to the kitchens of Babylon, nearly four thousand years ago.

SERVES 3 TO 4
1 tablespoon clarified butter or ghee
1 Cornish hen or small bird (roughly pigeon-sized), cut into thighs, breasts and drumsticks
1 small onion, chopped
2 cloves garlic, minced
1 leek, sliced
4 cups (1L) water
1 cup (235ml)  whole milk
1 teaspoon salt, or to taste
1 tablespoon all-purpose flour

INSTRUCTIONS
In a medium pot, heat the clarified butter over medium heat. Brown the bird pieces on all sides until lightly golden, then remove and set aside.

In the same pot, sauté the onion and garlic until softened and fragrant.

Return the bird to the pot and add the sliced leek and water. Bring to a gentle simmer and cook for about 20 minutes, until the meat is tender.

Stir in the milk and salt. Simmer gently for several minutes more.

In a small bowl, whisk the flour with a small amount of the broth to form a smooth paste, then stir it into the pot to lightly thicken the stew. Cook briefly until the broth takes on a soft, velvety texture. Serve warm.

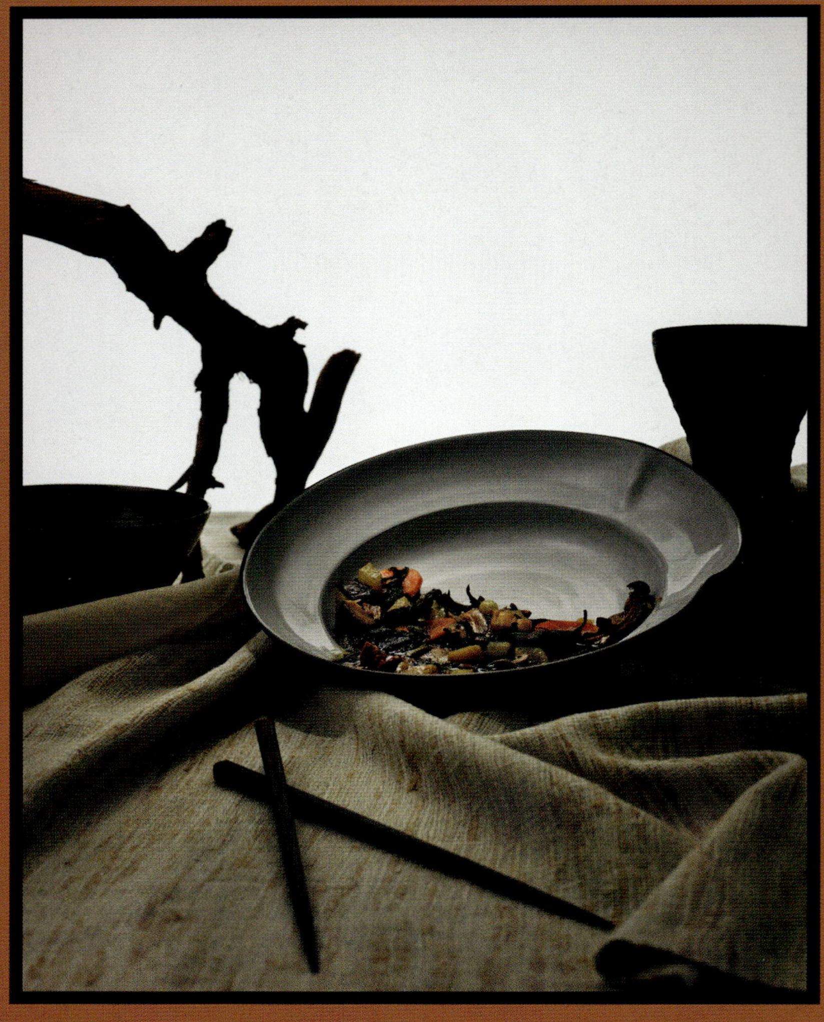

## 4.   TAOIST SOUP FOR THE SOUL

Taoist philosophy, traditionally traced to the 4th–3rd century B.C.E. and the teachings of Laozi in the *Tao Te Ching*, placed great emphasis on harmony between the body and the natural world. Later Taoist practitioners developed dietary practices intended to cultivate clarity, longevity and the smooth flow of chi, the body's vital energy. Some ascetics practiced *bigu*, or grain avoidance, favoring simple broths of roots, herbs and wild greens. This light vegetable soup reflects those principles: seasonal, restrained and nourishing without excess.

SERVES 2 TO 3
6 to 8 dried shiitake mushrooms
(or other dried mushrooms)
4 cups (1L) water or light vegetable broth
1 medium carrot, sliced
1 small daikon or turnip, diced
2 slices fresh ginger
2 to 3 roughly chopped sprigs
dandelion greens (or seasonal greens such
as spinach or nettles)
Salt, to taste
*Optional:* chopped chives or fresh
wild herbs

INSTRUCTIONS
In a small bowl, soak the dried mushrooms in warm water for 20 minutes. Remove, slice and set aside. Reserve the soaking liquid to add to the broth, if desired.

In a medium pot, bring the water or broth to a gentle simmer. Add the carrot, daikon, reserved mushrooms and ginger. Cook for 15 to 20 minutes, until the vegetables are tender. Add the greens and cook for another 3 to 5 minutes, just until wilted.

Season lightly with salt. Sprinkle with chives or wild herbs, if using. Serve warm, allowing the natural flavors to remain clean and subtle.

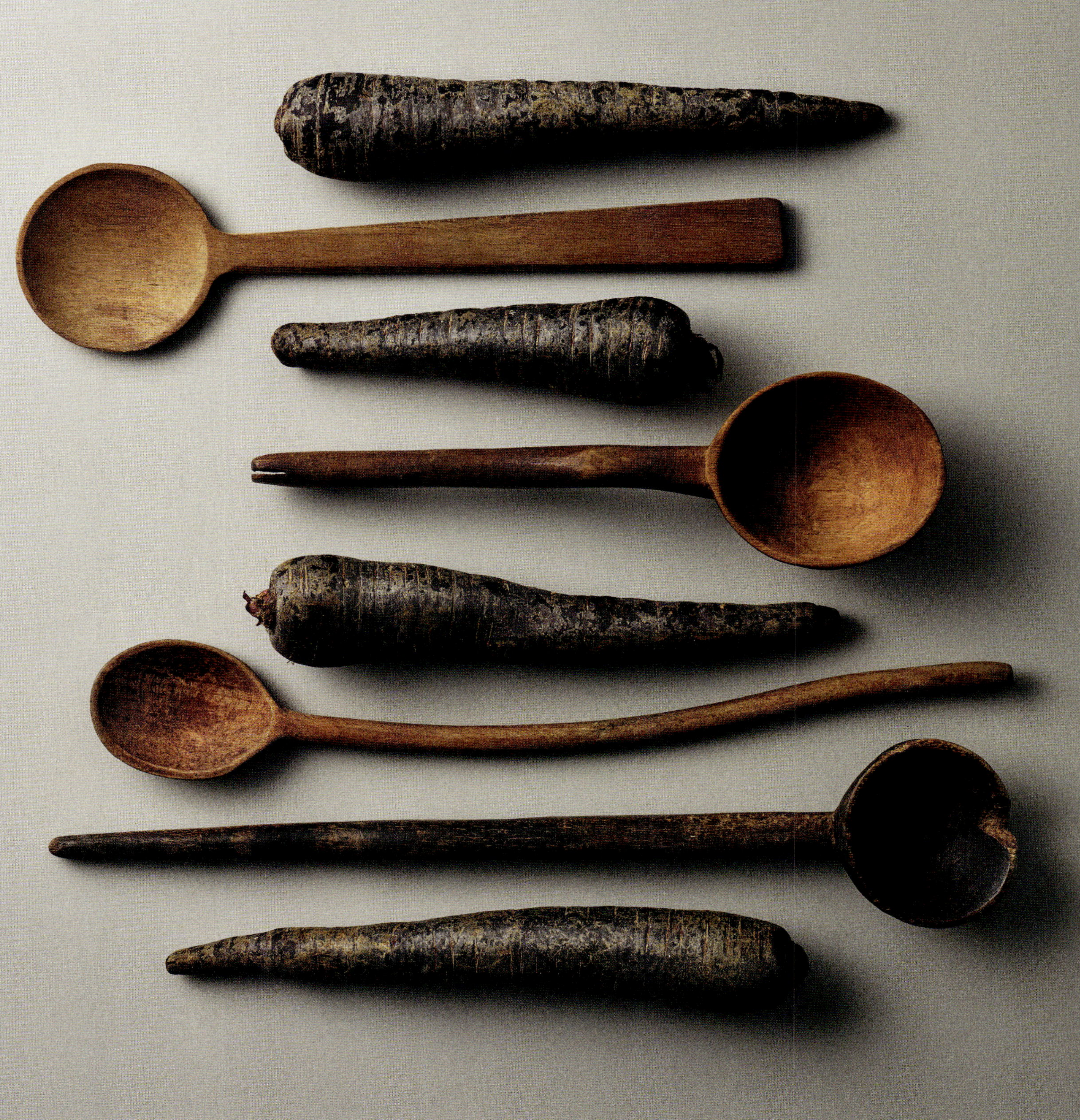

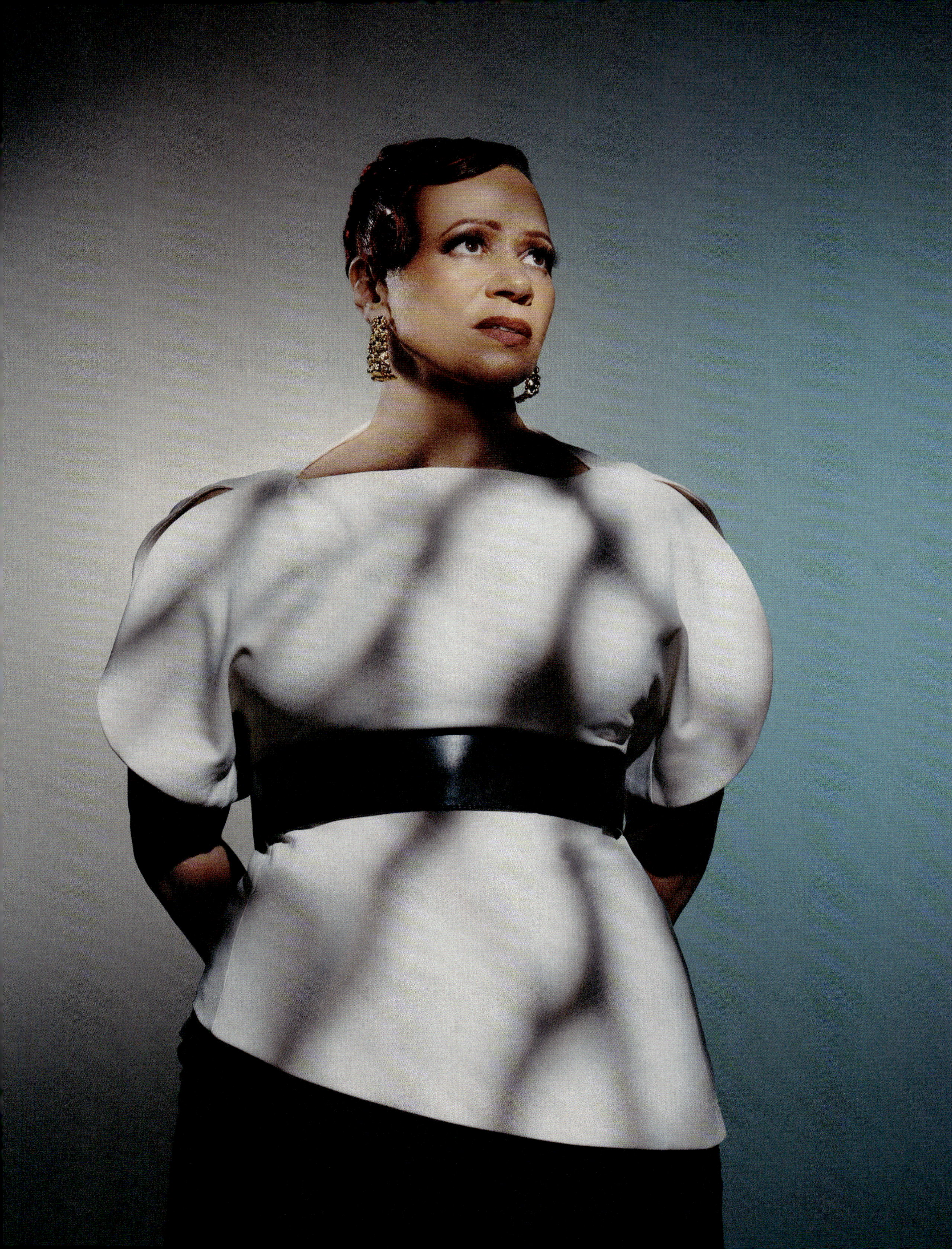

# V



## 1619:
## In proposing a new founding date for the United States, journalist Nikole Hannah-Jones challenged Americans to confront their national narrative.

*Words*
Sala Elise Patterson

*Photos*
Oyè Diran

*Styling*
Shola Shodipo



On July 23, 2020, Senator Tom Cotton introduced an act into Congress that sought to prohibit the use of federal funds to teach the 1619 Project in schools. The curriculum was based on a set of essays that had run in *The New York Times Magazine* in August 2019, on the 400th anniversary of the first enslaved Africans arriving in America. The project argued that the country's origins lay not in 1776, with the Declaration of Independence, but rather with the introduction of enslaved Africans into the British North American colonies in 1619. And that in predating America's birth story, we arrive at a more accurate history of the country, where slavery, racism and segregation play a central role—not equality, democracy and freedom.

The 1619 Project was the brainchild of Nikole Hannah-Jones, an award-winning investigative reporter at *The New York Times* who covers civil rights and racial inequality, and why it is so entrenched in America. "I have been obsessed with the year 1619 since I was 15, both as a symbolic date and for what it meant for the story of Black people in the United States," she explains.

Hannah-Jones grew up in a Black neighborhood "on the wrong side of the river" in Waterloo, Iowa, a town of about 70,000 in the middle of America. After she attended a predominantly Black, low-income elementary school until second grade, her parents enrolled her in a school desegregation program that bused working-class and Black children to schools in whiter, more affluent neighborhoods. She lived the stark contrast between the worlds—one Black and underserved, one white and academically stimulating. Soon Hannah-Jones was reflecting on the circumstances that gave birth to such a persistently segregated and unequal system. Journalism became a way for her to look for answers.

"With most investigative reporting on racial inequality, you're just cataloging maladies. But no one's |being held| responsible for all the wrongs. I became a journalist because I wanted to show that you could do investigative reporting about structural inequality and show that actual people are making decisions, that actual policies are being put in place," she says.

After obtaining a master's degree in mass communication, Hannah-Jones worked at newspapers in North Carolina and Oregon and at a nonprofit news agency from 2003–2015. It was during these

( below )    Hannah-Jones wears a dress by NAKED WARDROBE, jewelry by ALEXIS BITTAR and shoes by SCHUTZ.
( opposite )  She wears a jacket by NAKED WARDROBE and jewelry by ALEXIS BITTAR.
( previous )  She wears a top and belt (stylist's own) with jewelry by ALEXIS BITTAR.

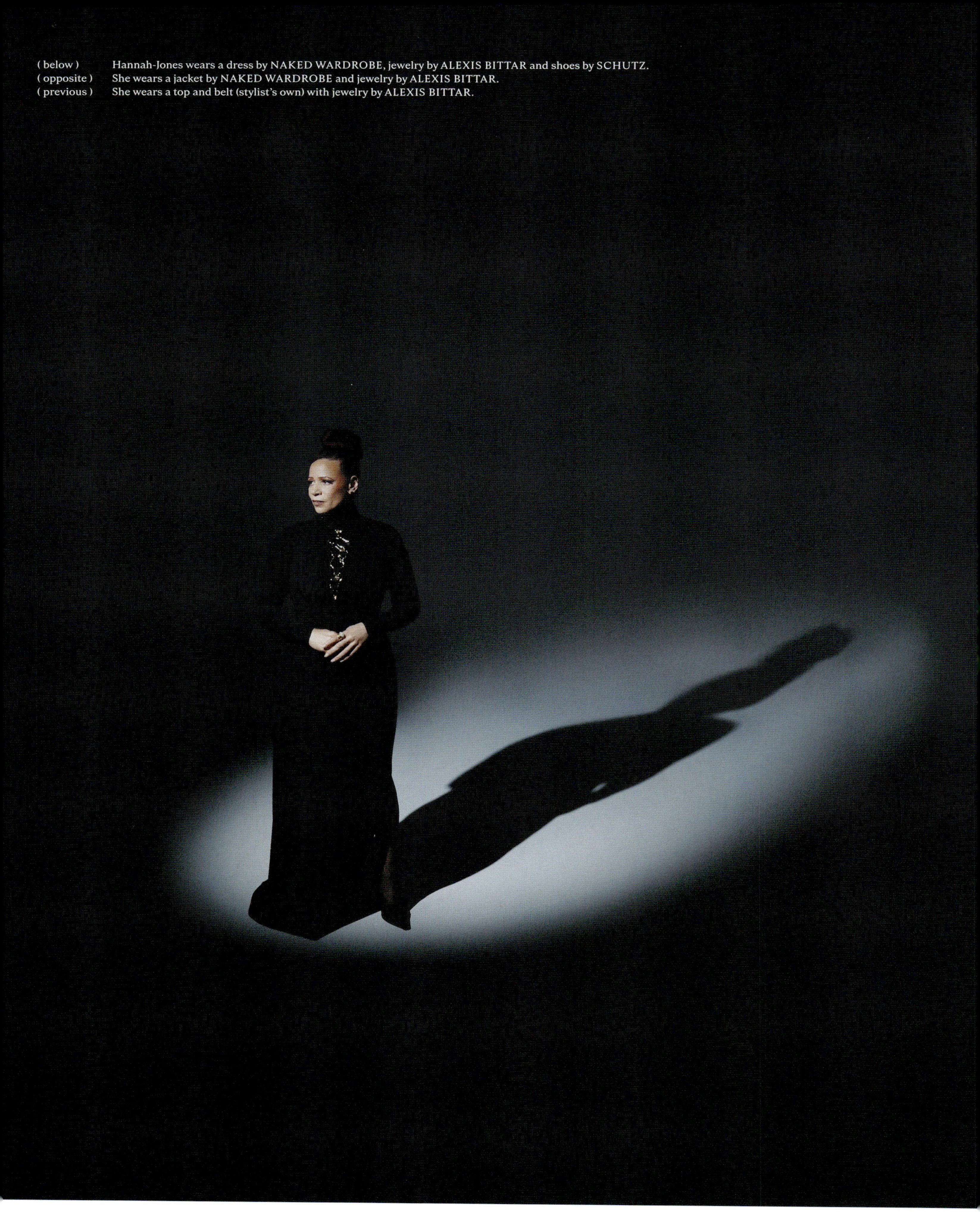

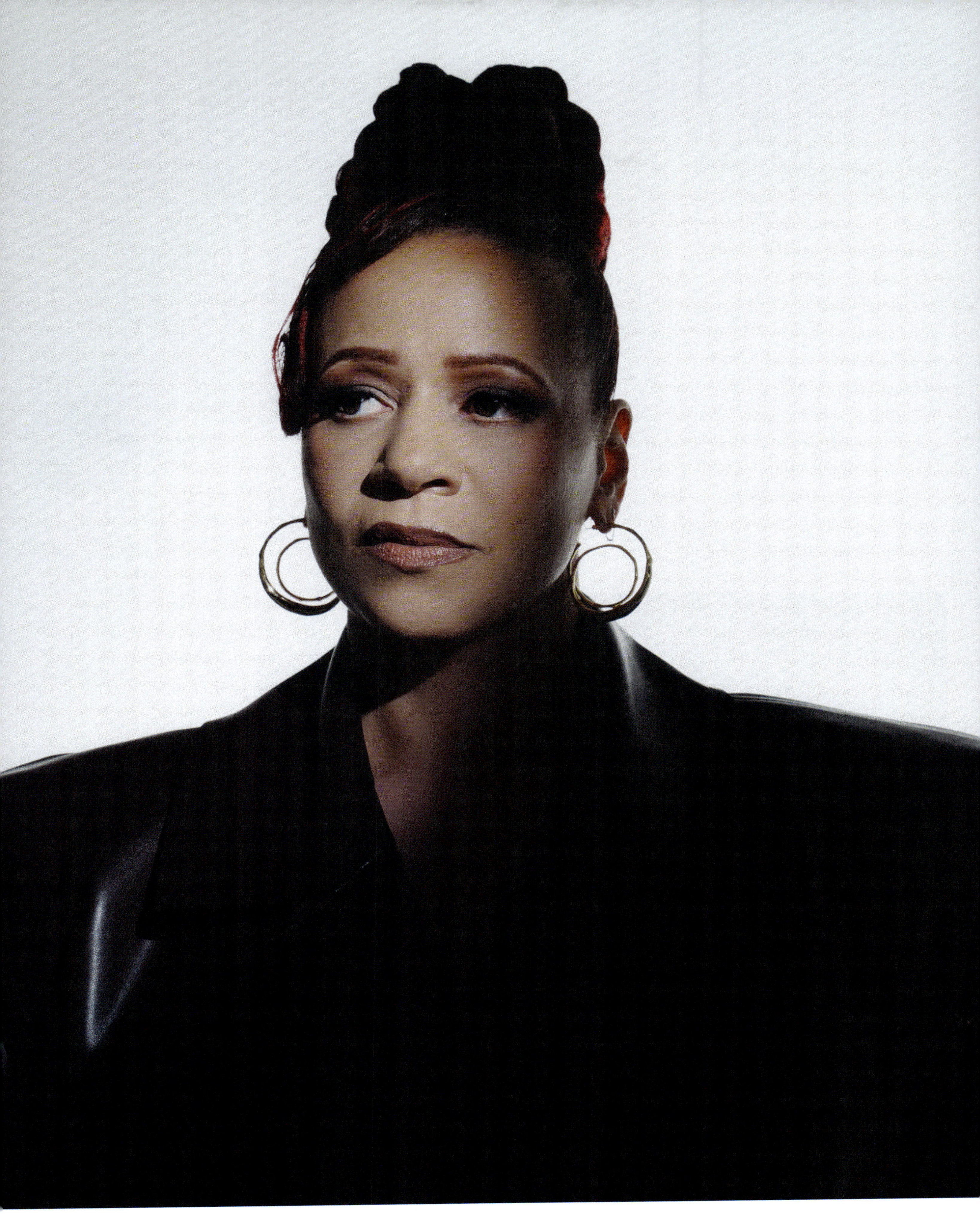

years that she honed a signature approach to writing about structural racism that relied on history, scholarship and policy. In 2015, she joined *The Times* and two years later was recognized with the prestigious "Genius" grant from the MacArthur Foundation for "bringing into sharp relief a problem that many are unwilling to acknowledge still exists."

For 2019 and the 400th anniversary of slavery, she decided to produce a piece of journalism about the root cause of what she had long been reporting on. "I wanted to use the platform of *The New York Times* to draw attention to that date and the way slavery shaped the United States in ways that were ongoing," Hannah-Jones says. She pitched a special issue on the topic at a weekly team meeting in early 2019—she knew that a single essay would not be enough. The magazine's editor, Jake Silverstein, committed to it on the spot.

Telling a version of the American story that originated from slavery and its descendants would be a radical proposition for Americans of all political persuasions. She would need to make the case across multiple articles, each addressing how one aspect of modern American life could be traced to slavery and its legacy. In the end, the issue featured ten essays, with Hannah-Jones writing the introductory piece: "The United States is a nation founded on both an ideal and a lie," she wrote. "Our Declaration of Independence, approved on July 4, 1776, proclaims that 'all men are created equal' and 'endowed by their Creator with certain unalienable rights.' But the white men who drafted those words did not believe them to be true for the hundreds of thousands of black people in their midst."

The other contributors explored topics as diverse as the link between American capitalism and slavery; persistent myths about physical differences between the races; Black music and its centrality to American music; slavery and the prison system; and the violent history behind America's addiction to sugar.

Silverstein later wrote that, upon publishing, "The issue was greeted with an enthusiastic response unlike any we had seen before." People had to visit multiple newsstands to find copies of the magazine. The issue sold out within hours online.

Hannah-Jones says that her aim with the project was to educate, disrupt and, above all, to surprise. And as time went on, the gravity of her thesis sunk in, provoking for many a sort of identity crisis. If America wasn't founded on the ideals of freedom and equality, how could it claim to be the greatest democracy on Earth? Embracing such a brutal origin story proved, for some, too uncomfortable to bear. Hannah-Jones describes how two camps formed among those for whom the arguments of the 1619 Project were new: In one, you had people who were shocked and hurt that no one had ever taught them this history before. In the other were those who couldn't accept her thesis because, were it true, they reasoned, they would already have known about it.

Conservatives, like Senator Cotton, were irate. To them, her premise was unpatriotic, offensive and simply a lie. Although Cotton's bill eventually died in Congress, it inspired other initiatives to debunk Hannah-Jones' narrative. The most notable was the 1776 Commission, an advisory committee President Donald Trump created in 2020 "to enable a rising generation to understand the history and principles of the founding of the United States in 1776."

The response did not surprise Hannah-Jones. "We were trying to be provocative, and if the 1619 Project had told a story that was acceptable to most conservatives and even a lot of moderates, it would have been unsuccessful to me," she says. But she was not prepared for the response to shift from a critique to a coordinated attack on the credibility of the project—and her. At one point Fox News had a reporter assigned just to cover her social media activity.

There was solace, however, in the response of Black Americans and progressives. For many, the 1619 Project was vindicating. It laid bare, with unprecedented breadth for a mainstream news platform, a history of America that centered the Black experience. "I've become a symbol for people who love me. I've become a symbol for people who hate me," Hannah-Jones reflects.

Seven years since it was first published, the legacy of the 1619

"It is absolutely revisionist history, because all historiography is revision."

Project is clear. Hannah-Jones won the Pulitzer Prize for Commentary in 2020, and the project gave birth to a documentary series, a podcast and a book, which stayed on *The New York Times* best-seller list for six months. But more important was the impact Hannah-Jones has left on journalism and the American consciousness.

First, she showed journalists how transformative their work can be—that they don't just report stories but *make* them. "We have tremendous power in determining what issues people care about, how they care about them, what they think about them, whether they support policies or don't, far more than any politician or think tank," she explains.

The 1619 Project also underscored that history is not an absolute truth but an interpretation of facts. And, like all stories, it carries a point of view, with winners and losers, rights and wrongs, all determined by the historian. Hannah-Jones explains: "The point of the project was to make this argument that the quote-unquote history we had all been taught, was a curated history," she says. "A lot of critics accused the project of being revisionist history, using that word as a slur. But it is absolutely revisionist history, because all historiography is revision."

Indeed, the 1619 Project sparked a narrative battle over the hearts and minds of Americans—a fight that persists. "Now we see it everywhere," Hannah-Jones says. "There is this understanding that you have to control the past—and how we remember it—to control the present." And that is apparent as America prepares to mark its 250th anniversary on July 4, 2026. What is celebrated, and how and why is an open and active debate. "If we want to grapple with the truth of who we are as a country in the 250th year, you almost couldn't have a better moment," says Hannah-Jones.

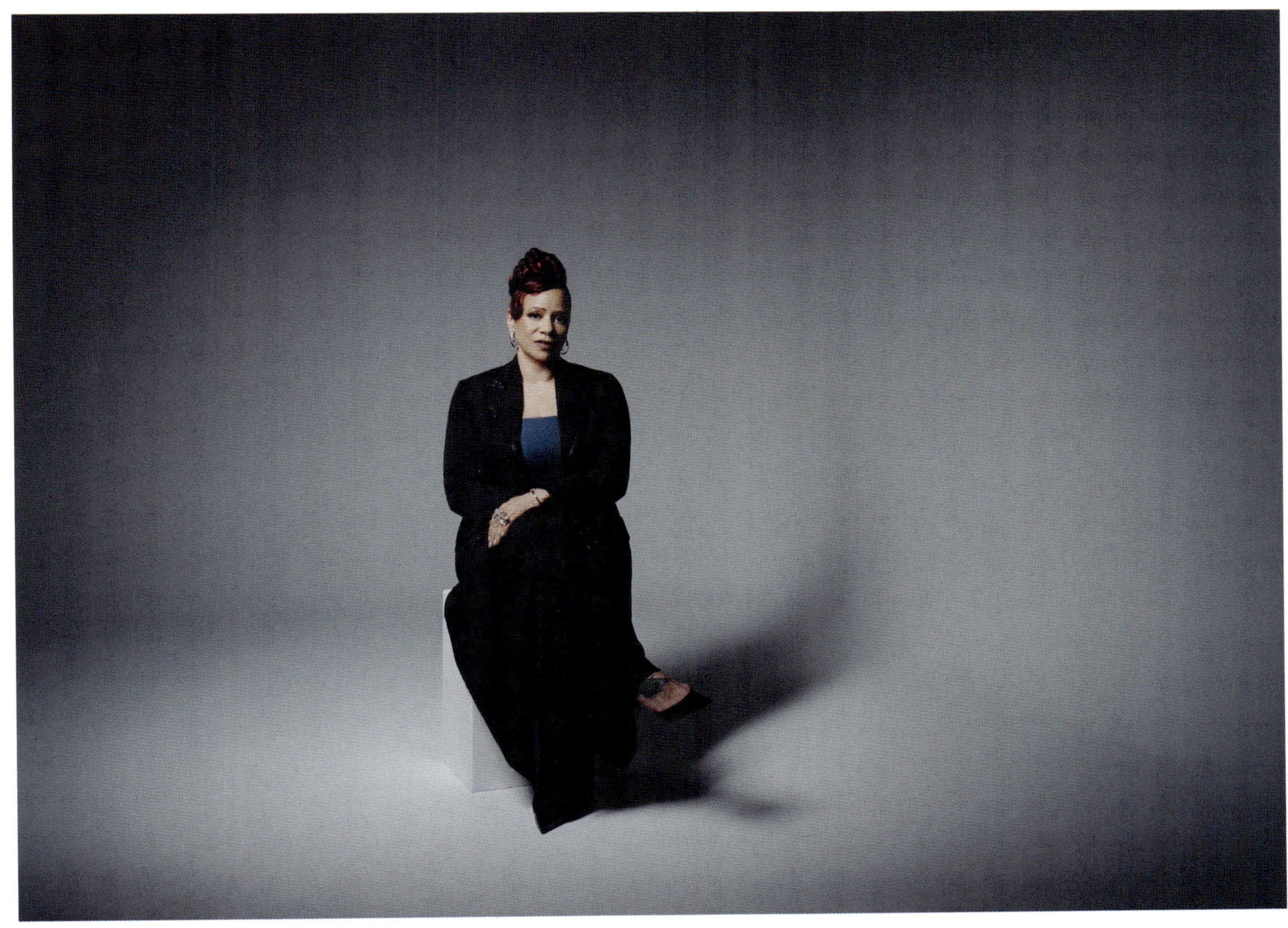

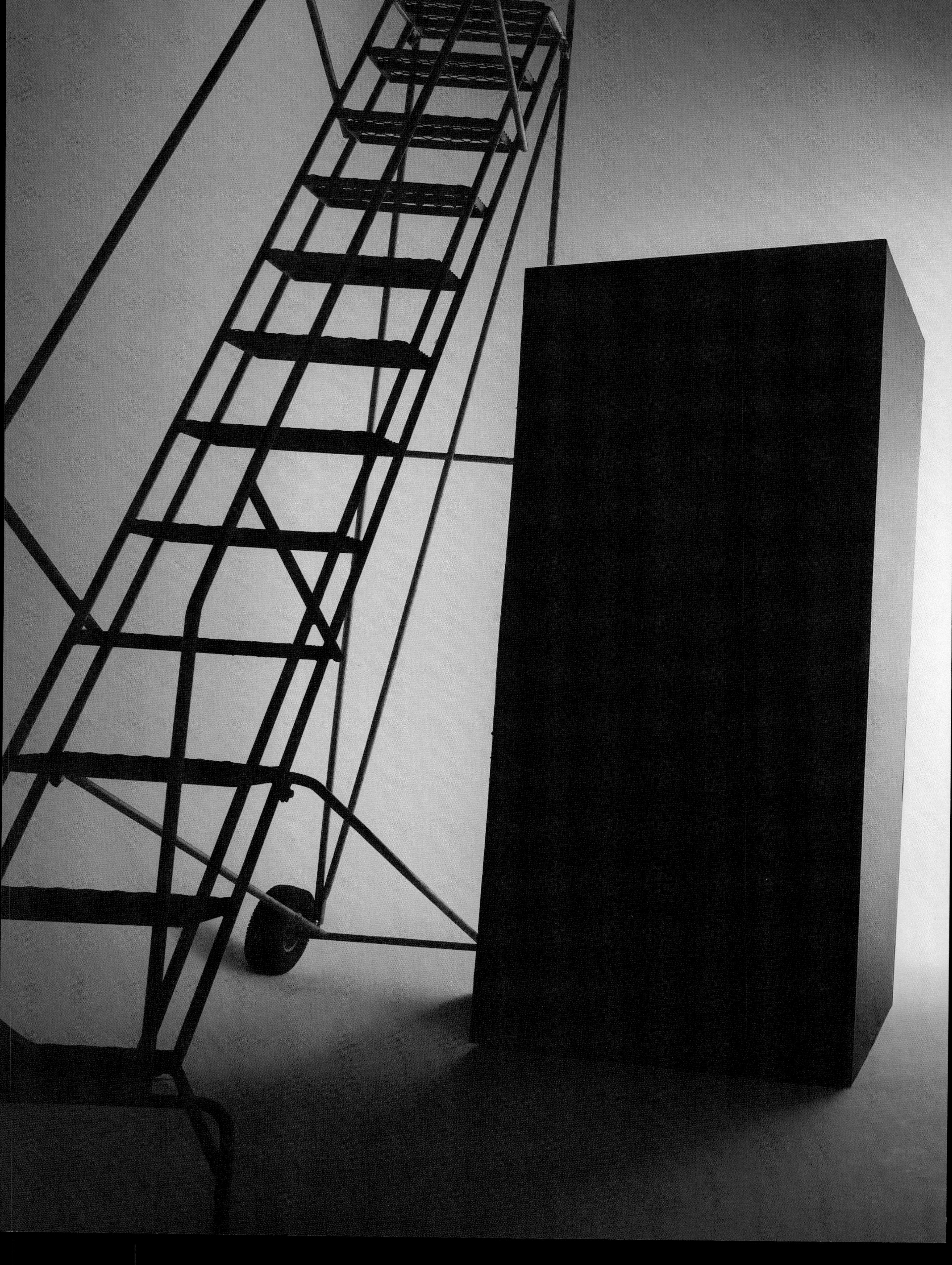

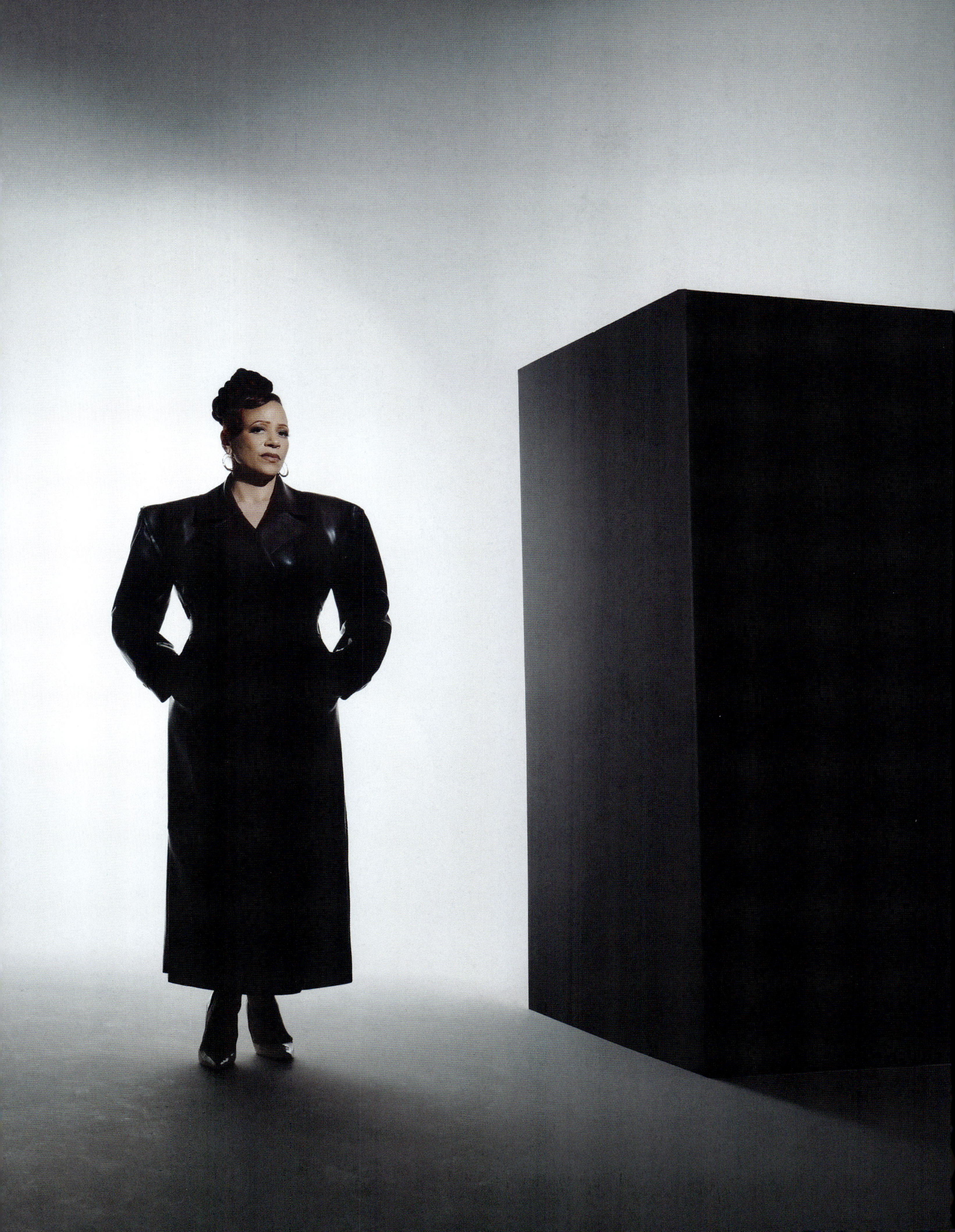

# VI

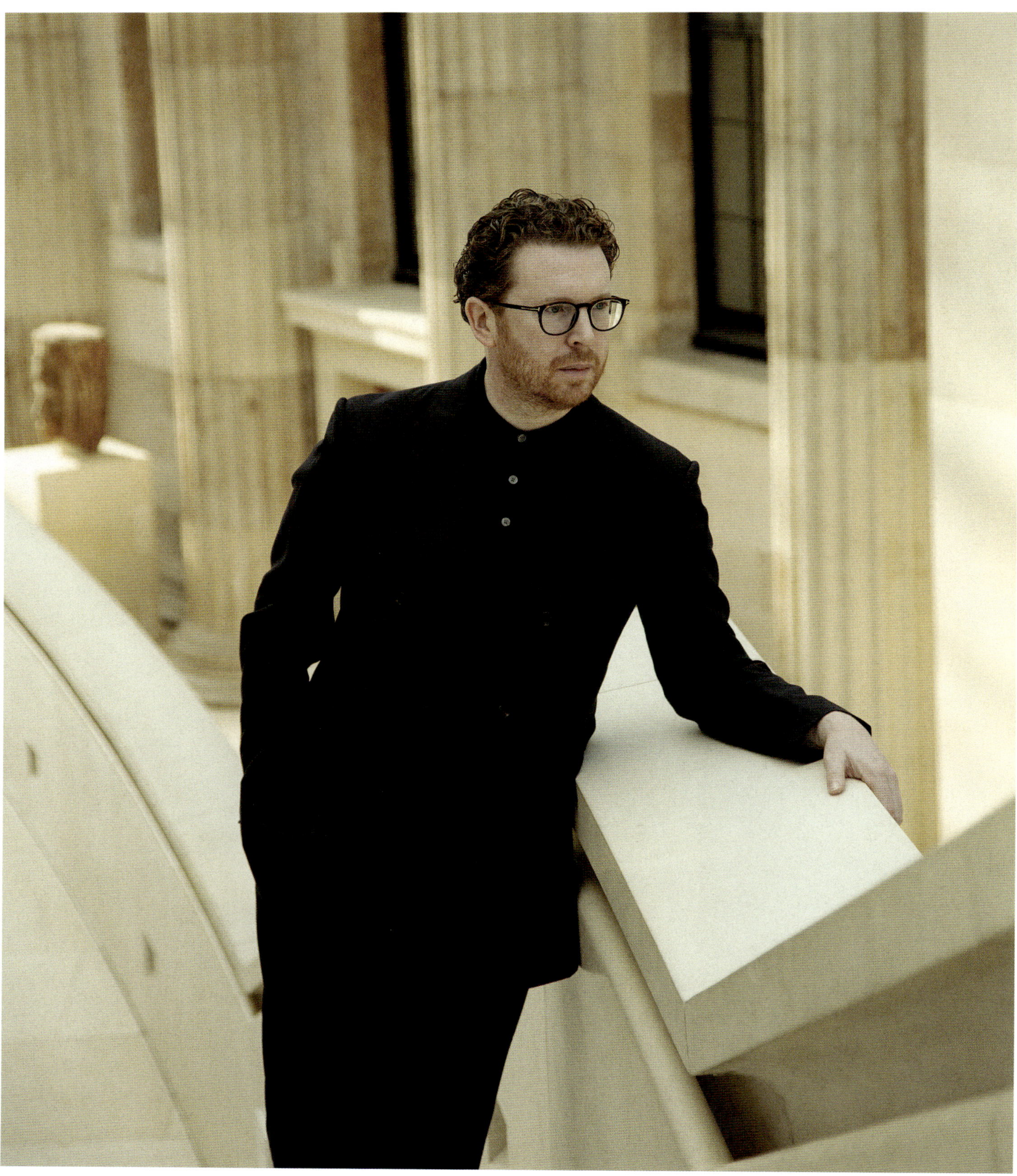

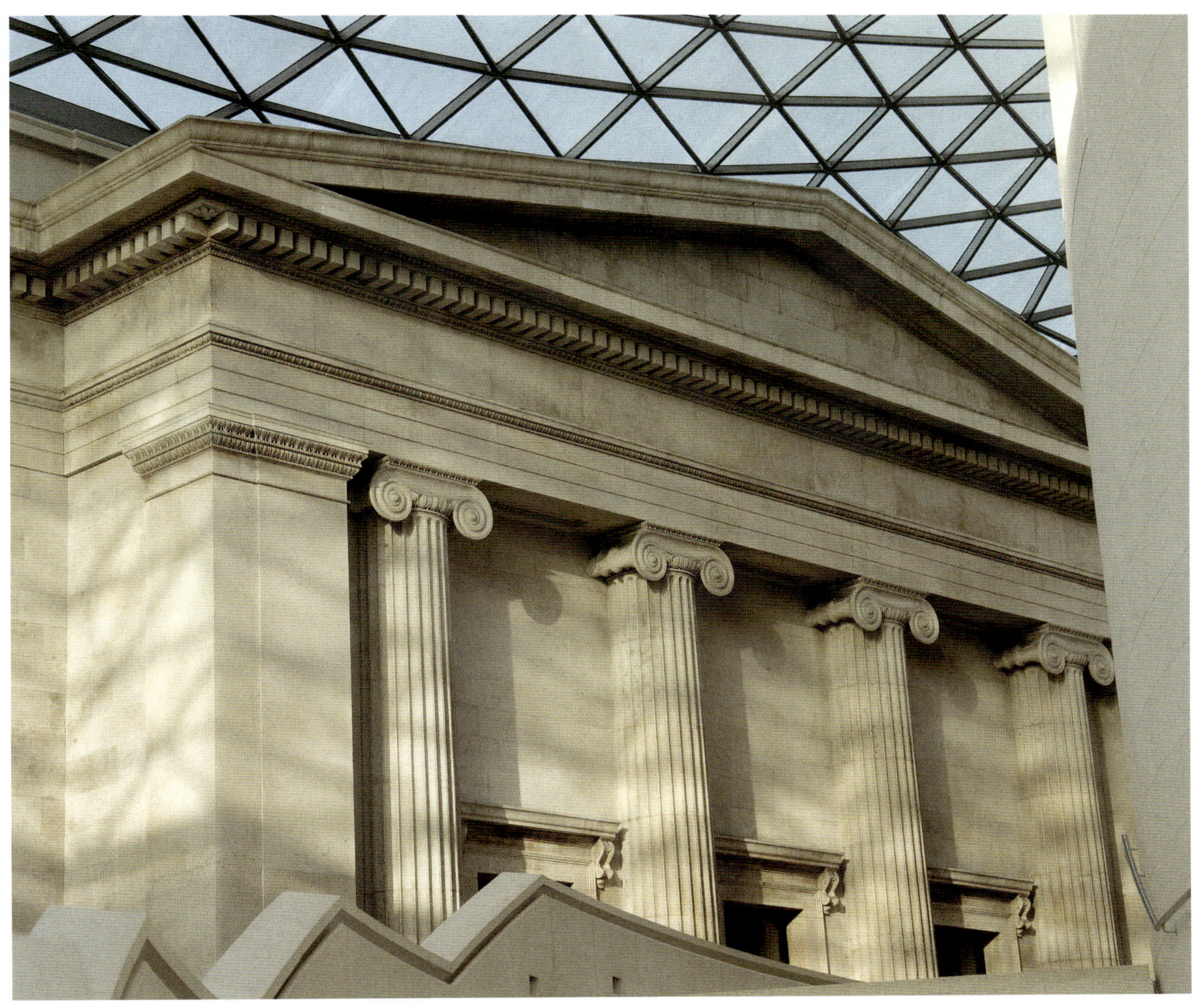

# NICHOLAS CULLINAN
## An audience with the director of the British Museum.

*Words*
Ellen Peirson-Hagger

*Photos*
Thea Løvstad

On a bright spring morning in the British Museum's Arched Room, Nicholas Cullinan gestures toward a bright red ladder—the same color as a London bus. "How about on there?" he asks the photographer. The director of one of the world's leading museums is excited about the prospect of shooting in the high-ceilinged space, normally used as a study room by the Department of the Middle East. It is one of his very favorites among the building's 3,500 rooms—though he admits that he has not had a chance to visit all of them yet.

Cullinan is two years into his directorate of the British Museum, whose permanent collection holds some eight million objects, making it the largest and most comprehensive in existence, and he is still thrilled to be there. "Look at those!" he exclaims, pointing toward fragments of cuneiform clay tablets—ancient Mesopotamian artifacts, which date back to between 3,200 B.C. and A.D. 80. Lining the walls are drawers containing 135,000 such fragments, while higher up still is a balcony full of books, accessible via a precarious-looking staircase. Cullinan, in a double-breasted navy suit and burgundy Nike sneakers, bounds through it all.

Later, sitting on a sofa in his office, the sounds of central London heard faintly through the open window, he explains his passion: "I do love encyclopedic museums," he says, speaking animatedly as he starts to set out his pitch for the museum in the 21st century. "I love making connections between different cultures, different times." Cullinan, who is 48, first visited the museum as a child. Born to British parents in Connecticut, he moved to the UK with his family when he was four. They settled in Hebden Bridge in Yorkshire, and while "financially, things were tough," he often went with his parents to museums in Manchester, Leeds and, occasionally, London. "I feel very lucky that I grew up with the understanding that culture is something that belongs to all of us," he says.

> "I feel very lucky that I grew up with the understanding that culture is something that belongs to all of us."

Cullinan studied history of art at the Courtauld Institute of Art in London, where he received a PhD in 2010. After working at the Metropolitan Museum of Art in New York, he moved to London's Tate Modern; in 2014, he co-curated an exhibition of Henri Matisse's cutouts that attracted more than 500,000 visitors, making it the most popular in the gallery's history. A year later, he was appointed the director of the National Portrait Gallery, where he oversaw a celebrated major refurbishment, and in June 2024, he took the reins at the British Museum. Today he lives close by, allowing him to walk to work and, when his schedule allows, to "pop home for lunch" with his husband, the art dealer Mattias Vendelmans, and their young daughter.

One of Cullinan's earliest memories is staying in a hotel on Gower Street, a short walk from the museum, after the family moved from the US. "I have this memory of being in the hotel room with my parents and my sister and everyone being freaked out that our whole life had been upended," he recalls. "I suppose they were thinking: 'Have we made the right decision?' And then my mum brought me to the British Museum, and I remember this feeling, as a small child who was aware they'd just been uprooted...." He pauses. The museum "gives you this sense of belonging. You understand you're part of a much bigger history."

( previous )
Cullinan in the Great Court of the British Museum, the largest covered square in Europe.

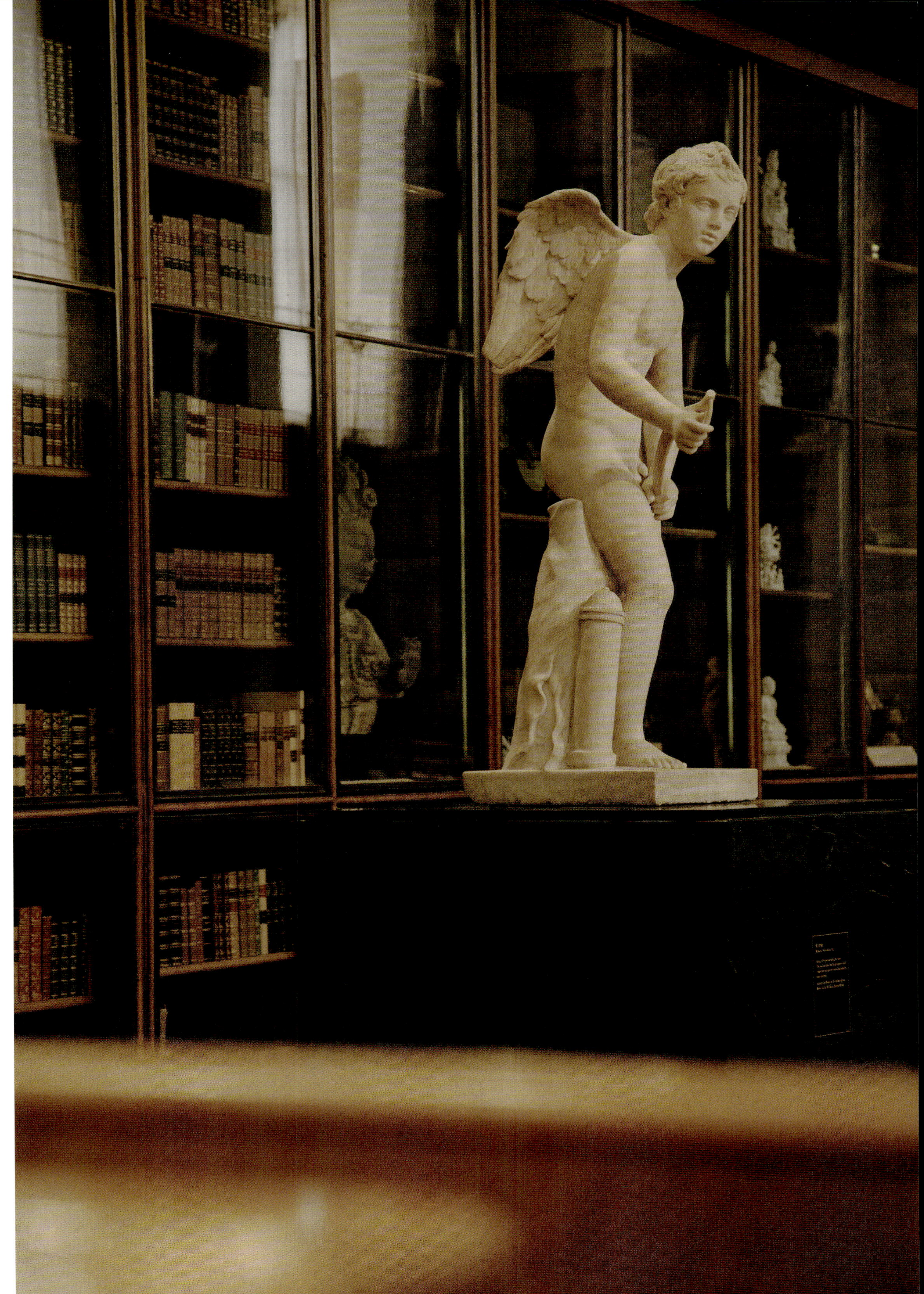

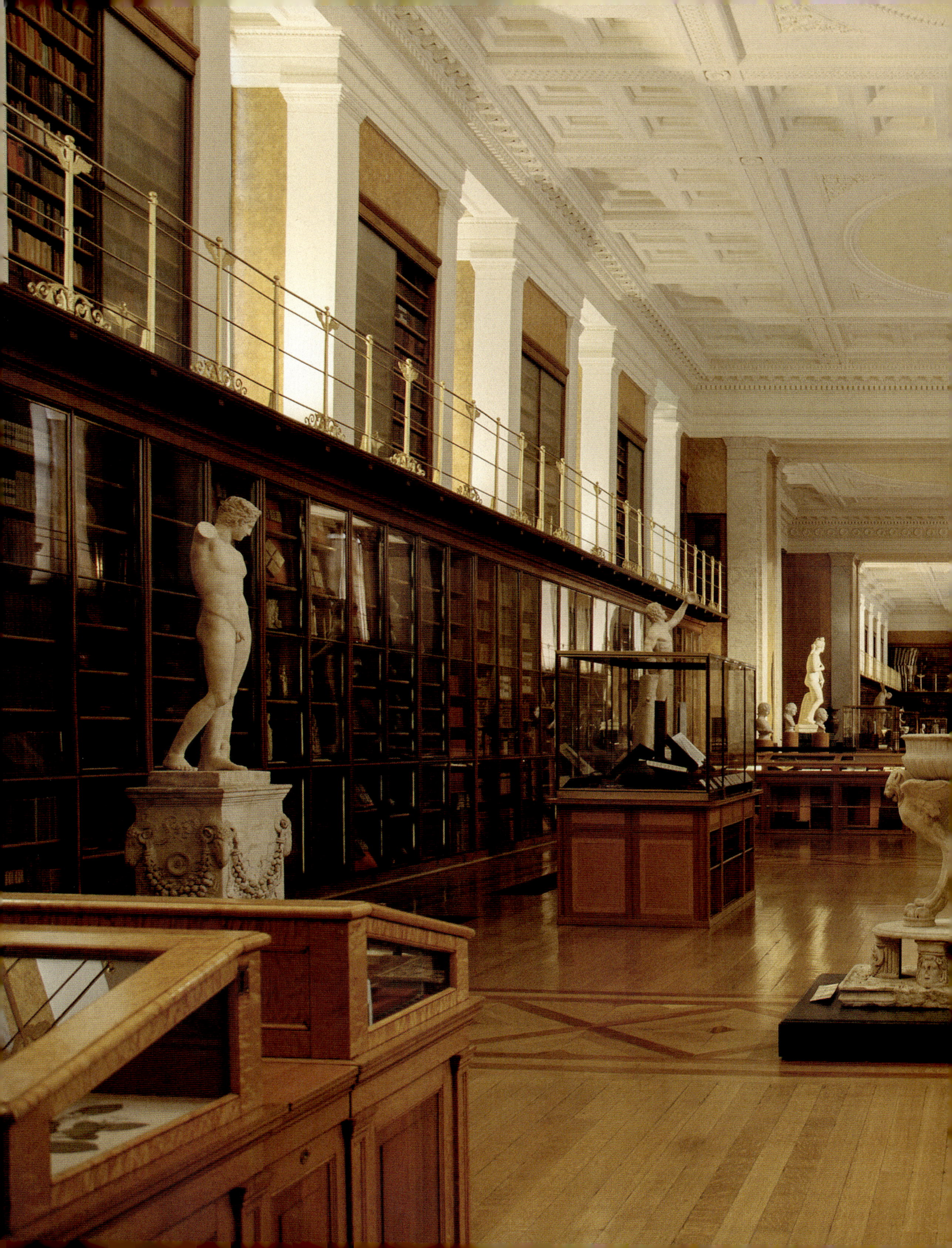

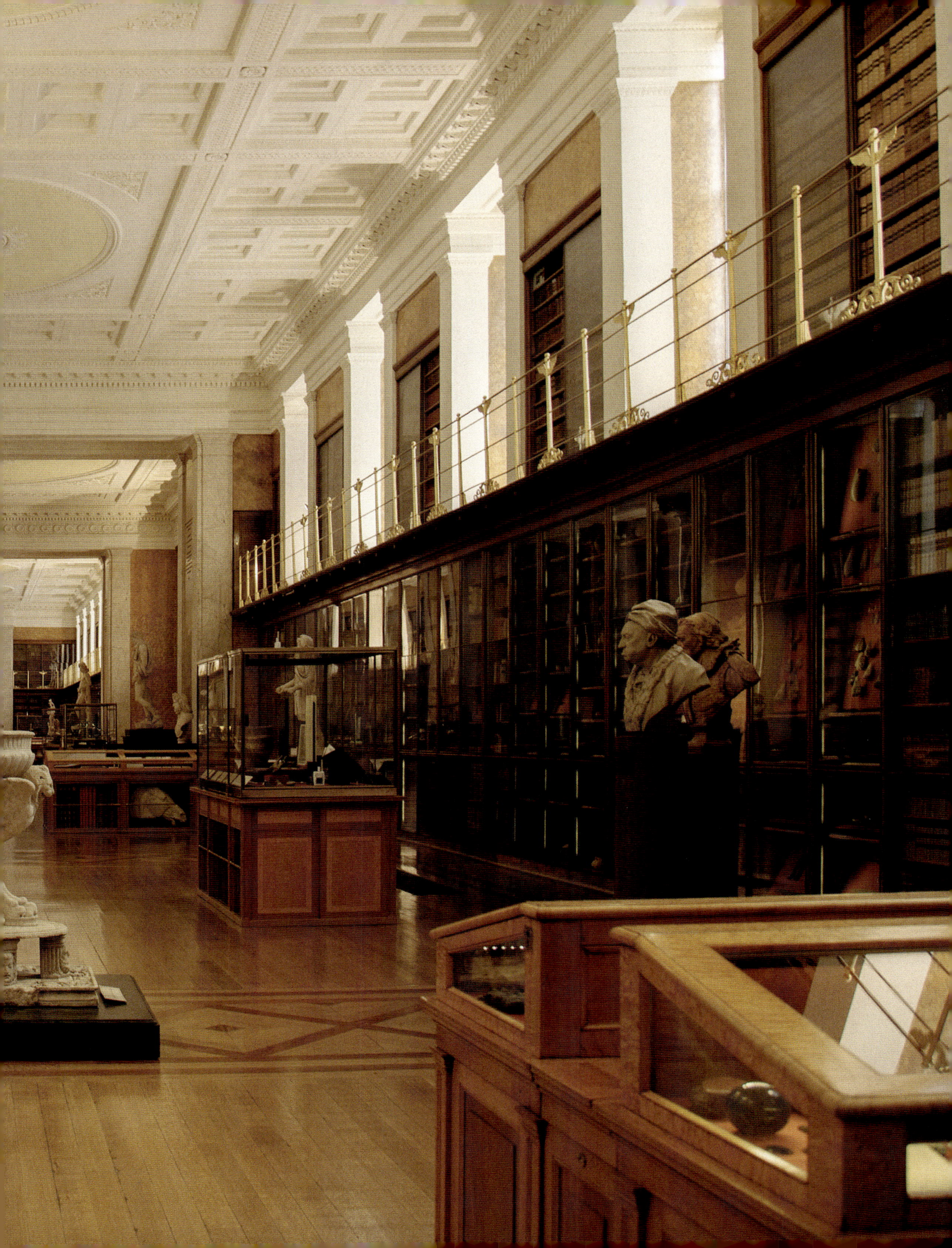

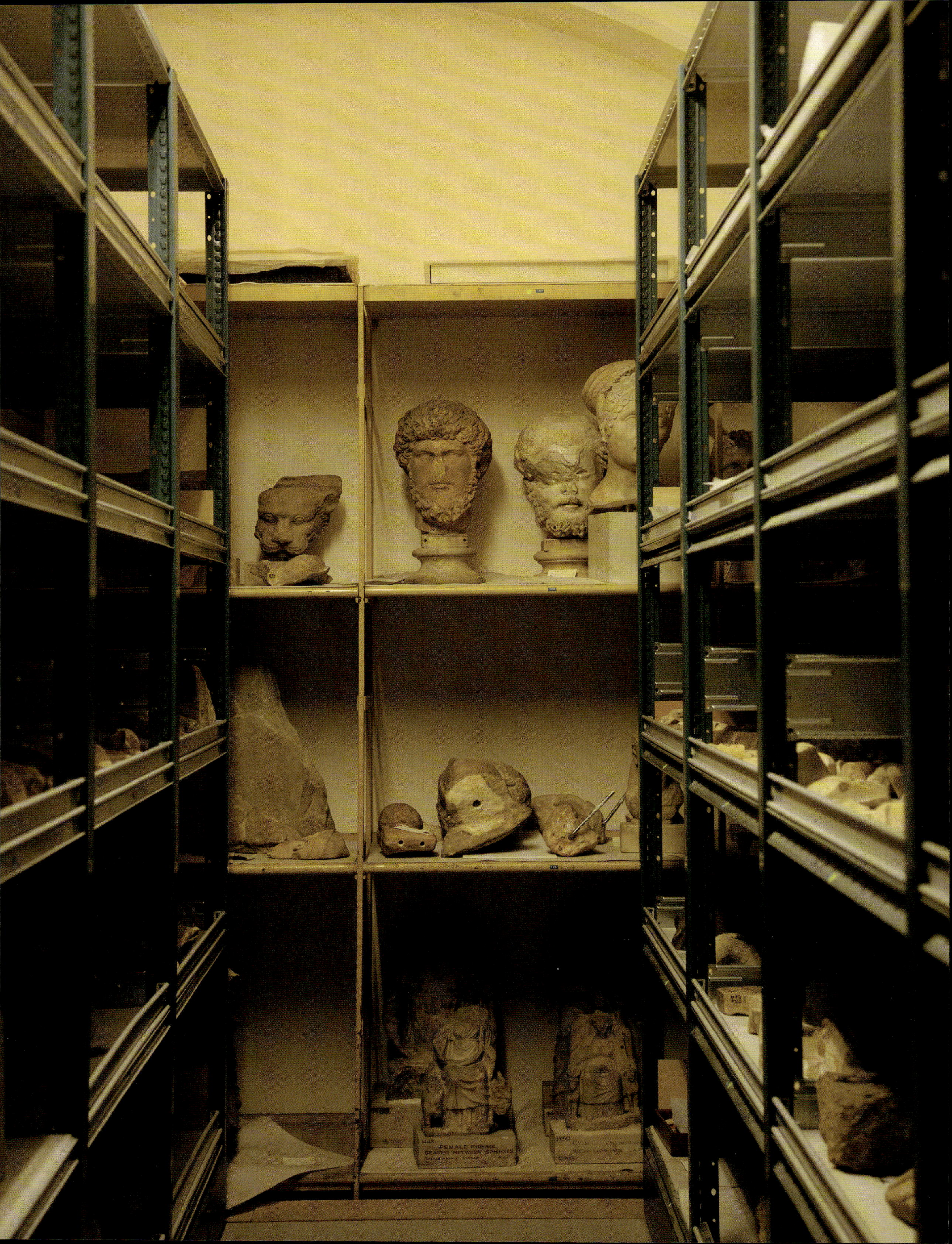

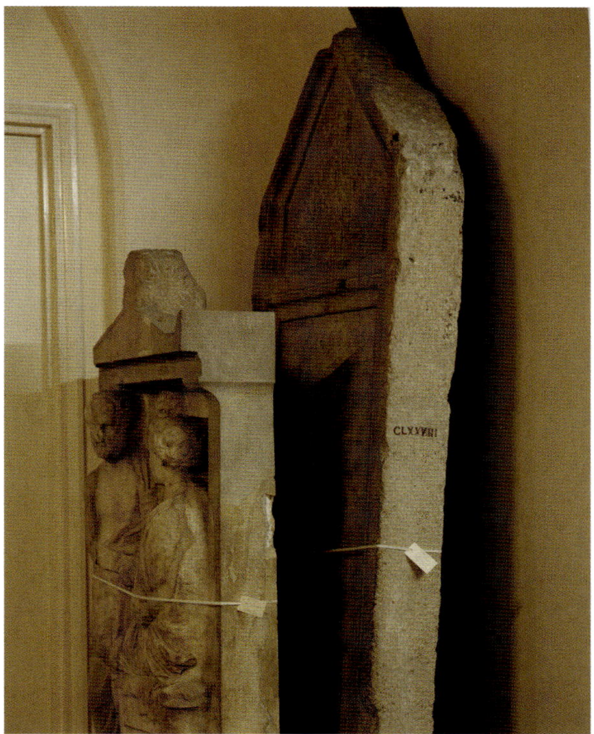

Back then, he was most taken by the mummies. "Children are fascinated by ancient Egypt," he says, gesturing toward a copy of the classicist Mary Beard's latest book, *Talking Classics: The Shock of the Old*, on his desk. "She describes this slightly ghoulish interest that children have in mummies. Obviously now we think about that carefully, because consciousness is evolving around the display of human remains. There's huge interest in mummies, and if that brings successive generations to Egyptology, then great, but it's about doing it in a respectful way."

These kinds of caveats—to do with the ethics of display, the politics of artifacts stolen during colonialism, the question of who gets to tell the story of the past—are second nature to Cullinan. Despite his enthusiasm for his institution, the museum is operating in an increasingly critical environment. After all, it was founded in 1753, when Britain ruled over the largest empire in history; its founder, Hans Sloane, partly owed his wealth to the forced labor of enslaved people on sugar plantations in Jamaica, and many of the objects in the collection were looted by British forces. In recent years, conversations around restitution—the return of objects to their countries of origin—have grown ever louder.

But the challenges facing the British Museum are not only ethical. Cullinan joined the museum after his predecessor resigned following the revelation that over 1,800 objects, mostly gems from the Greek and Roman collection, had been stolen over the course of a decade. Meanwhile, the institution is also grappling with practical issues: Its aging infrastructure is in urgent need of renovation. In the Western Range, which covers a third of the museum's galleries—including the Egyptian rooms, where the Rosetta Stone is located—the roof "doesn't have that long to go before it becomes perilous," as Cullinan explains. On top of all this comes the question of relevance: What, in the digital age, does a museum of history look like?

Cullinan is committed to facing these concerns head-on. A £1 billion transformation project is already underway, and having completed a similar, celebrated overhaul at the National Portrait Gallery, he is confident about his chances. "In a way, that's my special subject: how to take a much-loved historic institution, move it into the present, and make sure that it remains relevant and vital."

Under his tenure, progress has already been made. "A huge number, many more than was thought possible" of the stolen objects

> "We can't go back and change the past, and nor should we. I think the more interesting, more pressing question is: How do we therefore build something positive?"

have been recovered. It's a process that Cullinan describes as "very moving." "It's why people work in museums—to gather and protect. Being a curator is a bit like being a parent," he says. "You can't imagine doing anything that would harm your child. As a curator, you can't imagine doing anything that would harm the collection."

The effort has also given the museum the impetus to finally begin digitally documenting its collection—"an incredible resource," Cullinan says, "where anyone in the world with an internet connection will be able to access the whole collection of the British Museum." It's a project that, he says, is about "going back to the founding principles: this museum as meant to be for all persons." A free digital archive feels an appropriately 21st-century means of meeting that principle.

On the thorny topic of returning objects to their rightful owners, Cullinan is keen to clarify a "misunderstanding": "People say, 'There's nothing British in the British Museum.' Actually, the bulk of the collection is from the British Isles, from archaeological excavations." Indeed, parts of the collection have come to be there because of colonialism, he adds, arguing that "it's incumbent on all of us—not as people that work in museums, but as people that live in this country—to pan back and be honest about our history. We can't go back and change the past, and nor should we. I think the more interesting, more pressing question is: How do we therefore build something positive with that?"

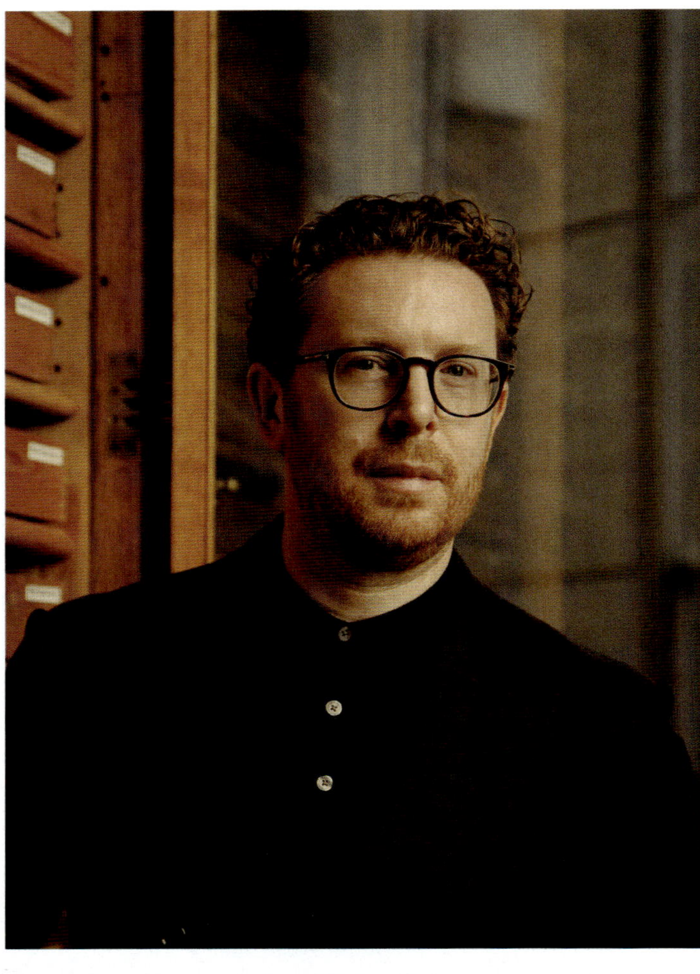

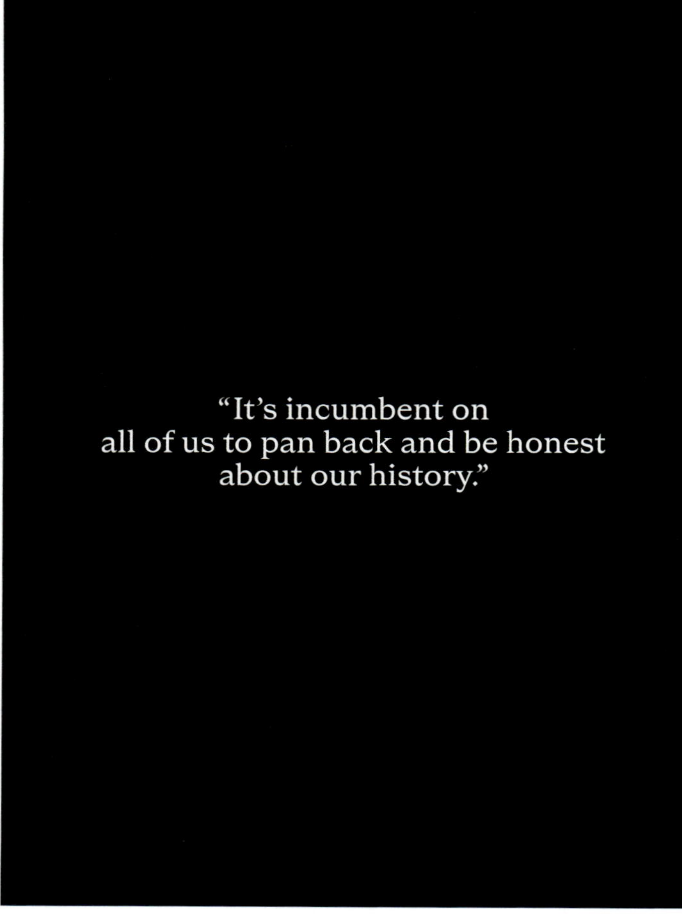



One such recent example is the Asante Ewer, a jug made in England during the 14th century that by the 1880s had ended up in a palace in Kumasi in present-day Ghana. In 1896, it was looted by British forces and purchased by the British Museum. Today the museum has a partnership with the Manhyia Palace Museum in Kumasi, and in 2024, contributed Asante gold jewelry to an exhibition at the Ghanaian institution, and invited the monarch of the Asante people to deliver a lecture in London. Cullinan says these kinds of efforts, that "create dialogue and foster understanding and build bridges, are more needed than ever before, because this trend of increasing nationalism and starting to think in silos and echo chambers is a real concern. We need things that force us to look at our shared history, to think about how it's incumbent on all of us to do something more positive in that history."

Restitution, meanwhile, is not straightforward: A 1963 law forbids the museum from deaccessioning objects in its care. "It's really out of our hands," Cullinan says. "If people feel strongly about it, then the correct thing to do is to lobby parliament for a change in law." Meanwhile, for objects such as the Parthenon Sculptures, which were taken from the acropolis in Athens by the British Lord Elgin in the early 19th century, he is more interested in finding a "third way" of restitution. "It would be great to find a partnership with Greece where the Parthenon Sculptures are lent on a rotating basis, but also to enter into research partnerships with Greece. Restitution is not just about objects. This shouldn't be about trophies. It needs to be about knowledge, understanding.... It shouldn't be a tug of war."

Cullinan is evidently used to feeling the burden of heading up such a significant cultural organization. In 2023, before he took up his role, the museum announced a new 10-year, £50 million deal with BP, which environmental activists called "morally indefensible." "The reality is we're all complicit in the way the world is today," Cullinan says, defending the deal. "We're all implicated. We all use petrochemicals. That has to change. But often museums now, because they're public-facing, are made to carry the can for certain issues. It's easier to target a museum than to really deal with the systemic problem."

For the British Museum, the reality is financial. Without a donation of the size only BP was willing to give, there would be no hope for the planned renovation of the Western Range by the architect Lina Ghotmeh. "If someone doesn't pay for it, within a few years, that whole wing has to be shut down. That's a big problem for the nation," Cullinan explains. The renovation will provide both infrastructural security and a "complete redisplay," including parts of the collection that aren't currently publicly represented, such as objects from the Caribbean and Indonesia. Long before that's ready, a whole museum rebranding is due to be unveiled in spring 2027 alongside a redesigned forecourt, which will become civic space.

Cullinan expects the transformation will take 20 years or more, and hopes to see it through himself. It will be one of the most significant cultural redevelopments ever—yet he does not seem daunted. "The timing feels really good," he says, even going so far as to remark that having a young child at home helps. "I've got two main things: working here and being with my family." It means "everything has become very clarified. And going home to a giggling baby puts it all in perspective."

Given his previous directorship, the project is also "not my first rodeo," he points out, playfully. "I feel equipped. And for most people who get this job, it is their final job before they retire, so it's maybe 10 years. But I'm not five or 10 years away from retirement. I've got a way to go."

( P. 142–143 )

The Enlightenment Gallery, curated to evoke an 18th-century museum experience. The more than 4,000 objects on display span periods and cultures, with the oldest dating back to prehistory.

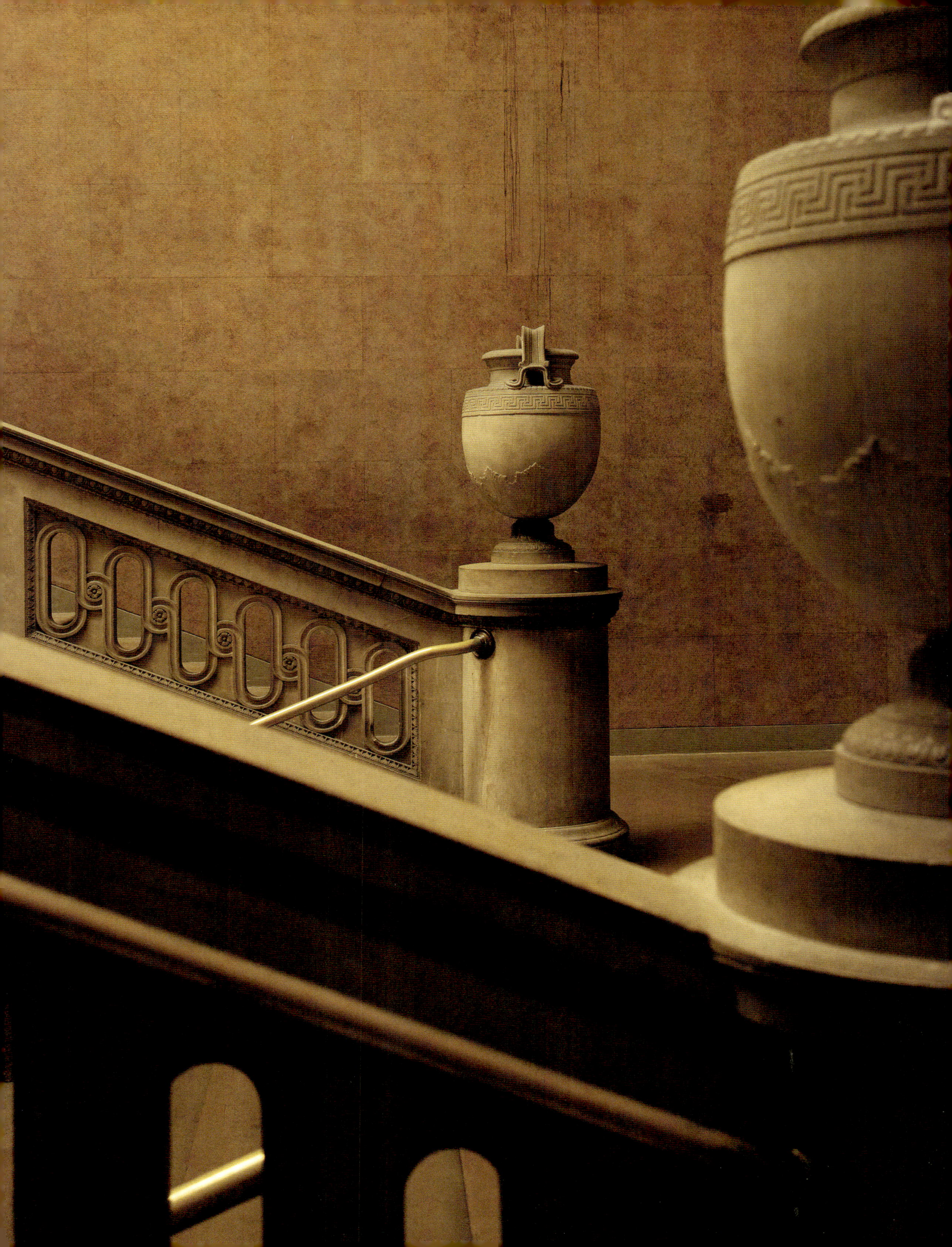

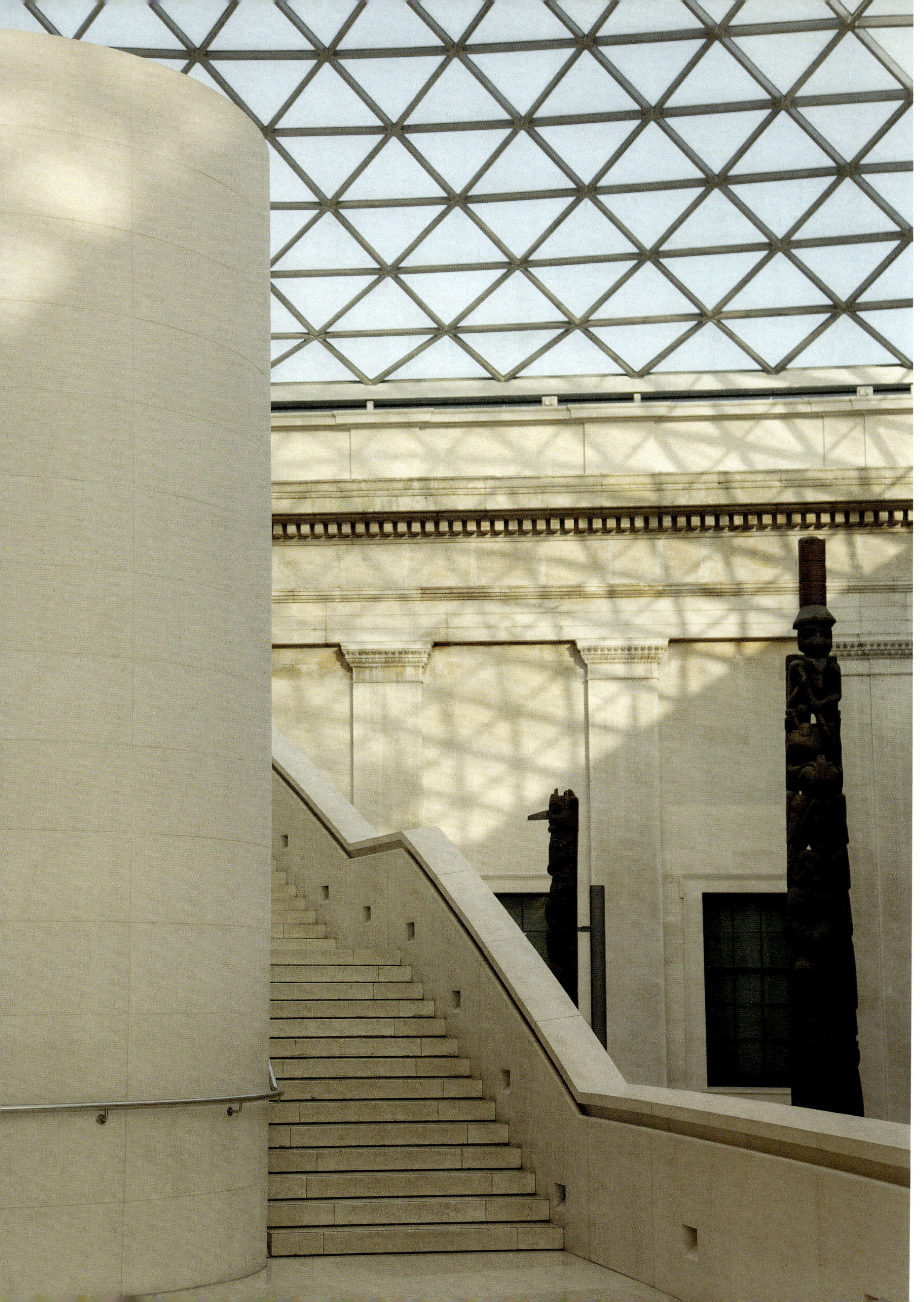

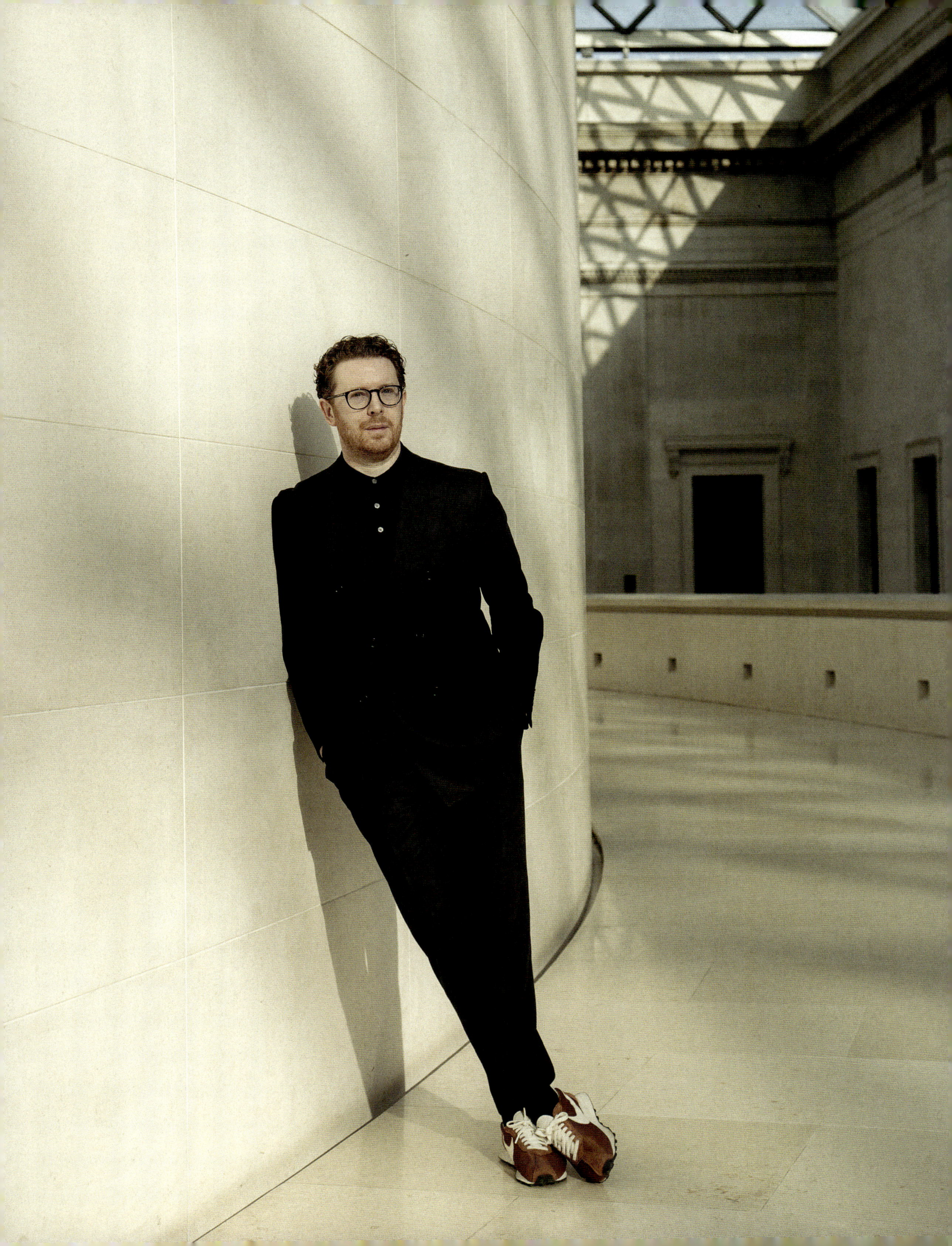

# VII

ESSAY: FORGET ME NOT
On the politics of remembering figures
hidden from history.

*Words*
Daphnée Denis

There is a haunted painting hanging in the Musée d'Orsay in Paris. *L'Atelier du Peintre* depicts the studio of the 19th-century realist painter Gustave Courbet: The artist at work is surrounded by his subjects—a mixture of working-class figures, female models and the Parisian cultural elite. On the far right of the monumental work is Charles Baudelaire, one of France's most celebrated poets. He appears to be sitting alone, staring at a book, but look hard enough and you might make out a faint silhouette next to him.

The ghost in the painting is the actor Jeanne Duval, a biracial woman from Haiti and the poet's longtime lover, who inspired some of his most famous verses. Until 2024, her origins, and even her full name remained largely a mystery—she was only remembered as "Jeanne" or "Black Venus" and described by racist critics of her time as rather unexceptional.[1] Legend has it that Courbet covered her up at Baudelaire's behest after their breakup. But over time, the fading paint has made her features reappear, as if the pigment itself rebelled against her erasure.

Jeanne Duval is just one example of an almost endless list of historical figures who were left out of the official record because they belonged to marginalized groups. Society's prejudice deemed some unremarkable; others were simply forgotten. Many who gained celebrity status when they were alive were actively kept out of the archives by the chroniclers of modern history in the West—mostly, white men.[2] "Many scholars and activists talk about these omissions from history as epistemic violence, the violence of what we're allowed to know, the suppression of certain knowledge," says Christy Pichichero, an associate professor of history, French, African, and African American studies at George Mason University. "Often, violence in the world, violence against enslaved women for example, is replicated in the archive, in the way that Black women are seen as fractured, trivialized or hypersexualized."

There have long been efforts from feminist and postcolonial scholars, educators and storytellers to rehabilitate these forgotten lives. Yet these initiatives only became mainstream after the 2010s, and the moments of reckoning brought by the Black Lives Matter and Me Too movements. #SayHerName—a movement launched in 2014 by critical race theorist Kimberlé Crenshaw to raise awareness about Black women victims of police brutality in the United States—highlighted how their identities went largely unacknowledged by the general public.

Some institutions are now beginning to atone for their failures. In 2018, for instance, *The New York Times* launched *Overlooked No More*, a series of obituaries of remarkable people whose deaths went unreported in the newspaper of record. The list includes journalist and civil rights leader Ida B. Wells, who famously fought against lynchings, Ada Lovelace, a mathematician who wrote the first computer program, and the ragtime composer Scott Joplin. A growing number of exhibitions, books and films aim to shed light on these untold stories, such as the Oscar-nominated movie *Hidden Figures*, about Katherine Johnson, Dorothy Vaughan and Mary Jackson, the Black mathematicians who significantly contributed to NASA's space program in the 1950s and '60s. As these endeavors grow, however, a question arises: Is it not reductive to always preface the histories of these exceptional people with the stories of their marginalization?

*"This type of work must be understood as a process rather than a one-off."*

"There is definitely a paradox in offering visibility that is, in part, structured around shadow—around discrimination and exclusion," says Alicia Knock, head curator for contemporary creation at the Centre Pompidou in Paris. In 2025, she spearheaded *Paris Noir*, a maximalist retrospective bringing together 150 African, African American, Caribbean and Afro-descendant artists who all lived and worked in the French capital during the second half of the 20th century. Their contributions to intellectual movements of their time were often glazed over, Knock says, and many of the works on show had, until then, largely been ignored by prominent art historians. For instance,

African American painters Beauford Delaney and Ed Clark, who came to Paris in the 1950s, were mostly excluded from the history of abstraction—not to mention the fact that abstraction itself, which is in part inspired by jazz improvisation, is rooted in Black culture.

"This type of work must be understood as a process rather than a one-off," Knock adds. "The moment of excavation—a large-scale exhibition restoring visibility—is just the beginning: what follows are the nuances, acquisitions, publications, singular trajectories explored in depth. That allows the work to move beyond the frame of marginalization."

*"Often, violence in the world is replicated in the archive."*

While invisibility itself should not take center stage, it is impossible to consider an effaced legacy without considering discrimination. Unfair as it may be, a person's omission from history becomes an indelible part of their story. "Framing the active process of erasure is important because sometimes, when we talk about the notion of hidden figures, we don't ask why or how they were hidden," says Pichichero.

It's a question that Pichichero had to grapple with while working on a biography of Joseph Bologne, Chevalier de Saint-Georges, a virtuoso violinist, composer, master fencer and the commander of the first all-Black unit in the French army during the French Revolution.[3] Often reductively referred to as "Black Mozart," the Chevalier de Saint-Georges was the son of a white planter father and an enslaved Senegalese woman, who rose to celebrity status in the 18th century. Still, he remains largely unknown in France, and there is little documentation about him. "I very deliberately advance that his erasure is a product of racism and social injustice," Pichichero explains. "He was a true polymath of the Enlightenment Age. The complex layers of his brilliance and genius fly in the face of stereotypes that our current societies, which remain structured on white male supremacy, still rely on."

Reasserting the position of figures like Saint-Georges requires perseverance. Many would be tempted to fill in the blanks, to pick and choose which life events to highlight, or elevate rumors as fact. That, Pichichero says, does more harm than good. *Chevalier*, an unsuccessful 2022 Hollywood biopic about Saint-Georges, focuses on an unverified love affair, and presents him as overtly sexual, short-tempered and unable to behave within social mores. The harmful stereotypes are inaccurate; these characteristics would have made it impossible for a biracial man to survive French high society. For Pichichero, "The restorative gesture becomes patience, taking the time to do careful research." She quotes the great postcolonial thinker Édouard Glissant's theory of a "right to opacity": the fact that some people or cultures refuse to be readily explained, or translated to fit dominant narratives.

Back at the *Paris Noir* exhibition, Knock points out how some artists in the show chose to use invisibility as a tool for artistic experimentation: Hessie, a Cuban textile artist, poked holes in beige fabric with needles. Her canvases, which can appear bare to the naked eye, only truly reveal themselves when they are correctly illuminated. Similarly, the work of shedding light on lives long kept in the dark may require accepting shadows and silences as part of the process. To remember these forgotten figures, we need to restore the complexity of their lives—erasure only becomes a spectacle if it is all we know about those we are memorializing.

(1) Research into Duval is recent and ongoing. Her name was confirmed as Florine Jeanne Gabrielle Prosper, and her place of birth as Port-au-Prince, by the historian Catherine Choupin in 2024. A year later, a photograph appeared on Duval's Wikipedia page: a *carte de visite* from the studio of the photographer Nadar, a close friend of Baudelaire. Following this lead to the Bibliothèque Nationale de France, Professor Maria Scott located a second portrait taken on the same date. They are the only confirmed photographs of Duval.

(2) The word "archive" comes from the Greek *arkheion*, meaning the house of the ruler. The philosopher Jacques Derrida argued that archives are never neutral—they are instruments of power, shaped by those who control what is preserved and what is discarded.

(3) Saint-Georges' regiment included Thomas-Alexandre Dumas, the son of a French nobleman and an enslaved Haitian woman, who rose to become a general before being betrayed and imprisoned in Naples. His son, the novelist Alexandre Dumas, drew on his father's story when writing the classic French novel *The Count of Monte Cristo*.



HISTORY

# IS IT NOT REDUCTIVE TO ALWAYS PREFACE THE HISTORIES OF THESE EXCEPTIONAL PEOPLE WITH THE STORIES OF THEIR MARGINALIZATION?

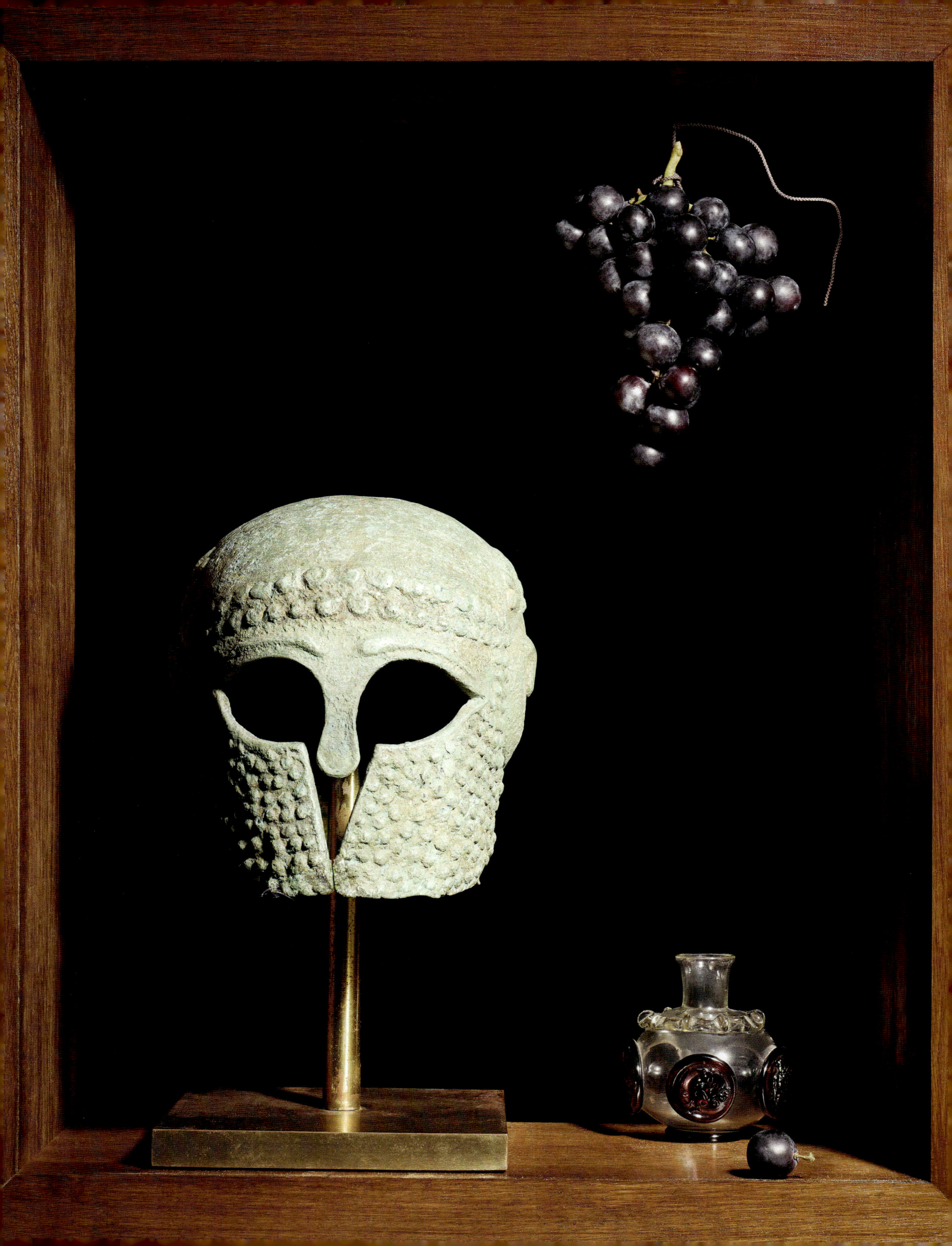

*Words*
George Upton

*Photos*
Aaron Tilley

*Set Design*
Carolina Mizrahi

# VIII

## MY ROMAN EMPIRE
Six historians share the factoid they can't stop thinking about.

# KEISHA N. BLAIN

Mittie Maude Lena Gordon was one of the most influential Black nationalist leaders in United States history. In 1932, while living in Chicago, she established an organization called the Peace Movement of Ethiopia, which promoted the repatriation of African Americans to Africa. A year later, Gordon initiated a nationwide campaign, resulting in a petition she submitted to President Franklin D. Roosevelt with hundreds of thousands of signatures of Black Americans desiring to leave the country in pursuit of a better life in West Africa. At its peak, the Peace Movement of Ethiopia attracted an estimated 300,000 supporters—working-class and impoverished Black men and women in Chicago and across the Midwest. During the Great Depression and World War II, it provided a vital space for Black nationalists to agitate for expanded political rights and economic power on a national and global scale, paving the way for the Black Power movement that would emerge during the 1960s and 1970s. However, Gordon—who also happened to be the great aunt of musician Prince—is little known today.

*Keisha N. Blain is a professor of Africana studies and history at Brown University, with interests in African American history, the African diaspora, and women's and gender studies. Her most recent book is* Without Fear: Black Women and the Making of Human Rights.

# CAMILLA TOWNSEND

It has long been said that the Spanish conquistador Hernán Cortés, arriving in the country of the Aztecs in the year One Reed (or 1519), just happened to get there in the very year that the god Quetzalcoatl was prophesied to return to earth, and so was welcomed as a returning deity. This purported coincidence was actually invented decades later by Spanish friars who found it an appealing story. In fact, the surviving Nahuatl-language sources demonstrate that there was no such prophecy, and that Quetzalcoatl was not even a terribly important god to the Aztecs. What actually happened was that the Indigenous people fought a long and brutal war against the newcomers. Sometimes historical anecdotes turn out to be more satisfying to posterity.

*Camilla Townsend is a professor of history at Rutgers University, focusing on Indigenous Mesoamerica. She is the author of* Fifth Sun: A New History of the Aztecs *and* The Aztec Myths: A Guide to the Ancient Stories and Legends.

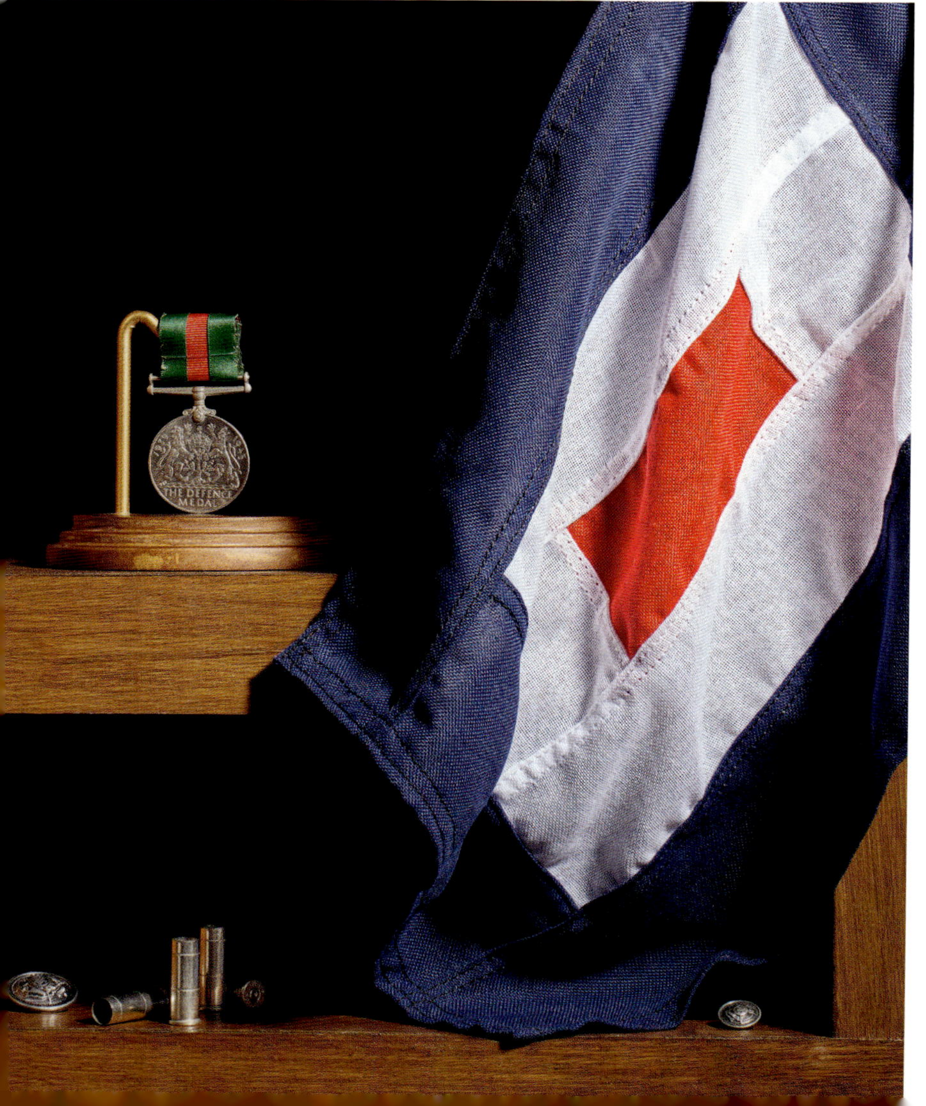

# ANTONY BEEVOR

Lady Victoria Cavendish-Bentinck, daughter of the 6th Duke of Portland and the last goddaughter of Queen Victoria, once recounted how in November 1913, the Archduke Franz Ferdinand of Austria-Hungary had been a guest at Welbeck Abbey, her father's country house, for a grand shooting weekend. Apparently, on one of the drives, the archduke narrowly avoided being shot when a loader fell, and the rest of the day was canceled. "Just think," said Lady Victoria. "What a missed opportunity. If he'd been more accurate, we could have avoided the whole of the First World War and who knows what else." When the story was mentioned later to her niece Lady Anne Bentinck who inherited the great house, Lady Victoria was not amused as the story was thought to have reflected badly on the shoot at Welbeck.

*Antony Beevor is a British military historian and the author of* Stalingrad, Berlin: The Downfall 1945 *and* Russia: Revolution and Civil War 1917–1921.

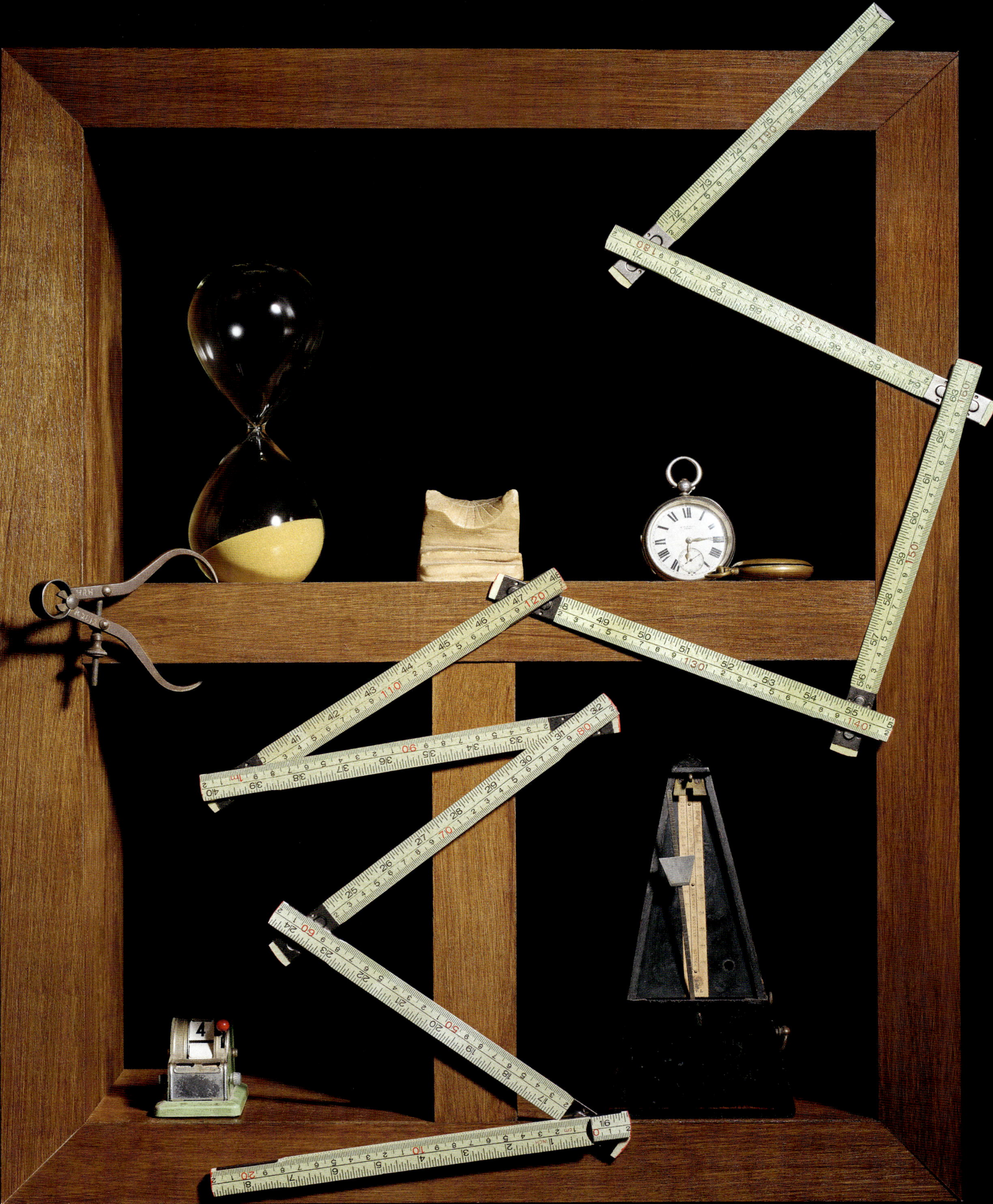

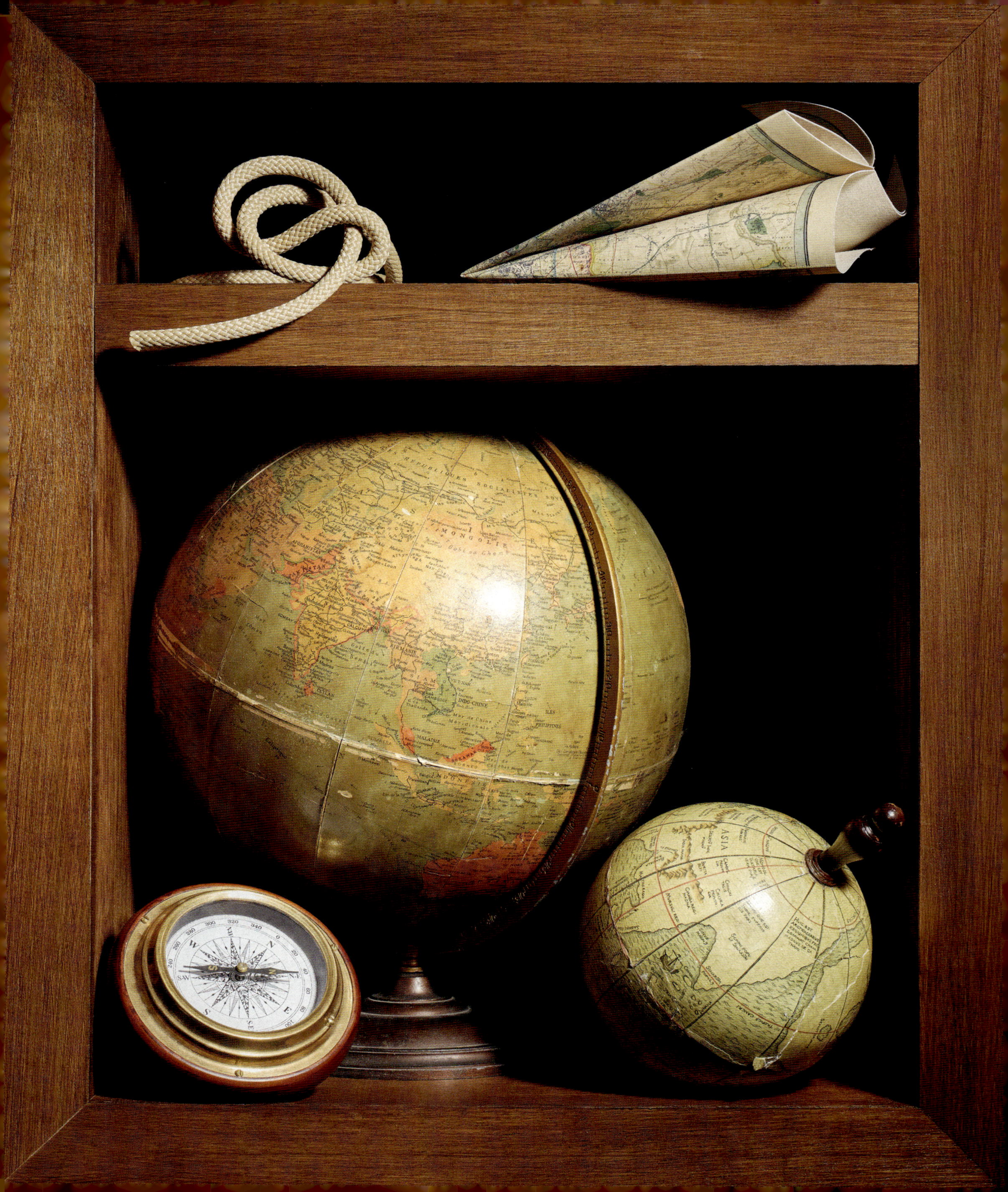

# MANU KARUKA

Friedrich Engels—the co-author, with Karl Marx, of *The Communist Manifesto*—was an avid swimmer. In 1840, he wrote to his sister Marie about swimming across the Weser River four times, "which no one in Bremen will so easily imitate." Two years later, his love for swimming cemented his bond with a spaniel he had received as a gift. "He is an excellent swimmer," Engels wrote to his sister, "but too crazy to learn any tricks. I have taught him one thing. When I say 'Namenloser' (that's his name)—'there's an aristocrat!'—he goes wild with rage and growls hideously at the person I show him."

*Manu Karuka is an associate professor of American studies at Barnard College. He is the author of* Empire's Tracks: Indigenous Nations, Chinese Workers, and the Transcontinental Railroad.

# ANDRÉS RESÉNDEZ

Ferdinand Magellan led the first circumnavigation of the world between 1519 and 1522. But securing support for such a risky and expensive enterprise had not been easy. Magellan, Portuguese by birth, went so far as to defect to the neighboring Iberian kingdom. In early 1518, he pitched his project in the city of Valladolid, where the Spanish king was holding court. Magellan's plan was to depart from Spain, sail across the Atlantic toward the tip of South America, cross into the Pacific, and finally navigate through the great ocean to the fabulous riches of the Far East. The main difficulty, however, was in finding a passage between the Atlantic and Pacific oceans—the alpha and omega of numerous Portuguese and Spanish expeditions to the Americas, all of which had failed.

On the day of the audience, Magellan presented not maps and nautical charts, as one would have expected, but "a globe that was very well painted and showed the entire world," according to one eyewitness, "and on it, Magellan traced the route that he would follow." Magellan said that he would cross from the Atlantic to the Pacific through "a certain strait" that he "already knew." But the portion of South America where the strait was supposed to exist had been left intentionally blank on the globe. Magellan implied that he was being cautious in case anyone present should wish to steal his project. But could Magellan really possess prior knowledge of the South American strait that now bears his name? Could there have been a now-lost chart in Portugal or an expedition prior to 1518 that reached the strait? Or was Magellan simply bluffing and was, in fact, a con artist who gambled everything to persuade a king, then turned out to be right? We may never know.

*Andrés Reséndez is a professor of history at the University of California, Davis, specializing in early European exploration and colonization of the Americas. His most recent book is* Conquering the Pacific: An Unknown Mariner and the Final Great Voyage of the Age of Discovery.

# ANNIKA NORMANN

In 1775, the Danish doctor, veterinarian and founder of one of the first veterinary schools in Europe, Peter Christian Abildgaard, carried out several experiments into the effect of electricity on animals. He wondered why lightning caused death when the animals' organs were rarely damaged. To find out, he gave a series of chickens electric shocks to the head to knock them out and revived them with shocks to the chest. He writes about these experiments: "However, after the experiment had been repeated quite a few times, the hen was clearly affected, walked with some difficulty, and did not eat for a day and a night, but later she was very well and even laid an egg."

It was not until 1899 that two physiologists, Jean-Louis Prévost and Frédéric Batelli from Geneva, described how small electric shocks can induce heart fibrillation—a rapid and irregular heartbeat—in dogs, and that larger charges intensify the condition. They also showed and described that with a new electric field they could stop the heart fibrillation and reestablish a regular rhythm, just as Abildgaard had done over 100 years earlier. Prévost and Batelli were the ones who finally described heart fibrillation using the meaning of the term the way we do today, paving the way for the invention of the modern defibrillator.

*Annika Normann is curator and conservator at the Veterinary Collections, University of Copenhagen.*

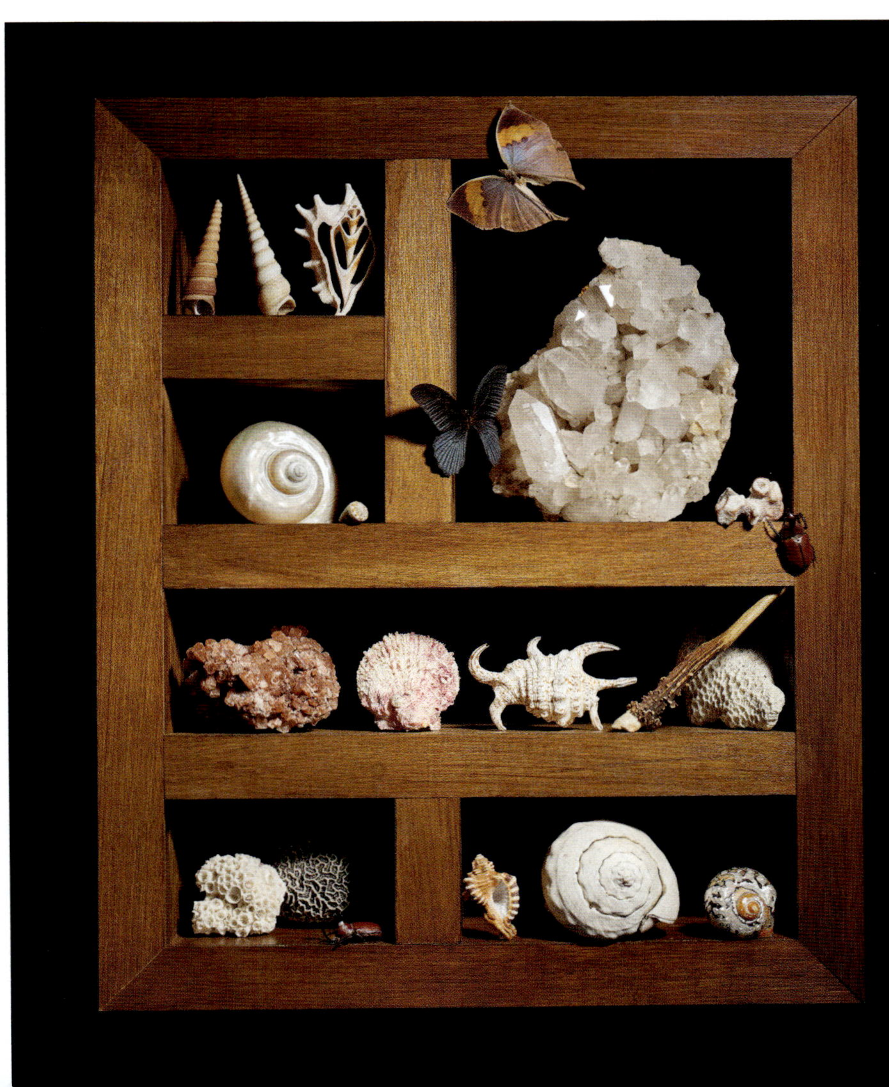

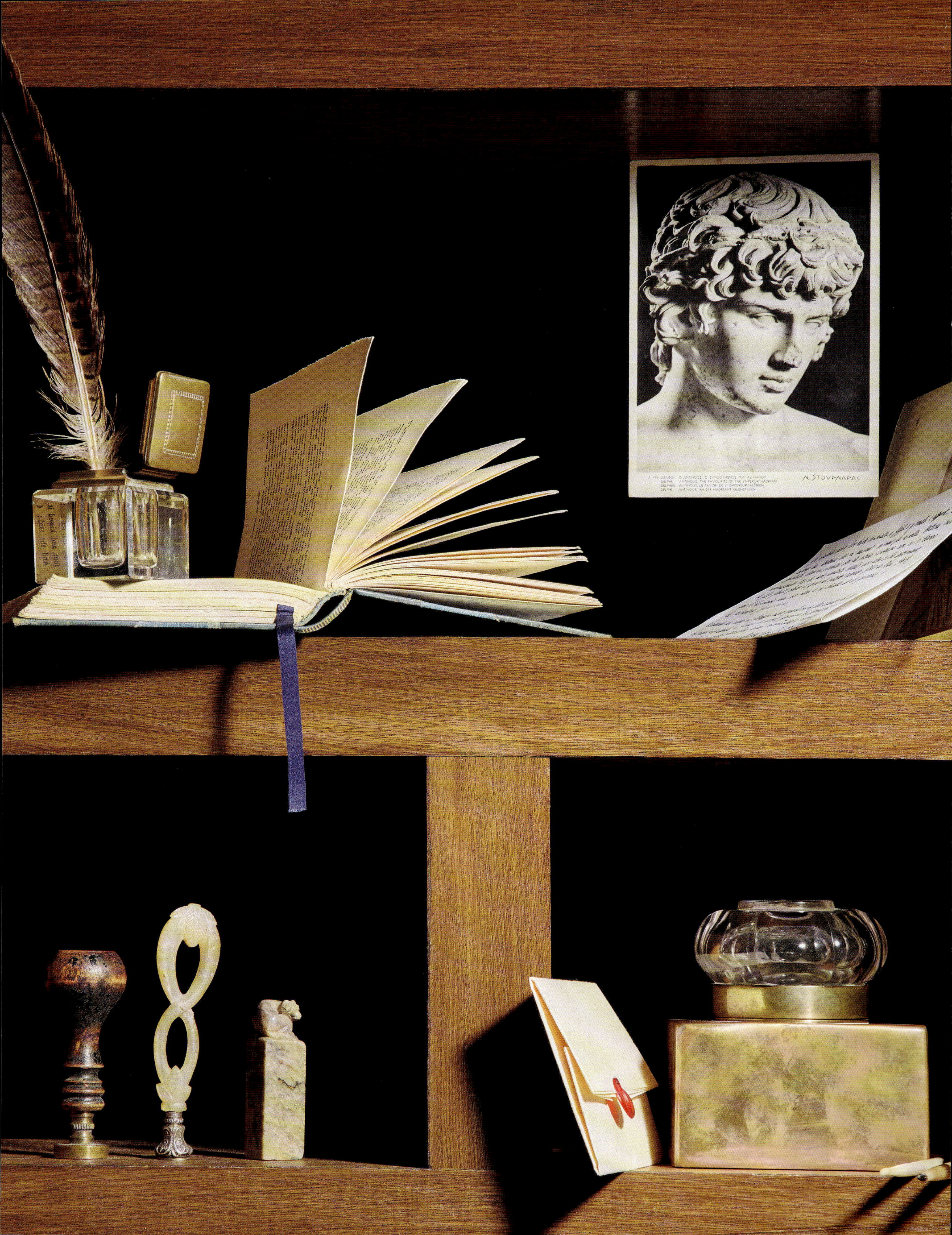
Α 419  ΔΕΛΦΟΙ    Ο ΑΝΤΙΝΟΟΣ Ο ΕΥΝΟΟΥΜΕΝΟΣ ΤΟΥ ΑΔΡΙΑΝΟΥ
DELPHI     ANTINOUS, THE FAVOURITE OF THE EMPEROR HADRIAN
DELPHES    ANTINOUS, LE FAVORI DE L' EMPEREUR HADRIEN
DELPHI     ANTINOUS, KAISER HADRIANS GUENSTLING
N. STOURNARAS

# Directory.

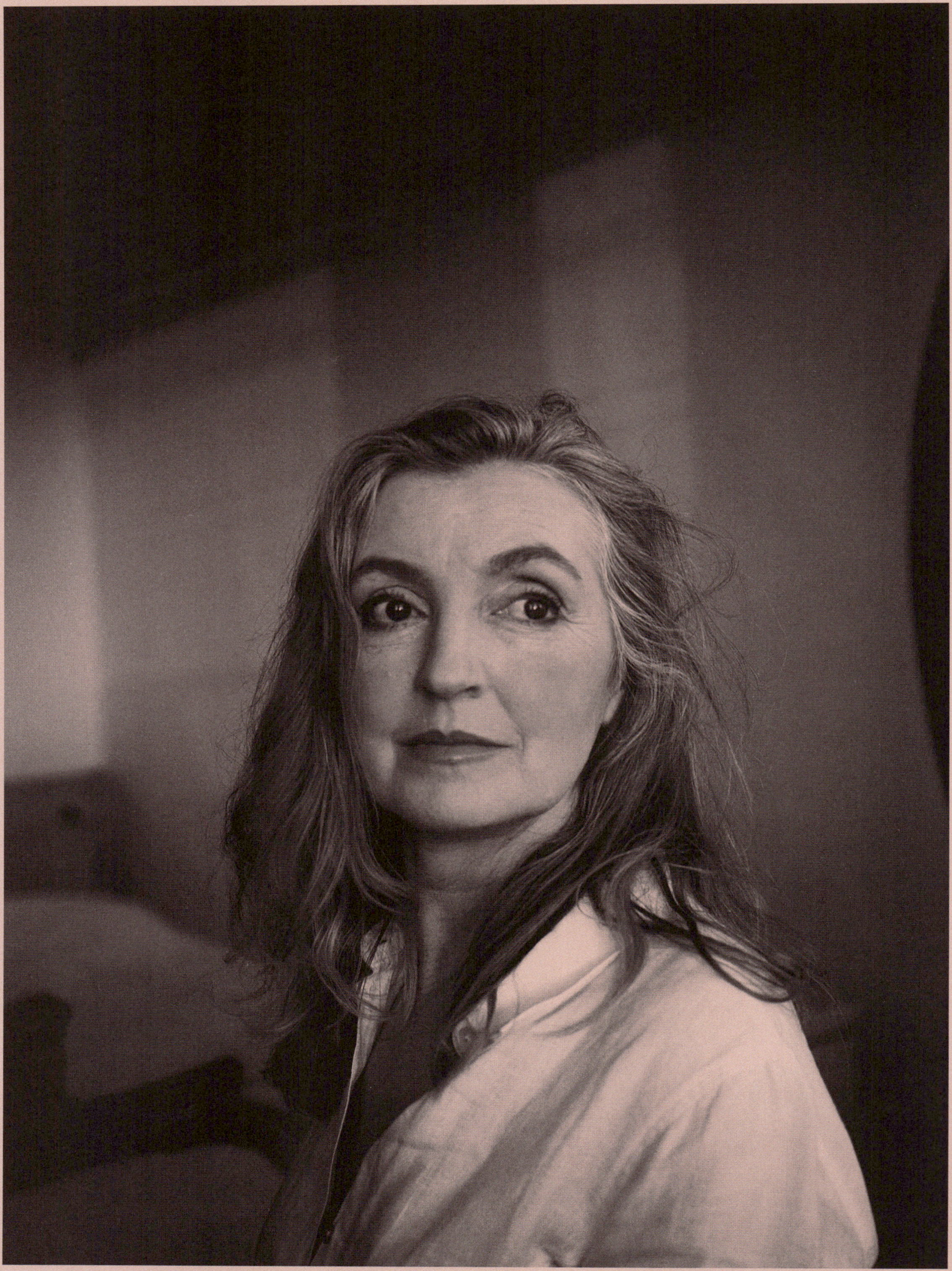

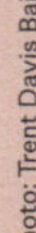




DIRECTORY

Words:
Rhian Sasseen

# Writer REBECCA SOLNIT reflects on a rapidly changing world, and the enduring power of collective action.

Across more than 25 books, the California-based writer Rebecca Solnit has cast her incisive eye over topics as diverse as long-distance walking, feminism, climate change, photography and Indigenous rights. Her latest, *The Beginning Comes After the End: Notes on a World of Change*, continues this approach, interweaving analysis of the contemporary American political landscape and the rise of the global hard right with meditations on the legacy of protest in the 20th century and on the relationship between the present and the past.

RHIAN SASSEEN: There's a particular urgency to this book's message. Did that impact your approach to writing it?

REBECCA SOLNIT: Yes. It was very much a book for this moment, and that meant that I wrote it fast. It feels like we are so embroiled in the horrors of this moment, and that pulling back to see how we got here would be really useful for people—useful to recognize that we live in a world that has been profoundly transformed, and is in the process of being transformed. And that all good things are the result of active engagement, whether intellectual or activist. That, of course,

becomes an exhortation to continue participating. People often feel to me like they live in a boundless present. If they feel confident that nothing bad will happen it's because they think that the world is stable; if they think we're all doomed, it's because all the negative things are somehow fixed and eternal. And that sense of a contextless present is very dangerous to this kind of active engagement.

RHIAN: Do you believe that the internet and digital media have changed our sense of time?

REBECCA: I think they have made it even worse. It got us very caught up in what *just* happened. There's a lot of things that contribute to that lack of context—a lack of intergenerational conversation, for example, and newspapers leaving context out because it's seen as editorializing. But saying what happened yesterday might not make sense unless you also mention what happened 10 years ago, and 50 years ago, or what the constitution says or what this amendment, passed in the 19th century, says.

RHIAN: In the book, you write about what you term "a secret history of kindness" and

cite a number of historical counterexamples against political cruelty. How might we use the value of kindness as a means of protest?

REBECCA: I feel like it's already so present in Minneapolis and St. Paul. One of the things that's fascinating about what's happening right now is that the current administration did not calculate correctly on who we are. They calculated in a way that elites and authorities often do—by thinking that ordinary human beings are selfish and cowardly. Solidarity is born not only out of courage, but out of what you could call compassion, empathy and kindness.

RHIAN: Are you optimistic about the future?

REBECCA: I always say optimism is like pessimism, cynicism, doomerism and despair—they assume they know what's going to happen. A lot of auspicious signs—not about the future, but about the past, over the last several decades—show us how profoundly the world has changed. And about how much power *we* have—people who believe in equality, and human rights, and dignity for all, and the rights of nature. With that knowledge, we can make the future, because the future is always something we're making in the present.

## Words:
## Francis Martin

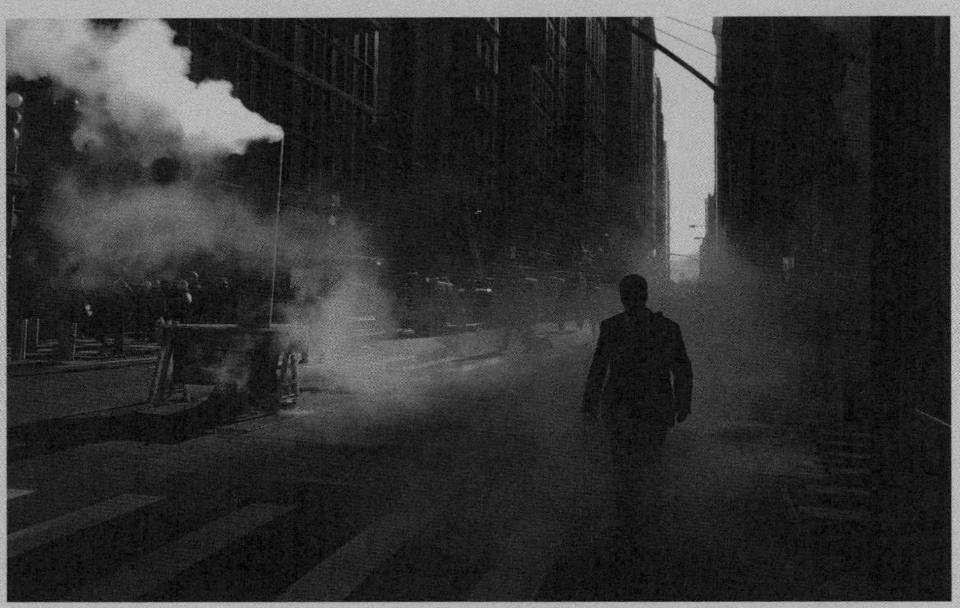

# To know a city, breathe it in.

Every city stinks, but no two cities stink in exactly the same way. It's not just how the different smells, pleasant and putrid, muddle together, but also how different noses experience them. No sense is as subjective as smell, and neither is anything such a potent trigger for memories—or as hard to capture. Unlike sight, sound and even taste, the scent of a city is something that cannot be experienced through vacation pics or recreated in your kitchen: You had to be there.

A city's odor evokes something of its essence and can offer a window into its past. Reflecting on the almost total transformation of Hong Kong, the city in which he grew up in the '60s, the writer John Lanchester marvels at how it nevertheless smells the same today. The main aromas, he writes, emanate from its harbor: "fish, oil, fish oil, live things and dead things; a humid, tropical, unmistakable smell." Walk through the streets of Sheung Wan or the island village of Cheung Chau, and you'll still encounter the pungency of dried shrimp, scallops and sheathlike fish maw. It's an old smell, one you would have experienced on these shores three hundred years ago.

Marseille, on the other hand, doesn't smell quite like it did a hundred years ago, when Walter Benjamin described the storied port city as smelling like "the yellow-studded maw of a seal with salt water running out between the teeth . . . it exhales a stink of oil, urine, and printer's ink." The printers have gone, the cargo ships now dock farther down the coast and sanitary, kiosk-like *toilettes publiques* dot the streets around the old port. But not all challenging olfactory experiences have been expunged: Step through a doorway on a narrow street near the central train station, as I once did, and you might be choked by the perfume of chicken manure and warm feathers, emanating from cages packed with live poultry.

Lanchester and Benjamin both, to some degree, write as outsiders, and it is perhaps the attentive visitor, or returning former inhabitant, who most keenly notices the scent of a city. Residents become habituated to the peculiarities of their environment; only the traveler is able to truly breathe it in. The next time you're somewhere new, take a moment to let the city's perfume swirl around you. You'll acquire the most potent souvenir.

## Words:
## Poppy Okotcha

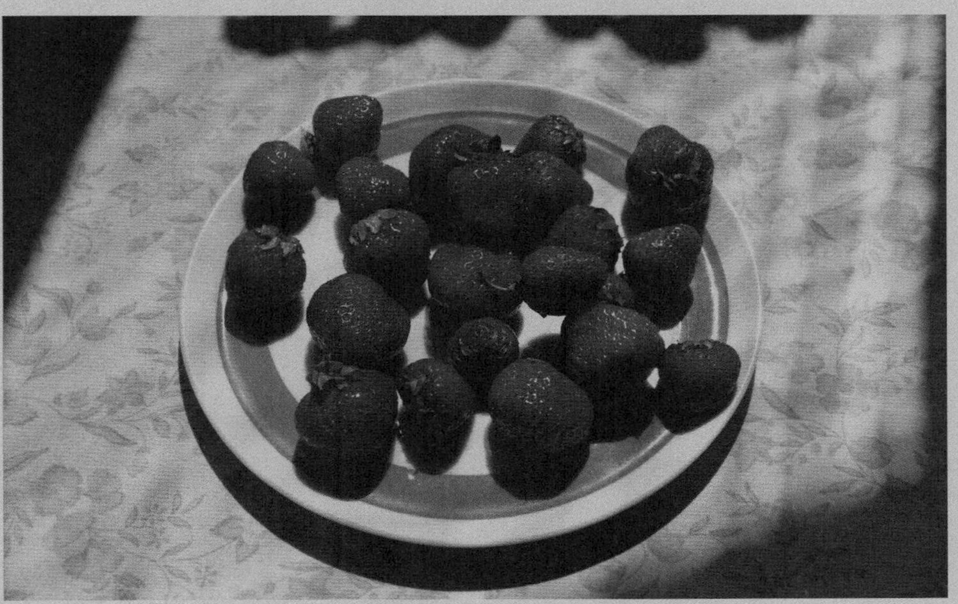

# An ode to the summer strawberry.

In his second summer out in the world, my son sat in the community garden strawberry patch and gorged. I had planted the patch two winters before; with a baby on the way, a strawberry patch suddenly became nonnegotiable.

That winter I ordered the young plants, known as runners, from an organic nursery. We prepared a 3-by-16-foot bed using the no-dig method and planted them about a foot apart. They produced only a modest crop in their first summer, but by their second had found their feet, and we harvested all through June.

At home, my strawberry patch contains plants given to me by my late mother-in-law from her own garden some five years ago. They have spread into the paths, and each year produce more fruit, a living reminder of her generosity. The sun beats down on my back as I weed, warming and comforting. I watch my little one maneuvering fruit toward his mouth. A bumblebee drones past.

Like all aggregate fruits, strawberries are especially vulnerable to the decline in insects caused by industrial farming and habitat loss. For a strawberry to form properly, each flower may need to be visited up to 15 times by pollinators. Crops like wheat and rice rely largely on the wind; strawberries depend on living helpers.

When grown industrially, strawberries are often heavily treated with toxic chemicals; pesticides, fungicides and soil fumigants protect the delicate fruits from pests and disease. Out of season, they are often flown long distances to stay fresh, giving them a hefty carbon footprint. But in an organic garden, we grow with nature: favoring diversity over monoculture to limit disease, welcoming predators such as beetles that prey on slugs and using simple barriers like bird netting.

Strawberries can be multiplied for free by removing the runners that form along the long, thin stems the parent plants send out. Planted in a pot or strawberry tower, they make delicious gifts for friends and family.

So, grow some strawberries in a pot or a patch. They need little more than good soil, sunlight, moisture and protection from slugs and birds. Harvesting organic, sun-warmed strawberries is one of life's greatest pleasures—a simple and wonderful way to mark the arrival of summer.

# PERIOD PIECES
## Here's a puzzle to help you while away the time.

## Mark Halpin

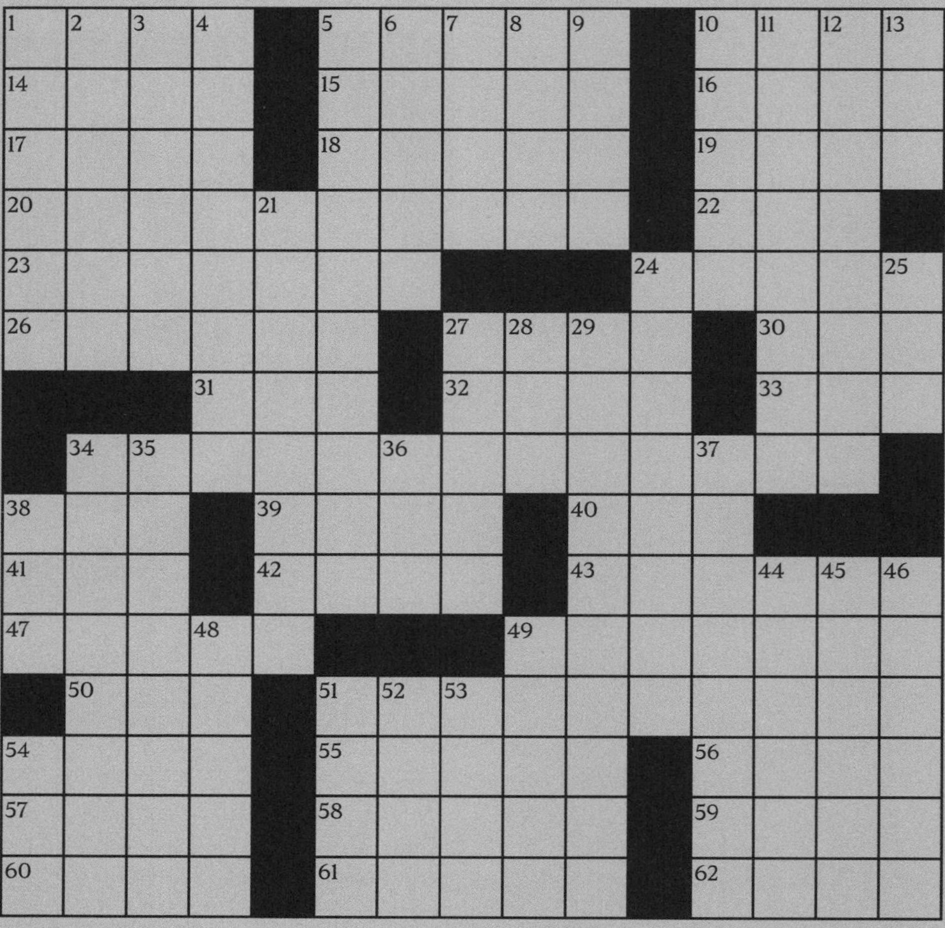

ACROSS

1. Mister in Münster
5. Back-up strategy
10. Tie
14. Intestinal parts
15. Wild party, in slang
16. Character in Norse lore
17. Feeling blue
18. "____ vincit amor"
19. R&B great Redding
20. Time period's legendary disasters?
22. Flee
23. Five colors locale in a McFly song
24. Music or picture collection
26. Most bizarre
27. Portent
30. "___ general rule…"
31. Issa of "Insecure"
32. Sword handle
33. Word before X, Y, or Z
34. Time periods on ludicrous display?
38. Ripen
39. One of the Great Lakes
40. Poem of praise
41. Rapper Tecca or Naz X
42. Certain vipers
43. Thrilling rafting locales
47. Even now
49. Embassy employee
50. Presidential nickname of the 1800s
51. Concealed one's boredom with time periods?
54. Coup d'____
55. Squander
56. Star Trek android
57. Himalayan monster
58. Car wheel connectors
59. Egress
60. Pristine nature spot
61. Some landings
62. Not those, in Brooklyn

# TABLE

Words:
Ruby Tandoh

## The cucumber—smashing the limits of a summer staple.

A person can go a lifetime without having a single nice thought about the cucumber. It might be bulking up salads or smuggled into sandwiches, kebabs and sushi rolls, but for most people, if they do spare the cucumber a thought, it is only to nudge it to the side of the plate. Dr. Johnson, the English essayist who had an opinion on just about everything, recommended that it should be "well sliced, and dressed with vinegar and pepper, and then thrown out as good for nothing."

It does not help that cucumbers are approximately 95% water, making them (particularly those suggestively large supermarket ones) somewhat insipid and texturally treacherous. Meanwhile, the skin—where all of that recognizably "cucumber" flavor concentrates—tends toward chlorophyllic bitterness.[1] Yet even those who can't stand that electric flavor can be turned. You just need to do the unthinkable: You need to cook it.

Broadly speaking, American cooks do

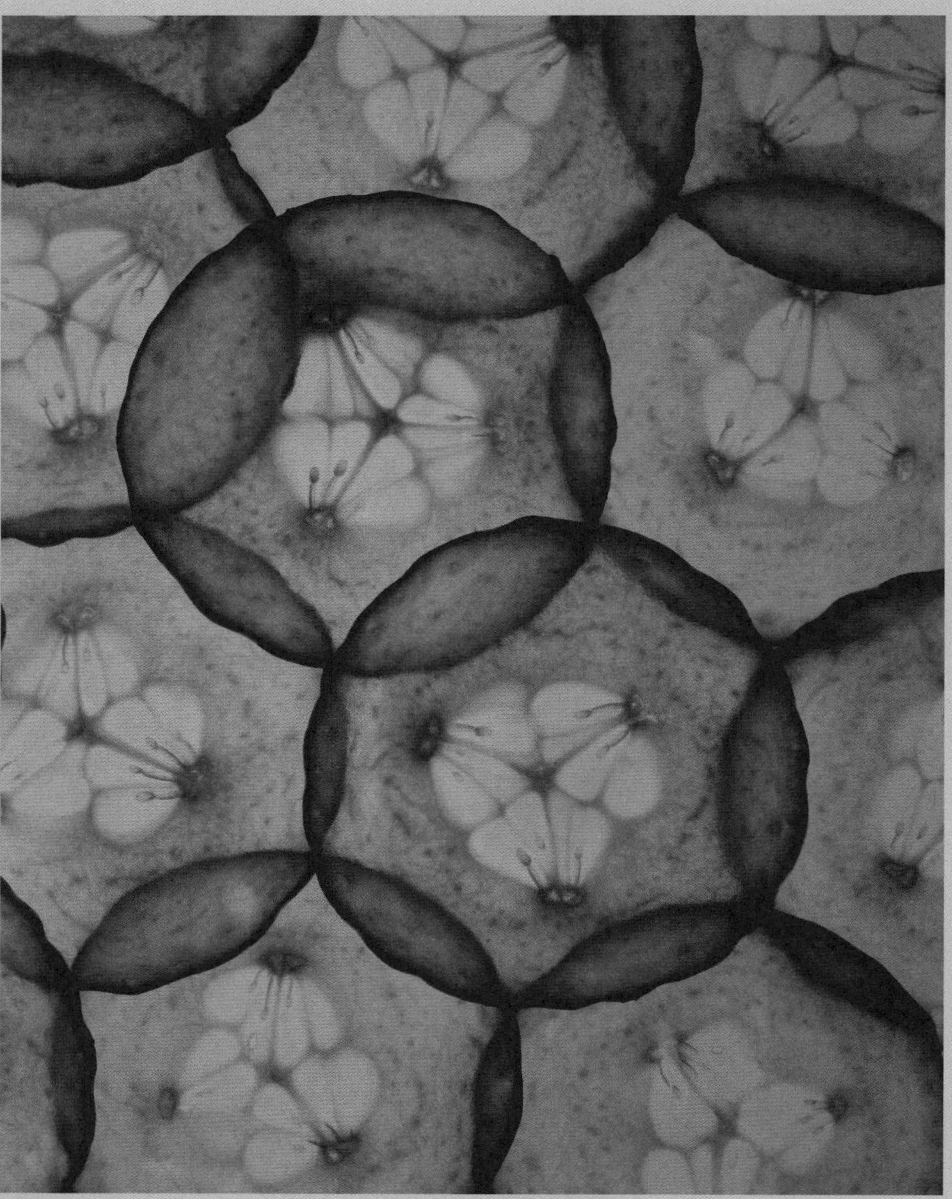

not dare to warm the cucumber. To heat vegetables is to break them down, to make them softer and wetter, and it is hard to think of a vegetable (technically a fruit, but let's not quibble) that needs this less. But cucumbers also like to confound and surprise. German cooks know that if you peel and then gently stew cucumbers, they will develop the mellow sweetness of summer squash. Toss them with a mustard sauce and you have *schmorgurken*, an unimpeachable side dish for beef or pork.

France also offers a masterclass in this unlikely art. Take Jane Grigson's cucumber ragôut, in which little jade coins of cucumber slip in a thickened butter sauce, or Julia Child's braised cucumbers, peeled and cut into batons, cooked, then seasoned with lemon and dried mint. The secret to these recipes is to blanch the cucumber first in well-salted water—counterintuitively, this is what stops it from turning to mush.

Most special of all is a summery rabbit stew I had last year, a Richard Olney recipe with cucumbers and tomatoes. I was against the idea at first—I thought that the cucumber would interrupt, interjecting when it was least welcome. But shucked of its rind and subjected to the acid of the tomatoes and the simmering heat, it lost its attitude. It was so sweet-tempered. In the end, it was the best part of the meal. The cucumber carried its flavor—sweet, green, redolent of bok choy— as lightly as a summer breeze.

(1) Cucumbers can taste bitter because of cucurbitacins, compounds the plant produces when stressed by drought or temperature extremes. These compounds are concentrated in the skin and stem end and evolved to deter herbivores. Modern varieties have been bred to suppress them, though the trait can resurface under adverse growing conditions.

## Words:
## Emily May

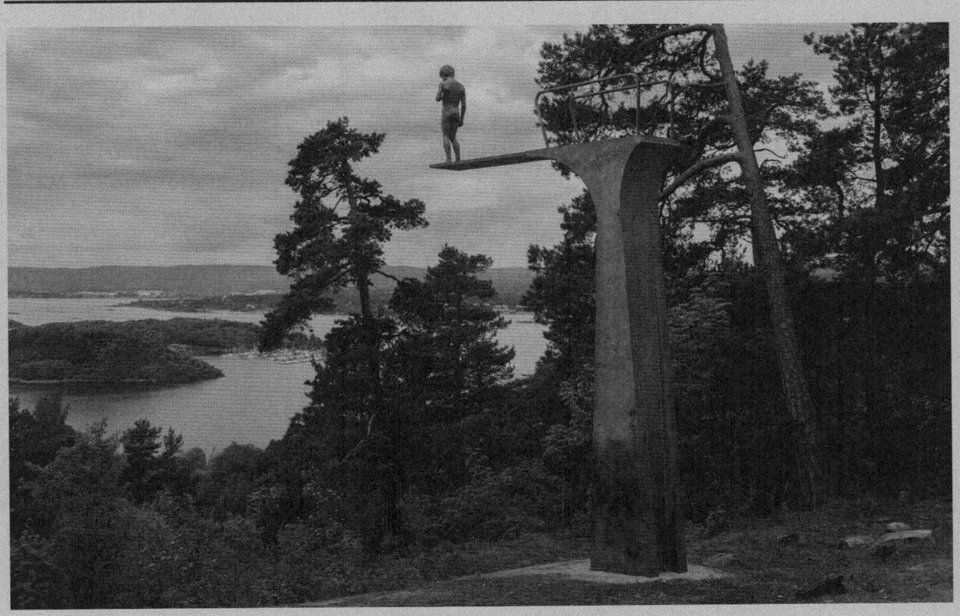



# What does an art fabricator do?

Sandra Stemmer and Holger Hönck founded their Berlin-based art fabrication agency, Stop Making Art, in 2018. While many fabricators specialize in a particular skill, such as casting bronze sculptures, Stemmer and Hönck see themselves more as consultants and advisors— they work hands-on to create the sculptures and installations that artists are unable to make themselves, but a big part of their role is as project managers, connecting the dots between artists, institutions and engineers. It's an approach that was shaped through years of collaboration with the renowned duo Elmgreen & Dragset, particularly on *Van Gogh's Ear*—a monumental swimming pool installed upright at Rockefeller Center in New York. "We thought, if we were able to do this, we can do it for other artists too," says Stemmer.

EMILY MAY: What kind of conversations do you have with artists? How much creative input do you have?

SANDRA STEMMER: The conversations are very technical and about the aesthetic outcomes artists are looking for: "What material would you like to use? Do you know that's very heavy? Did you know that if you want to polish stainless steel to look like a mirror, there are different grades of polishing that can be very expensive?" We work for the artists, so if they come with a crazy idea, we really try to make it happen.

HOLGER HÖNCK: We won't say an idea is stupid or great. Our role is to be neutral. It's really important for artists to have space to find their creations, and not to be pushed in a certain direction.

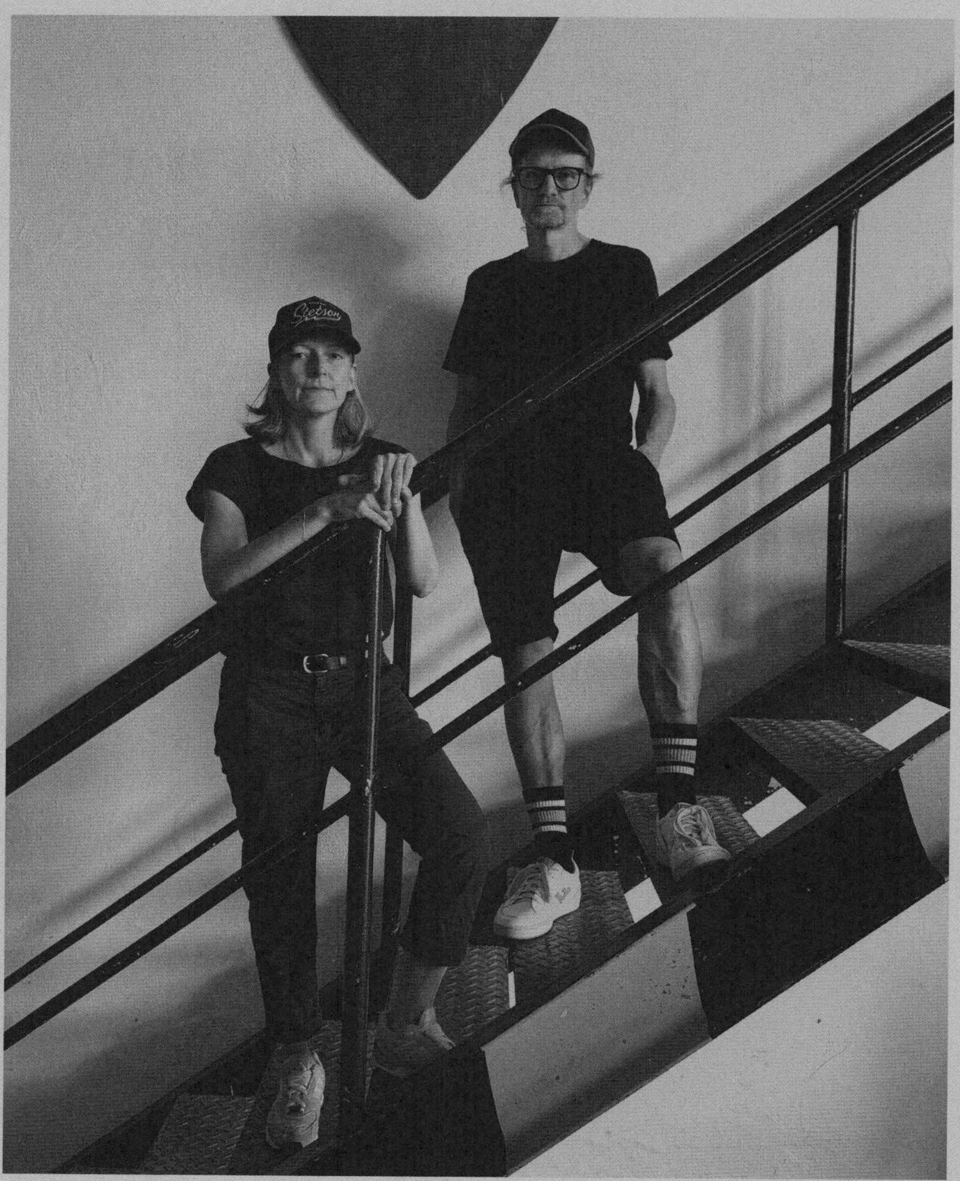

---

EM: What are some of the most challenging projects you've worked on recently?

SS: One of the toughest things we've had to do is mounting a massive, curved film screen for a showing of Lucy Raven's *Ready Mix* (2021) at Berlin's Neue Nationalgalerie in 2024. We had to cover it with several layers of special reflective paint in situ. After the first layer, it seemed as if there had been a fog machine in the gallery—it activated an alarm and the fire service came! The museum was very supportive, but it was really stressful to be in an institution with so many valuable works and create such a mess.

HH: Last October, we installed a light sculpture by Monica Bonvicini in a university hospital in Denmark. Change to "It's about 16 feet long, has almost 650 LED tubes and hangs in a stairwell. The structure was pretty lightweight, but the main problem was ensuring that switching it on didn't trip the fuse in the entire building!

EM: Have you encountered any misconceptions about art fabrication?

HH: Sometimes people are disappointed to hear that artists don't do everything by themselves.[1] But the ideas come from the artists—that is the most important thing. They can't produce 30-foot-high sculptures with their bare hands.

SS: The nature of artistic projects has become more expansive. Artists are expected to come up with big, room-filling concepts. It's not just about making a painting that hangs on the wall anymore.

---

(1) While contemporary artists such as Jeff Koons and Damien Hirst have faced criticism for employing fabrication teams, collaboration and delegation have been central to artistic production for centuries. Renaissance painters such as Michelangelo and Titian relied on assistants for large-scale commissions and, as today, the arrangement provided both practical employment and a form of artistic education for emerging artists.

# FILM

## Words:
## Hester Underhill

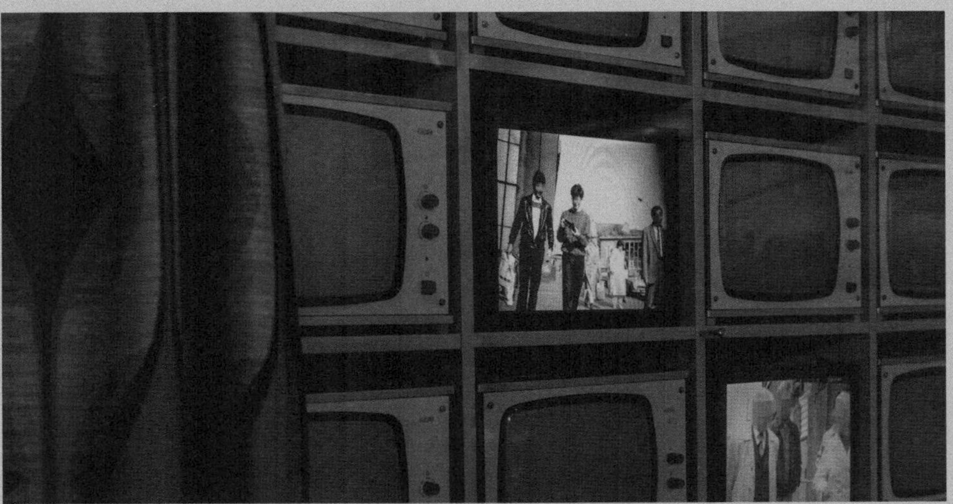

# The trouble with the modern biopic.

When the Bob Dylan biopic *A Complete Unknown* hit theaters in 2024, critics were quick to jump on its historical inaccuracies. Dylan, they noted, did not meet folk music legend Woody Guthrie in a psychiatric hospital, nor did he ever date a woman named Sylvie Russo. The list of ways in which the movie had subverted the historical record was long, forcing director James Mangold to spring to his film's defense—claiming he had always set out to make a "fable," not a documentary.

As director Martin Scorsese once put it, "cinema is emotional truth, not factual truth." But the idea that veracity must be sacrificed on the altar of entertainment would be far more acceptable if these biopics were actually worth watching. Recent additions to the genre generally amount to little more than toothless hagiographies (think *Elvis* or *Bohemian Rhapsody*) or reductive tales of tragic heroines (think Marilyn Monroe in *Blonde* and Judy Garland in *Judy*); and rarely do filmmakers acknowledge accountability for the way in which their work will inevitably shape popular conceptions of history.

With the film industry today relying almost entirely on reworking familiar stories to get audiences into movie theaters, executives are more keen than ever to give celebrity lives' cinematic treatment. Elon Musk, Michael Jackson and Madonna biopics are all in the pipeline—not to mention the four upcoming films about the lives of each individual Beatle. If Hollywood is going to insist on churning out these cine-portraits, directors would do well to think long and hard about what their film can do that a documentary never could. Which complex emotional truths can it reveal? What can they tell us about the true nature of genius?

Some filmmakers have attempted to achieve this by leaning into the impossibility of ever reaching full historical accuracy. Sofia Coppola's 2006 film, *Marie Antoinette*, shows the queen running around Versailles in Converse sneakers and tracks her rise and fall with music from the likes of Aphex Twin and the Strokes. A year after the film's release, Todd Haynes took Coppola's experimental approach a step further with *I'm Not There*—enlisting six actors (including Cate Blanchett and Christian Bale) to portray different facets of Bob Dylan's identity.

These films attempted to push the genre in new directions, and while they may not have been huge critical and commercial successes upon release, the intervening decades have propelled them to cult status. And rightly so; they deserve to be celebrated for their playful embrace of ambiguity, contradiction and myth. In acknowledging that a life can never be fully captured, only interpreted, they turn the genre's greatest limitation into its greatest strength.

Words:
Salomé Gómez-Upegui

# JOHN ZABAWA on painting the liminal.

In another life, John Zabawa may have been a philosopher. In this one, his existential inquiries unfold in luminous paintings that pull viewers into the present. A graphic designer turned artist, Zabawa grounds his work in technical precision and an acute understanding of color, yet his practice hovers into more elusive territory, where nothing is certain and everything seems possible.

SALOMÉ GÓMEZ-UPEGUI: You move fluidly between abstraction and figuration. How does a painting reveal the form it wants to take?

JOHN ZABAWA: I think it comes from my experience working as a designer and thinking deeply about visual communication. As a designer, you're usually responding to someone else's needs. Over time, that trained me to listen closely to the brief and to focus on finding the clearest solution within an infinite field of creative possibilities. It's a way of setting aside ego.

I think that's how I approach painting as well. When an idea arrives, I try to listen to it. The paintings in my latest series, *Crashing Waves*, for instance, are rendered in a figurative style, but I've explored the same motif abstractly too. It's about giving the idea what it asks for. I see myself as a passenger, trying not to get in my own way.

SGU: The sky is another motif that appears in your work. What keeps drawing you back to it?

JZ: One person I give credit to for really changing the way I look at the sky is Yoko Ono.[1] When I was just starting college, I was deeply inspired by her work. I even have one of her postcards with the hole cut out to see the sky through. I'm also very interested in Stoicism, Buddhism—all of that, and for me, the sky is a reminder of how to live. It's hard to articulate, but it reminds you of where you are: a planet spinning through this fast, expanding, infinite universe.

You would think that reminding yourself you're this tiny, insignificant grain of sand would create anxiety, but

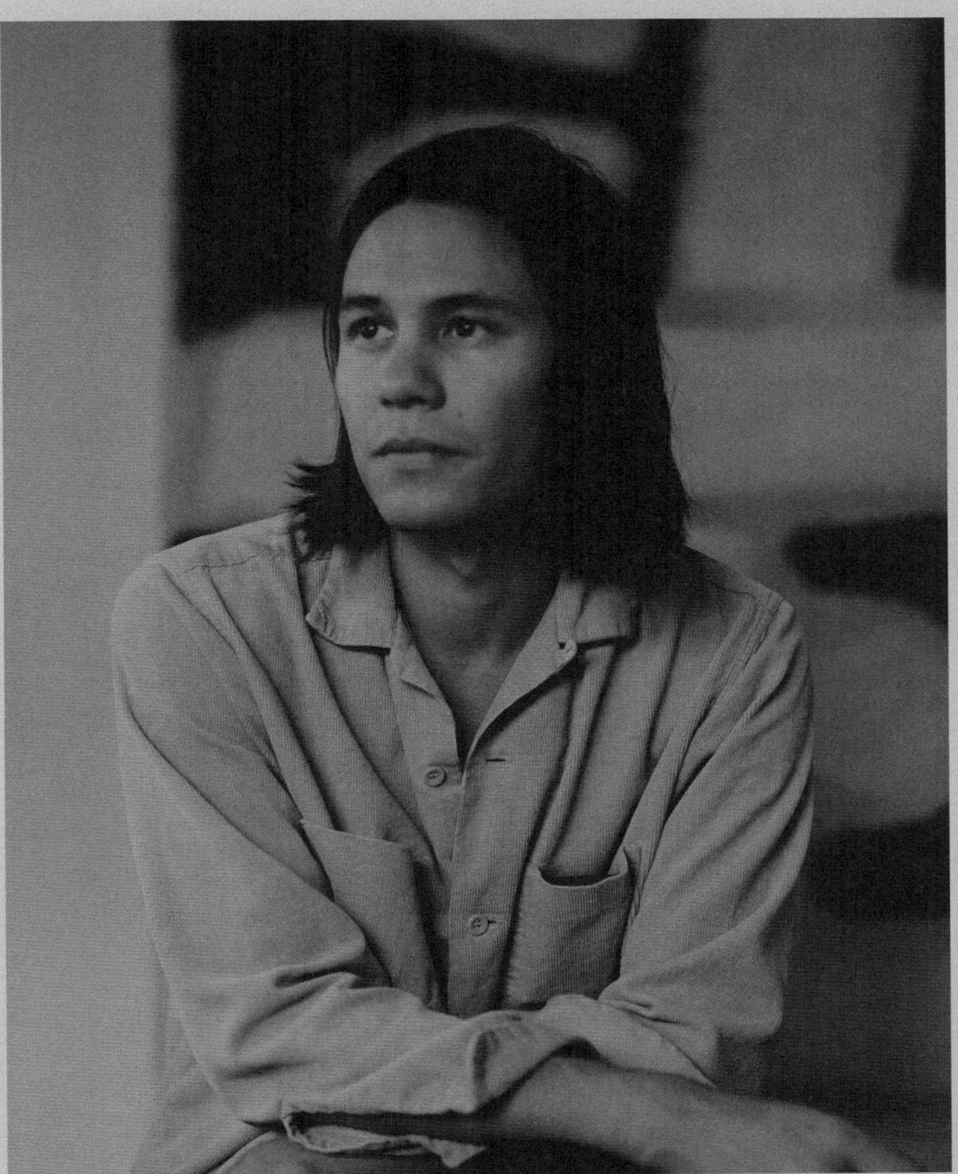

it gives me a purpose. Knowing how small and temporary we are makes me want to make the best of life.

SGU: Is there an existential question or concern that's currently driving your practice?

JZ: Most recently—over the past year especially—everything I've made has shifted. After the LA fires, my father passed away, and it really rocked our family. We didn't have a close relationship, but it changed something in me. I wouldn't say the work has been a direct response to his death, but it altered where the work comes from. Before, I was collecting ideas, circling around topics and themes. After he passed, I started pulling more directly from my own life.

SGU: How do you know a painting is finished?

JZ: A painting feels complete when it carries certain dualities. As I get older, I'm more interested in that balance: light and darkness, speed and slowness, something studied and something loose. It has to hold both the analytical mind and the free mind. Intention and naivete. Control and surrender.

I think that desire for duality also comes from being biracial. My mother is Korean and my father is white, and I've often felt between two worlds. That in-between space has shaped how I see everything. My work lives there too. It's not fully abstract or fully figurative; it exists somewhere in the middle. That middle space is challenging, but it's where I want to be.

(1) Most people know Yoko Ono as John Lennon's partner, but she is an accomplished artist whose seven-decade career spans conceptual, performance and multimedia practices. Her work includes *Cut Piece* (1964), an influential performance in which audience members were invited to cut away her clothing with scissors, and the ongoing *Wish Tree* series (from 1996), where visitors tie handwritten wishes to the branches of living trees.

# CREDITS

<table>
<tr><td>COVER:</td><td>PHOTOGRAPHER:<br>STYLIST:<br>SET DESIGNER:<br>HAIR:<br>MAKEUP:<br>PRODUCER:<br>CASTING DIRECTOR:<br>MODEL:</td><td>Gregory Chong<br>Una Ho<br>Owen Lo Yuk Chi<br>Cooney Lai<br>Jenny Shih<br>Una Ho<br>Summer Chen<br>Tong Aojun at Sparkling Models<br><br>Tong wears a look by LOUIS VUITTON.</td></tr>
<tr><td>TIMELESS:</td><td>PHOTOGRAPHY ASSISTANT:<br>STYLING ASSISTANT:<br>SET DESIGN ASSISTANT:</td><td>Bo<br>Tiffany Tsui<br>Laam Tsang</td></tr>
<tr><td>WORKING OUT<br>WITH NINA<br>CRISTANTE:</td><td>PHOTOGRAPHY ASSISTANTS:<br>STYLING ASSISTANT:</td><td>Antonio Savignano and George Tomlinson<br>Tilly Hopcraft</td></tr>
<tr><td>1619:</td><td>PRODUCTION ASSISTANT:<br>DIGITAL TECH:</td><td>Olayinka Ehi<br>Obinna Obioma</td></tr>
<tr><td>SPECIAL THANKS:</td><td></td><td>Lilly Babirye<br>Ted Barrow<br>Maxine Brangwyn<br>Adeline Collingwoode<br>Claudine Eccleston<br>Sol Elibol<br>Bevali Francis<br>Lorna Hamilton-Brown MBE<br>David O'Brien<br>Erica Tate<br>Ann Tucker<br>Emily Wilson<br>Patricia Fullerton<br>—<br>Ace Hotel Toronto<br>Norwich Making Space<br>Stow Studio</td></tr>
</table>

<table>
<tr><td>A</td><td>ALEXIS BITTAR</td><td>alexisbittar.com</td></tr>
<tr><td>C</td><td>CARL HANSEN & SØN</td><td>carlhansen.com</td></tr>
<tr><td>F</td><td>FLAMINGO ESTATE</td><td>flamingoestate.com</td></tr>
<tr><td>G</td><td>GRYTHYTTAN STÅLMÖBLER</td><td>grythyttanstalmobler.com</td></tr>
<tr><td>H</td><td>HERMÈS</td><td>hermes.com</td></tr>
<tr><td></td><td>HOUSE OF FINN JUHL</td><td>finnjuhl.com</td></tr>
<tr><td>I</td><td>INTERMEZZO</td><td>intermezzodancewear.com</td></tr>
<tr><td>J</td><td>JOHANNES WARNKE</td><td>johanneswarnke.com</td></tr>
<tr><td>K</td><td>KALDA</td><td>kalda.com</td></tr>
<tr><td></td><td>KARMUEL YOUNG</td><td>karmuelyoung.com</td></tr>
<tr><td>L</td><td>LE MANDORLE</td><td>lemandorle.com</td></tr>
<tr><td></td><td>LOUIS VUITTON</td><td>louisvuitton.com</td></tr>
<tr><td>M</td><td>MALOA</td><td>maloaofficial.com</td></tr>
<tr><td></td><td>MATT HUI</td><td>matthui.co</td></tr>
<tr><td></td><td>MUGLER</td><td>mugler.com</td></tr>
<tr><td>N</td><td>NAKED WARDROBE</td><td>nakedwardrobe.com</td></tr>
<tr><td>O</td><td>OMEGA</td><td>omegawatches.com</td></tr>
<tr><td>P</td><td>PRADA</td><td>prada.com</td></tr>
<tr><td>R</td><td>RICHARD MILLE</td><td>richardmille.com</td></tr>
<tr><td></td><td>ROLEX</td><td>rolex.com</td></tr>
<tr><td>S</td><td>SCHUTZ</td><td>schutz-shoes.com</td></tr>
<tr><td></td><td>STRING</td><td>stringfurniture.com</td></tr>
<tr><td>T</td><td>TINA FREY</td><td>tinafreydesigns.com</td></tr>
</table>

## Words:
## Sala Elise Patterson

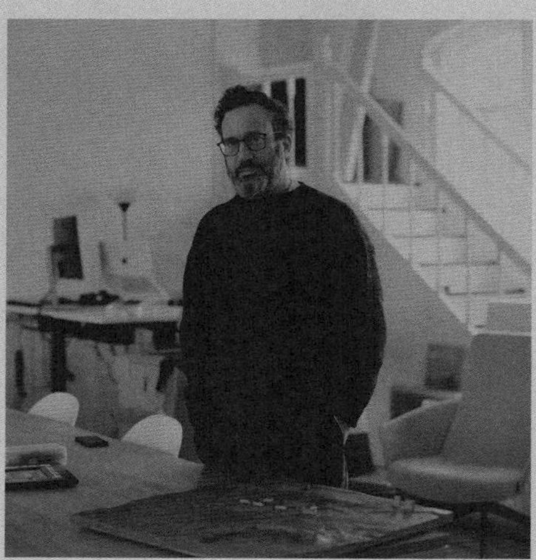

# EYAL WEIZMAN on turning architecture into evidence.

I'm in Forensic Architecture's offices at Goldsmiths University, south of the Thames—one of the last areas of London that has not been gentrified. In front of me, I see a huge open-space studio with about 20 colleagues. There's paper everywhere, there are models, there are maps and photographs pinned to the walls, there are people speaking on phones, trying to verify information. It looks like a hybrid between an architecture studio and a newsroom.

I founded the Centre for Research Architecture in 2005 as an alternative to conventional architectural education, and in 2010 I established Forensic Architecture. We investigate state and corporate violence in the UK and around the world through a multidisciplinary practice that blends the arts, architecture and investigative journalism.

We practice the art of attention, a form of aesthetic expertise. When I talk about aesthetics, I refer to the original Greek meaning of the word: what is in the realm of the senses. We are attentive to visuals, to images, to spaces, to faint traces that others cannot see. We believe architecture is not merely a way of designing and constructing buildings but a field of knowledge, a way of looking at the world.

I moved to London after a period of activism in occupied Palestine, having experienced, as an Israeli-born person, how architecture can be used as a weapon. When you start understanding that banal features of the landscape, like roads, hilltop settlements, bridges, fields and orchards, are part of a process of colonization, you understand that you are actually looking at a battlefield. Whoever gets to draw the space controls the space.

The construction of all these architectural elements is a form of slow violence. Israeli settlements strangulate Palestinian built fabric. Forests erase the remnants of Palestinian villages that were evicted in 1948. Roads enact an apartheid: highways for Israelis; meandering roads for Palestinians.

After the Hamas-led attacks on Israel on October 7, 2023, that slow violence accelerated rapidly. Seen from an architectural perspective, the genocide is not only an act of demolition. It is a construction site where a settler-colonial reality is being built. It reveals how architecture is political forces slowing into form.